Gerda Boyesen

Between Psyche and Soma

Healing the Soul through the Body

Biodynamic Psychology & Psychotherapy

I dedicate this book to all who serve Mankind
and to the giants on whose shoulders I am carried.

I also dedicate it to my family, to those who are close to me,
and to the patients whose psychological truth has enabled me
to make these discoveries.

Between Psyche and Soma: Healing the Soul through the Body by Gerda Boyesen
Published by Dorian Boyesen
Boyesen Publishing | Boyesen Verlag
Leipzig, Germany

Photography by the familiy Boyesen
Designed in cooperation
Ebba Boyesen, Mona Lisa Boyesen, Dorian Boyesen
Photo by Raspopova Marina on Unsplash

ISBN: 978-3-944225-03-6 (Print)
ISBN: 978-3-944225-04-3 (PDF)
ISBN: 978-3-944225-05-0 (EPUB)

Printed in Germany 1st Edition 2026

Prologue

Gerda Boyesen's Biodynamic Psychology is one of the earliest forms of bodypsychotherapy to be developed, based in part on Willhelm Reich's Vegetotherapy, Gerda introduced the concept of "psycho-peristalsis": the inner digestive organs respond directly to the rhythms or stresses of emotional life. Gerda worked directly on the body using soft, non-invasive forms of massage in order to loosen tensions and restore vitality.

Biodynamic Psychology works with the expressive language of the body and the pulsations of the organism, in order to reduce neurosis. Even psychotic states can be helped, through learning to trust the body again and to start to manage the charge of strong emotions. Gerda's methods strengthen the "motoric ego" through subtle somatic forms of communication, which help to restore the natural flow of libido in the body.

Gerda was a close colleague of mine, ever since she left Norway in 1968 and moved to London, where I organised her first lectures to introduce her work to the public, and became a visiting guest trainer in her Institute.

I experienced that Biodynamic Psychology is a method which is sensitive, compassionate, and rich at times with a healing sense of humour.

David Boadella, Co-director, Institut for Biosynthesis

Introduction to Gerda Boyesen's book "Between Psyche & Soma"
by Ebba and Mona Lisa Boyesen

We are pleased to publish Gerda Boyesen's first edition in english of her long-awaited book: "Between Psyche & Soma" with the subtitle that could be "Healing the Soul through the Body". This classic within Body-oriented Psychotherapy introduces the theory, methods and practice of Biodynamic Psychology.

It was published in France in co-operation with Jean-Paul Gerome drs. and Lucien Bailly-Maître in 1985 titled : "Entre Psyché et Soma" followed by the german republication 1987 under the title: "Über den Körper die Seele heilen", where it has been a bestseller within its field for the last 30 years.

In a way it is miraculous that this book has been republished consistently all these years, and even the publishers were amazed! In another way it is very just that it is so; while in "Between Psyche & Soma" Gerda Boyesen is going straight to the core of Bodyoriented Psychotherapy, initiated in the late 40s by Dr. Wilhelm Reich.
A great number of people have ventured through the both personal and educational "magic" of Gerda's book towards a profound exploration of their sense-of-self, bridging in subtle ways the Psyche with its Soma.

G. Boyesen speaks directly to the "bio-logic" of the unconscious. Her theory, (in a nutshell) which she explores throughout her book, is, that the enteric system of the guts - namely, the smooth muscles of the intestinal walls - with their multitude of neurons, has the innate capacity to digest and discharge surplus stress.

Her theory was developed in 1955 (Oslo) long before the american neurobiologist, dr. Michael Gerson in his research in neurogastroenterology presented the enteric system as "The Second Brain" (HarperCollins, New York. 1998.) This neurodigestive functioning is what G. Boyesen refers to as "Psychoperistaltic selfregulation". An essential part of Biodynamic Psychology methods aims to help the person to regain this organic ability of restoring balance on both physical, emotional and energetic level.

Gerda Boyesen, a pioneer before her time, never tired of advocating that the body ‚has a mind of its own' and that the gut-feelings have their own intelligence !
By drawing this conclusion, and by the way she applied this knowledge in her therapeutic work, she has been bridging an essential gap in the understanding of psyche-and-soma.
G. Boyesen's discoveries, revealed in this book, can be regarded as an ‚appendix' to medicine. By following her through the jungle in the network of man's mind and

emotions, it may become evident to each reader, that G. Boyesen has helped to evoke a revolution in human biology.

In 1969, after our respective studies, Ebba Boyesen, 24 years old arrived from the USA, Mona Lisa, 23, coming from Oslo, and Paul, 20 years old, already was studying in the UK, we all joined Gerda in London in 1969.

We trained in our mother's methods, became her apprentices, and later her colleges and staff members. We were all actively involved in building up the Biodynamic Training Centers both in the UK as well as on the continent.
By time, her life-work became also ours. Here, in this book, is her story: How Gerda became a disciplined scientist, an inventor with the courage and curiosity to go beyond conventional and compartmental thinking.

Until 1973, Gerda had called her work "The Method of Bioenergy", as was the first Centre in London called "Centre for Bioenergy" and the work with the stethoscope she called "Stomach Wrumblings Work-Out/Discharge"

Mona Lisa Boyesen coined it with the term "Psychoperistalsis" in summer 1972 and further "Biodynamic Psychology" in 1973. Gerda liked the terms and it has remained. She had by that time finished working and researching on Gerda's theoretical papers, which circulated in Energy & Character, published by David Boadella. Her special contribution to the work is "BioRelease", "Alpha Nursing", working with the infant and the Eros/Oedipal constellation work. Paul Boyesen developed "Psycho-Organic Analysis" and started his own School in France. Ebba Boyesen focuses her work on "Birth Release" and Segmental Vegetotherapy: extended methods of the segments in the body from the 7 segments in the body from Reich/Lowen to 12, so as to include the whole leg and feet segment.

Ebba and Mona Lisa Boyesen established the European School of Biodynamic Psychology in Germany in 1993, accredited members of the EABP and EAP. They further specialized in developed the various psychoperistaltic massages, which is being taught in their School.

Psychoperistalsis as a concept was introduced in David Boadellas's Journal of Bioenergetic Research): "Energy and Character" by Mona Lisa Boyesen in 1974.

Biodynamic Psychology as a concept was founded by Mona Lisa Boyesen in spring 1973, and presented as a Training Department in The Institute Of Unitive Psychology in Utrecht (The Netherlands), which Mona Lisa was directing (1973-1979) together with Jay Stattmann. Biodynamic Psychology as concept - with Theory and Foundation of Gerda Boyesen's work - was introduced in Energy and Character in 1977*. Since 1974 Ebba and Mona Lisa Boyesen have developed Biodynamic Psychology and Psychotherapy further in both theory, praxis and in the Training Aspect of the method.

---

* There are two papers of Mona Lisa and Gerda that have been published 1977 in E&C under the headline: Foundation for Bio-dynamic Psychology. Part 1 is: Spontaneous Movement and Visceral Armour, in E&C, Vol.8, No.1, Jan 1977, 32-41. Part 2 is: Cries from the Guts, in: E&C, Vol 8, No.2, May 1977, 62-69.

* These two articles focus on the therapeutic effect of working out nervous tension and stress through the biodynamic massage, which by the use of the stetoscope makes the immediate response of the intestines audible for the therapists to follow the reaction of the guts throughout the massage. In this way the process is helping to provide the required condition for internal stressrelief and emotional discharge - activating the person's (patient's) organic capacity to obtain stress-relief and homeostasis. After several sessions, the patient's organism is better equipped to regulate and discharge internal tensions, and by improvement of the peristaltic regulation - spontaneous "neuro- digestion" is leading way to the person's organic selfregulation, emotional balance and revitalization.

Ebba and Mona Lisa Boyesen

Foreword to the first english edition by Thomas Haudel

It's a great pleasure for me and all in the GBP organized Biodynamic Therapists, that this classical book of bodypsychotherapie 25 years after his first edition now is published in English language.

I had the luck to be trained personally from Gerda Boyesen directly over a period of several years towards the end of her long live. She has influenced my psychotherapeutic work very strong till today. I don´t know any others psychotherapist, that found such a deep and healingful approach to the embodied emotional complaints of man like Gerda Boyesen.

Her psychotherapeutic methods have a certain simplicity and yet they are brilliant. They reach everyone, who has the personal courage to look and dwell within oneself.

The book has not lost his actuality. More and more people worldwide fall in psychic deseases. It is a great challenge to find therapeutic treatments to healing this deseases. This book introduce a method, that has the capacity to solve many of this problems. A lot of scientific studys after the first publication of "Between psyche and soma" confirm her theory, that the small intestine digest not only food but also emotions. That's why the small intestine is the most important organ for the biofeedback during the Biodynamic massage. The effectiveness of this massage in cases of depressive clients would be proved in a scientific study published by the german Biodynamic society GBP. Besides the touch as a neglected treatment in the modern psychotherapy would be appreciate in the book "touch" by Müller-Oerlinghausen and Kiebgis.

It is high time, that the Biodynamic Psychotherapy would be applicated in more hospitals and ambulant psychotherapeutic centers and would be payed by the health insurances. That would be suitable in reflection of the high effectiveness and the humanistic appproach of the Biodynamic Psychotherapy. Only on this way could be more people get a chance for application this method to heal their psychic deseases.

Berlin in September 2021 Thomas Haudel

The Birth of the term Biodynamic Psychology

In 1973 Mona Lisa joined forces with the american body-psychotherapist, Jay Stattmann, with whom she were to set up the first body oriented training center in The Netherlands (Utrecht 1974). Before they came that far, they decided to make a holiday together in Spain, and rented a flat in the village Mijas, in the south of Spain. At this time Mona Lisa was occupied with writing on an article series for David Boadella's Journal: "Energy and Character". In this series she presented her mother's work, which so far was known as Gerda Boyesen Methods.

For this purpose, Gerda came to Mijas and spent about 2 weeks with Mona Lisa exclusively writing on two articles of the series. Mona Lisa spent a lot of time interviewing Gerda in order to understand and write down the different theoretical steps, which involved Gerda's personally and professionally processes in the development of her metods.

It was during one of these intensive discussions, that Mona Lisa exclaimed: "But, Gerda !!!! Everything you talk about is soooo bio-dynamically !!!! Let's call your work: Biodynamic Psychology !!" Gerda was immediately content with this word ! and the new term for her work was born !!

It was in Mijas, spring 1973 that Biodynamic Psychology found its frame with name, theories and practical application! After this day, Biodynamic Psychology became the overall concept for Gerda's methods, - and within this frame, her children/colleagues, Ebba, Mona Lisa and Paul put their own therapy and training contributions within this new concept.

The first official use of Biodynamic Psychology took place few months after Mijas; when Jay Stattmann and Mona Lisa founded the Institute for Unitive Psychology in Utrecht (the Netherlands) autumn 1973 and set up their training program respectively: Unitive Psychology by Jay Stattmann and the Boyesen method of Biodynamic Psychology.

In the article Mona Lisa was working on in Mijas, Biodynamic Psychology as a term was for the first time introduced in written form in her article: "Foundation for Biodynamic Psychology", Part. 1., subtitle: "Spontaneous Movements and Visceral Armour" (*Energy and Character, The Journal of Bioenergetic Research*, Vol 8. No. 1, 1977, p. 32-41). But, as previously mentioned, the official use of the name appeared already in Jay's and Mona Lisa's training programs in their institute in Utrecht in 1973. "Psycho-Peristalsis" was first mentioned in 1974 by Mona Lisa (E&C, Vol. 5, 1).

In 1975, Gerda, Paul and Ebba Boyesen created in Paris (Le Center de Bioénergie, Rue des Plantes in Paris, founded by Paul, Joëlle and Ebba) and in Geneva 1976 the first two training groups of what would be called Biodynamic Psychology. The name „Biodynamic Psychology" is coined by Mona-Lisa Boyesen, who was settled in the Netherlands at the time, to designate the body of work of the four Boyesen.

BETWEEN PSYCHE AND SOMA

An Introduction to
Biodynamic Psychology and Psychotherapy

by

Gerda Boyesen

ACKNOWLEDGEMENTS

First of all, I want to thank my parents for having unwittingly made me neurotic. Without them, none of my discoveries could have been made. I also thank them for all the love they gave me. And I want to thank my children for the inspiration they gave me when they were small, and for their support and co-operation as adults.

I thank my therapy students for their trust, their help and their personal contributions. I also thank everyone who welcomed and supported me when I moved to London.

I owe especial thanks to the late Dr Ola Raknes, who introduced me to the world of body-oriented psychotherapy. I am also eternally grateful to Aadel Bülow-Hansen for all that she taught me. And I thank Dr Lowen for all that he taught me without knowing it (I have only met him once).

I thank Dr Wilhelm Reich for his pioneering work, and David Boadella, who published my first articles in his journal Energy & Medicine. I greatly appreciate the exceptional support that he gave me.

I thank Dr Paul Gérôme for suggesting to me that I should write this book, and for his practical assistance, his valuable advice and the immense effort that he invested to prepare this book for publication. And I thank Lucien Bailly-Maî-tre, who revised the French edition of this book with such thoroughness and dedication.

TABLE OF CONTENTS

I THE ORIGINS OF BIODYNAMIC PSYCHOTHERAPY

WILHELM REICH AND OLA RAKNES

In 1934, not long before the war, Wilhelm Reich came to Norway. He had left Germany to flee the Nazis, and had actually wanted to settle in Denmark. But the Danish Ministry of Health demanded that he provide proof that he was a member of the International Psychoanalysis Association, for which he would have needed a reference from Freud. It was a bitter blow to Reich when Freud refused to give him this document, and his dormant pleurisy broke out again. He then went to Norway, where Dr Evans, the Director of Health in Oslo, showed great interest in his work. A group began to form around Reich, a real little movement, in which artists played an important role. Sigurd Hoel, one of Norway's most famous poets and writers, was one of the people who was passionately interested in Reich's work. His wife Nic Waal, a respected psychiatrist and psychoanalyst, and Ola Raknes, who was introduced into this artists' circle as her friend, also became members. Ola Raknes was an outstanding philologist and the husband of Aslaug Vaa, one of Norway's best poets who was later awarded a state pension for life for her work. I myself was too young at that time to belong to this group.

The little "family" became very close, and Reich expounded many of his theories in this circle. It was around this time that he discovered and described the orgone, the unit of cosmic energy, and began integrating it into his work. He also investigated the movements of the tiny energy particles which he called "bions". He set up a large laboratory in the basement of a house on Drammen Road in Oslo, and began carrying out a host of biological experiments on animals. All of this came to a very abrupt end, however with his expulsion from Norway. Reich had wanted to measure the sexual energies in men and women during coitus, using patients in psychiatric hospitals, which sparked off a press smear campaign against the "King of the Orgasm" that ultimately brought the affair to the attention of the Norwegian Parliament. As it turned out, Reich's expulsion in fact saved his life, since the Nazis invaded Norway shortly afterwards. He emigrated to America, and so gained valuable years in which to continue his work.

Reich had trained a small number of character analysts, three of whom proved to be true Reichians; the others disappeared after the press campaign. The three who remained were outstanding personalities: Ola Raknes, Nic Waal and Dr Havrevoll. All of them were exceptional psychotherapists who genuinely continued Reich's work. At that time there were only a handful of psychoanalysts in Norway, all of whom lived in Oslo. Professor Schelderup practised a technique he called global analysis; Ola Raknes, Nic

Waal and Dr Havrevoll worked with character analysis and vegetotherapy. I remember that Nic Waal once prefaced a remark about the past with the words: "When I was still a psychiatrist...". She meant that when she began practising vegetotherapy, she stopped regarding herself as a psychiatrist.

After Reich's departure, these three therapists courageously carried on working according to his methods. Ola Raknes, for one, was a man used to weathering storms. All the same, it was some years before the quality of his work was recognised. Students were the first to show an interest in this novel form of therapy. Raknes formerly taught at the university, and now had a private practice.

He was an extraordinarily hard worker. At the age of 85, shortly before he died, he said to me: "I believe I must be getting old; I can't work more than eight hours a day any more." He was a very warm-hearted, powerful person who loved his work and his patients. He came from the "sober" part of Norway; the puritanical region around Bergen. Raknes had undergone psychoanalysis training at the Berlin Institute, and had also worked with Dr Karen Horney. Before he met Reich he had already notched up countless sessions of analysis, but he said that everything really began when he started his therapy training with Reich. He was astonished by the depth and intensity of this form of therapy, with which he could penetrate into regions that psychoanalysis had never touched. Raknes had enormous respect for Reich, and nothing that anyone said or wrote about Reich could shake his faith. Many Reichians deserted Reich during the press smear campaign, but Raknes never doubted his integrity or his genius. He often spoke of Reich as a warm-hearted man. He kept a photo in his therapy room of Reich surrounded by children, which clearly showed how full of life, how vibrant with orgone energy this man was. Raknes liked to boast a little by telling the following story: Reich's colleagues measured the orgone energy in the red blood cells of various people, and so determined the time it normally took for maximum contraction to occur; in other words, how long the red blood cells were able to store orgone energy. But in both Reich's and Raknes's blood this process took twice as long, purely because of the high orgone charge. After Reich emigrated to America, Raknes visited him every year to work with him. He also proudly related how Reich once said to him: "If I ever decide to enter into therapy again to work on my father complex with Freud, I want you to be my therapist!"

Nic Waal's situation was somewhat different. She set up an institute with the aim of providing not only vegetotherapy for children and parents, but also vegetotherapy training. A considerable number of psychotherapists were trained by her.

Reich was a man of such abundant creativity that the people surrounding him could only either follow him or oppose him, according to their individual character structures. For example, his lectures about the orgasm, in which he drew curves to illustrat the duration of a "normal" orgasm, only succeeded in provoking hostility since few peo ple were able to live up to this ideal. Furthermore, even the scientists who took part i Reich's experiments with bions, who could have confirmed the accuracy of his claims refused to act as witnesses and denied every word of his experiments.

These are just a few details to illustrate the mood of the times and the situation o the Reichians in Norway.

MY ENCOUNTER WITH OLA RAKNES

In 1947 I was a young wife and mother of two small daughters. I came across a book b Harold Schelderup entitled: "Neurosis and the Neurotic Character", which mentione both psychoanalysis and vegetotherapy. As I read Schelderup's description of neurosis I became aware of my own neurotic structure. I immediately went into town, looked u his address in the telephone book, hurried to his consulting rooms and rang the bell. H opened the door himself, and I told him that I had read his book and wanted to ente into psychoanalysis with him. I was greatly surprised when, instead of welcoming m with open arms, he replied that he did not have time, and suggested that I should g to Ola Raknes or Dr Havrevoll instead. I believe Nic Waal was in America at the time touring hospitals to demonstrate the muscle test that bears her name; with this test diagnosis could be made in under an hour in cases where a three month long investiga tion was normally needed.

At that time I had no idea what vegetotherapy actually was. I wanted to underg analysis, so I forgot Ola Raknes's name and made an appointment with Dr Havrevol There I told him that I was neurotic and wanted to undergo psychoanalytic treatment At some point I also mentioned the fact that I played tennis. He immediately asked m to show him my style of playing: how I made a serve, a left-handed return shot, etc. gave him a demonstration there in his treatment room - I was crazy about tennis - unti after ten minutes, I suddenly realised how ridiculous it was to be pretending to play ten nis here. Why was he asking me to do this? I had certainly not come to him for that! Bu he just told me to carry on, and then, after a while, he suddenly announced that I wa very stubborn. I felt that he was really going too far, and told him that it was nonsense I said that I was not the slightest bit stubborn; on the contrary, I was always accommo dating and friendly, and all my friends were forever telling me so. "That doesn't matte in the least", he said. "You're stubborn." "I'm not stubborn!" I exclaimed, but he insiste that he could tell by looking at my jaws while I was playing tennis. Still I maintained tha I was not stubborn: I was very proud of being friendly and accommodating. And all th way home, the same sentence kept on repeating itself in my head: "I'm not stubborn! He's wrong, I'm not stubborn!".

When I got home, nobody was there. Luckily for me! Before I knew what was happening, I felt my jaws clenching together. Suddenly I began to scream, and found myself transported back to the age of six, lying on my stomach on the sofa. I had done something which annoyed my father, and he had given me a spanking. I howled, and he warned me, "I won't stop until you behave yourself and stop crying!" I was crying very hard, and I had absolutely no desire to behave myself; all the same, I managed to mumble through my tears, "I'll be good! I'll be good! I'll stop crying! I'll never cry again if you love me!" In spite of the distress and the effort it cost me to stifle my tears, I managed to hold them back by breathing in short gasps. I promised my father that I would always be a good, obedient little girl, if he would only love me.

This was an extraordinary experience! The memories and the tears really seemed to have come out of nowhere. I was particularly astonished because I had not cried since childhood. Then, two days later, something else extra-ordinary happened. I was sitting in the living room reading a story about a dog that climbed up a tree, when suddenly I heard somebody roaring with laughter. To my amazement, I realised that the laughter was my own! That was when I realised that I had never been able to laugh properly either, and indeed I had thought that people who could laugh when they heard something funny were rather odd. All I could do was smile, or permit a little chuckle, a tiny sound to escape from my throat. And now a single hour of therapy had released all this! But, sadly, Dr Havrevoll could not take me on as a patient, because his waiting list was two years long.

I sensed that this outburst of sobbing after my session with Dr Havrevoll had released the tension in my diaphragm, so that my tears and laughter could finally escape. Simply reading a book about neurosis and a single visit to a character analyst had given me an experience that utterly changed my life! From that day onwards I became passionately involved with the ideas to which Dr Havrevoll had introduced me: I was utterly determined that my children should be allowed to cry freely without being repressed. Now all my attention became focused on my children: what must I do to prevent them from becoming neurotic? I wanted to study psychology, so I requested an interview with the lecturer in child psychology at the University of Oslo. She advised me to start my studies at once by reading (the psychology course was still being organised at that time). I read and read, but I did not gain anything from it.

Then, in the autumn of 1947, I heard about a lecture to be given by a psychiatrist whose special interest was body-oriented psychotherapy: Dr Trygve Braatöy. This connection later yielded the second foundation of the theoretical structure of Biodynamic Psychology - the first and most important being Wilhelm Reich, of course. In his lecture Dr Braatöy declared that a vegetotherapist first needed to train in either medicine or physiotherapy. His words remained with me long after the lecture, and I decided to become a physiotherapist after completing my psychology degree. Dr Braatöy was a brilliant psychiatrist, who sadly died too soon. His lecture was about psychotherapeutic work on the body; he did not talk about Wilhelm Reich. His enthusiasm was so infectious that my desire to become a therapist became even stronger.

In that same autumn of 1947 I began my psychology studies at the University of Oslo. At the end of the first week of the course, we heard that the medical students were inviting the psychology and law students to a lecture by Ola Raknes on the subject of "The German Character".

Before I describe what happened at this lecture, I must first briefly describe my everyday life. My husband had old-fashioned, authoritarian views about child-rearing, and it was not easy for me to constantly stand up for my children's freedom to express their emotions. For example, I was busy laying the table when my younger daughter Mona Lisa, then one-and-a-half years old, suddenly threw herself onto the carpet in a tantrum, screaming and stamping her feet in a fit of rage. My husband was furious, threatened to hit her, and told me to put her to bed without dinner. I picked her up in my arms and carried her upstairs. She was trembling, and kept gasping between each breath: "I only want to be nice, be nice to my mummy." I was very moved to see how deeply this little being was shaken by her emotions, and how full of love she was. I had protected her. Now I realised that she was unhappy, that she became so furious because I had not had enough time for her, because she could not show me and give me all her love. Similarly, on many other occasions, I discovered my compassion for children who are not understood and are overcome by their emotions. These daily experiences confirmed and strengthened my urge to protect the emotional life that was so seldom respected.

And so I went to hear Ola Raknes's lecture. I was immediately impressed by this huge bear of a man with his direct and natural way of expressing himself. He was not only an established psychoanalyst, but also enjoyed a reputation as an eminent philologist. As I listened to his analysis of the German character, I was surprised to realise that his remarks could apply equally well to my own family. That was it in a nutshell: the authoritarian character! Then, at the end of the lecture, a law student got up and declared that all Raknes's ideas were worthless: classical education was a good thing, our society was built on solid foundations, and past centuries had proved the value of the authoritarian educational system. He added that no one had the right to carry out "experiments" on children.

I was swept by an irrepressible anger, because the truth was exactly the opposite: throughout all those past years people had been carrying out "experiments" on children to turn them into miniature adults. But Ola Raknes's progressive ideas would give children the chance to grow up without having their spirits broken. Before I even realised what I was doing, I found myself standing on the platform, waiting to speak. For a young wife and mother like myself, speaking in public was something unheard of. The president of the association of medical students applauded and exclaimed: "A woman! Extraordinary!" But as I stood there facing the audience, I found that I had no idea what to say! My compassion, my enthusiasm, my anger at this law student who did not understand anything at all had brought me to this point, and now I was lost for words! The only image that came into my head was some plants I had put in the dining room that afternoon.

So I looked at all those students and said to them: "You describe the new methods of child education described by Ola Raknes as "experiments", but the truth is exactly the opposite: during all those centuries you talk about you have been destroying children, you have crushed them instead of helping them to develop into free human beings. That's why there are so many social problems! It's as if you have a seedling and you cover the place where it is meant to grow with stones; it will push its way up bent and twisted." I was greeted by thunderous applause. Ola Raknes declared that he was very impressed by my answer and by the profound understanding that I had shown. He thanked me publicly. After the lecture we talked for some time, and I confided in him that I wanted to become a vegetotherapist. He told me: "You can begin training with me whenever you like. I do have a two year waiting list, but you will be welcome." So Raknes opened the door to me; and when he learned my name, he revealed that he was also a friend and neighbour of my grandfather.

I began my training just a few days later, since I was extremely eager to become a vegetotherapist - even though I actually had very little idea of what vegetotherapy was! But I was still inspired by the fantastic experience which I described earlier. And in the end it was all very simple, for the personal therapy itself was the training - the best training that a therapist can have.

Ola Raknes lived in a very beautiful spot near the harbour. He worked from home, in a small room (with a gigantic couch) which could only be reached by going through the bathroom. Later I realised that this was to help reduce the noise - for noise is always a problem for vegetotherapy practitioners. Such a small room and such a huge man - everything conspired to create an intimate atmosphere. I had married young and had had no sexual experience before my marriage; I had simply moved from my father's protection to that of my husband. Now I felt the strange sensation of being a young girl alone with a man in a small room. I did not feel very comfortable. He told me to lie down, which did not help matters. Next he added that many clients took off their clothes. Things were going from bad to worse! Then the therapy began, with Raknes encouraging me to talk about myself. Next we concentrated on my breathing: "Imagine that you are a jellyfish", he suggested. And with these simple instructions he set the process in motion. "Imagine that you are a jellyfish... let the breathing and the movement come..."

Two things made a lasting impression on me. The first was the personality of Ola Raknes himself: he was a man capable of accepting everything, and he radiated a sense of absolute security. He had the gift of understanding everything, loving everything, he was tolerant and non-judgmental, and he had infinite warmth and patience. To me he was the healthiest person I had ever met. The second thing which so astonished me was being told to let my body breathe and move like a jellyfish. I had read a certain amount about a psycho- analysis, but I had never imagined that the therapy could be anything like this.

So I let my body move with my breathing, and I found that my head moved forward and my chest sank down as I breathed out. It seemed to be a movement of pulsation, and although I found it difficult to begin with, I gradually entered into an intense dynamic process. I was truly amazed to discover that I was absolutely free to do or say whatever I liked. Indeed, one of the instructions that Raknes gave me during my therapy was: "Try to find out what you want to say or do, and simply let it express itself. But if you want to break the window, you will have to pay for it!" This was an unimaginable possibility: I could even break his window without being rejected. I would simply have to get it mended.

Ola Raknes was a man in whom the qualities of understanding and love were coupled with a good grasp of reality. At the same time he was blessed with such stature that nothing could throw him off balance. During the therapy sessions he would often place his hand on my stomach - but only later did I realise that he had the hands of a healer, radiating currents of energy. At the time, though, it occurred to me that my father-in-law was paying for my therapy, while in my mind what was actually going on was close to adultery! I imagined that Raknes had only one thing in mind: to seduce me. In Freudian terms, this was a typical example of transference. But then Raknes told me the following story: while treating a woman patient, he had touched her with his hands, but had avoided all contact with her chest. Later he regretted his caution, because she developed breast cancer. He believed that if he had also treated his patient's chest, the energy there would have circulated and the cancer could have been prevented. At that time I was not aware of the crucial importance of these phenomena, but I was soon to learn more. The dynamic process which had been unleashed in me progressed further with every session. Until then I had had an absolutely rigid body, without a trace of emotion; but since I thought that everyone else was like me, it did not worry me. Now I was completely amazed by everything that happened to me both during and after the sessions.

On one occasion I felt such an intense sensation of aggression and rage in my jaws that I literally felt like a wild animal. This was of course a further consequence of the "analysis" of my stubbornness. But while the emotional discharge did not arrive until a little while after the "tennis" episode in my first vegetotherapist's therapy room, here everything came to the surface during the session itself, in a totally direct physical reaction. Conscious memories arose later, aroused by the movements of my body. I later read in a book by Raknes that this was precisely the criterion that distinguished Reich's approach from Freud's. According to Freud the memories emerge first, to be followed (often, but not always) by emotions. Conversely, according to Reich's method memories and consciousness are activated through physical expression. I was certainly astounded to discover how many feelings surfaced in me in every session. How could a single body contain so much tension, so much consternation, so many old feelings?

While I was undergoing my therapy with Raknes I also began a period of practical training in a psychiatric clinic as part of my psychology course. The psychiatrists there knew that I was training in Reichian therapy with Ola Raknes, and were very curious to know what exactly it was all about. They associated vegetotherapy with psychoanalysis, and so were particularly eager to know whether my training caused any difficulties in my relationship with my husband. I told them that it did not, but that if I had still been living with my parents I would have had real difficulties there, because my therapeutic process was focused chiefly on my inner liberation from my father, on resolving my conflicts with him. I was extremely glad not to be living with him any longer.

On the other hand, my relationship with my husband was largely protected by the advice that Raknes gave me when my therapy first began: "Never talk to anyone about what goes on during the sessions." My first reaction was one of alarm: "Oh no, something's going to happen here that mustn't be talked about!" But then Raknes allayed my suspicions by adding: "Later on you can talk about anything to do with your therapy to anyone you like; but for the time being you will only get into difficulties in discussions if you do. And don't get involved in theoretical arguments either, because you don't know enough about the subject yet to be sure of avoiding mistakes." Another important principle that he established at the start - and one also employed in psychoanalysis - was not to make any major decisions about changes to marriage, work or life in general during the course of the therapy.

So my life was divided between my children, my husband, my training with Ola

Raknes, my psychology course and my period of practical training at the clinic. But the things I learned in my personal therapy were far more important than anything that I was learning at the university. My work with Raknes turned my views about life, society, child-rearing, human beings and interpersonal relationships completely upside down. The essence of everything I learned was a deep respect for all living beings, all humanity. Raknes never talked about these things; rather, my awareness of them emerged from within me, as I came to comprehend what had been done to me and what people did to children. I saw more and more clearly how things could have been, and how they had actually turned out. I recognised the beauty and simplicity of the heart, and I developed a vision of a society in which every individual, parents and children, superiors and inferiors alike would meet each other in this same tolerance and deep understanding. Even politics could be like this, it seemed to me, if it sprang from the depths of the living, feeling body rather than reflecting a mechanical, rigid system of education and human relationships.

I completed my training with Ola Raknes in 1952, the same year in which I also received my psychology degree. My love for my children had motivated me very strongly to study psychology; but the course material seemed to get more and more theoretical each year, without any scope for practical application. My everyday life with my children and the practical problems which constantly arose taught me how irrelevant theoretical knowledge alone was in practice. On the other hand, I found it even more difficult to apply the things I discovered and learned with Raknes in my everyday life. All my attempts to do so met with determined resistance from my husband and his family. The deep rift between the authoritarian method of child- rearing and the way of self-regulation showed itself most clearly here. For example, my mother-in-law dictated the times at which the baby should be fed, and pressed on me all the rigid advice in which paediatricians believed at the time.

At this point I must explain what exactly is meant by self- regulation. I really came to grasp this concept through a number of practical experiences. For example, I found it virtually impossible to understand the distinction between self-regulation and the educational style known as "laissez-faire". My own behavioural structure was neurotic in that I could not express my own needs directly nor assert myself, and so I adopted a "laissez-faire" attitude towards my children.

But one day I learned a very important lesson. We were in the living room and the children were running completely wild, jumping on the chairs and knocking them over. I could feel anger mounting in me, but in the same breath I was thinking, "I must let them do what they like, otherwise I'll make them neurotic!" I didn't know what they really needed; all I knew was that I must not create any neuroses! I was utterly convinced that if children were not allowed to shout and let off steam freely, they would inevitably become neurotic. So on this occasion, I allowed them total freedom and suppressed my anger. I must mention that I was lucky enough to have a woman working for me as a home help at the time, which made it much easier for me to go through my therapeutic process. I was generally very happy with my daughters and they were very happy with me, but I do wonder how I would have managed if I had had nobody to help me cope with all my family's constant demands. At any rate, the unbelievable chaos in the living room that day was one demand too many and I blew my top. I seized my daughter by the hair and lifted her off the ground. She howled from the pain, and I felt as if all my plans for educating my children were an utter failure, which only increased my rage and despair. I was literally unrecognisable as I shook my daughter in every direction. Finally I became so distressed that I sank onto my knees in floods of tears and begged her to forgive me. At that moment my mother came into the room and calmly asked, "Whatever is going on here? Everybody's in tears and you're all so unhappy! Ebba, you tidy up the cushions; Mona, help me put the chairs back where they belong; Gerda, you straighten out the curtains." And all of a sudden I saw this drama that I had created through my impotence and my "laissez-faire" approach transformed into a co-ordinated activity in which we all co-operated cheerfully. My misunderstanding of psychology and of the right way to avoid creating neuroses had in fact made my children unhappy and neurotic. This episode taught me far more at the time than all my therapy and the psychology books that insisted that children should be allowed total freedom. The dilemma with which I was faced at that time is perfectly illustrated by a drawing published in a psychology journal: it showed a young mother with her baby in her lap and a psychology book in her hand, which was raised in readiness to spank the baby. The caption underneath it read: "To spank or not to spank?" I knew that one was not supposed to spank children... but my family thought otherwise... there seemed to be no solution. But then I realised that it was my own neurosis that made me insist on this "laissez- faire" style of child-rearing that led to so many problems. Once my neurosis began to dissolve, everything became much easier.

After finishing my psychology course, I stayed at home with my children for six months. Later I read a book by the anthropologist Margaret Mead on the culture of the Trobriand Islands, where it was customary for mothers who had been away for a while to spend extra time with their children and give them special attention upon their return, to make up for the time they had spent apart.

Not long after this, I began working in a psychiatric clinic where I was concerned with severe cases of mental illness: schizophrenia, paranoia, epilepsy, hebephrenia (a form of schizophrenia occurring in young people)... this was an important step for me, because I had only encountered milder cases of neurosis during my period of practical training as a psychology student. But now I was working as a clinical psychologist. During this period, Nic Waal founded her institute, where I would have loved to work.

But it was far from easy to get a chance to meet her. Finally I did manage to arrange an appointment with her. She invited me to her home, where she lived with a young doctor, and they were both very kind to me. She also advised me to study physiotherapy, because it was really the best way of getting to know the body in depth. To be sure, I had already completed my training with Raknes, but she still felt that I would find it very useful to know exactly what I was holding in my hands when I was working with a human body. She in fact gave me the same advice I had received from Trygve Braatöy after his lecture, even though I really wanted to become a vegetotherapist. Nic Waal suggested that I might work with the parents of children receiving treatment at her clinic after completing my physiotherapy training. Things did not work out that way; I never did work with Nic Waal.

Instead, I applied for a place to study physiotherapy. There was only one school of physiotherapy in the whole of Norway, and 160 people applied for just 40 places. The fact that I was admitted aroused a certain amount of hostility in various quarters. For one thing, it was a "step backwards" for a psychologist to embark on a course of this kind; and furthermore, some people felt that because I came from a rich family, I should not have taken the place of someone poorer who needed to work far more badly than I did. On top of this, I was so passionately interested in my work and my research that I came into conflict with my bourgeois family over and over again. I often felt as if their narrow views were suffocating me. But I was completely determined to work in this area - to liberate the personality and allow children to develop in freedom. So from then on I went to physiotherapy school from eight in the morning until three in the afternoon, and attended anatomy lectures at the university in the evenings. This did not create any real problems with my children, because I knew it was not the quantity but the quality of the time we spent together that counted. I was so happy to be able to study and make progress in my understanding of the body that I had far more to give to my children. I felt tremendously privileged to be able to study: after all, I had married so young! And the fact that I was ten years older than the other students only made me more conscious every day of this unhoped - for gift.

One day one of my fellow students, Anna, hurt her back doing gymnastics. She was given the customary physiotherapy treatment, but it failed to help her. Then she went to the Bülow-Hansen Institute, and when I met her shortly afterwards she was a great deal better. But when I asked her what they had done to her there, she replied: "I can't tell you!" All she would add when I pressed her was: "Anything I could tell you about it would only lead you into difficulties with your examinations and your daily life at the school." I was agog with curiosity about this method of treatment.

THE BÜLOW-HANSEN INSTITUTE

After passing my examinations I received my physiotherapist's diploma. I had originally planned to go and work for Nic Waal at this point, but now it occurred to me that perhaps I should first go to the Bülow-Hansen Institute for two or three months, to learn the strange techniques they taught there. I had almost forgotten this idea when I met a friend who invited me to a reunion at the School of Physiotherapy. Normally I did not go to these meetings, but that evening I went along. I sat next to Anna, who said to me: "Gerda, I'm going to get married. Would you like to take my place at the Bülow-Hansen Institute, where I've been working for some time?" My answer was an unhesitating: "Yes." To me, the things that went on at the Bülow-Hansen Institute were still a complete mystery, but I could see that the results were excellent.

Aadel Bülow-Hansen had a fine reputation, and so anyone wanting to train or enter into therapy with her generally had to join a long waiting list. I was invited to appear before a kind of jury made up of her staff and Aadel herself. She was very demanding, and although I had imagined that my psychology degree - which represented six years of study - and my training with Raknes would weigh in my favour, they actually had the opposite effect. I believe she finally decided to accept me because she was favourably impressed by what I told her about my methods of child-rearing. Now a whole new world opened up to me: exploring the body, but in a totally different way from physiotherapy. What was more, in order to grasp the very distinctive techniques developed by Aadel Bülow-Hansen I had to put everything I had learned previously out of my mind. She urged me to forget psychology and vegetotherapy, and had very firm views about how a Bülow-Hansen therapist should behave. But the background to all of this should not be forgotten: Reich had been expelled from Norway after a scurrilous press smear campaign and Raknes was his disciple, while Aadel Bülow-Hansen was a very professional, conventional single woman.

Aadel Bülow-Hansen was a physiotherapist and the daughter of a doctor renowned in the most exalted circles. She had been chief physiotherapist at the hospital, in the department headed by Dr Trygve Braatöy, an unusually open-minded psychiatrist. One day she went to see Dr Braatöy and said to him: "I don't know what to do: one of my patients is refusing to do her exercises!" (At that time, physiotherapy was based mainly on physical exercises, not on massage.) "She says she has been going through the same rigmarole for seventeen years with no results. She flatly refuses to start doing them again. What shall I do, Doctor Braatöy?" "Do whatever you think best", was the only advice the psychiatrist would give her.

Aadel Bülow-Hansen returned to her treatment room, at a loss to know what to do with this patient. So she asked the woman to lie on her back, and began to massage her. The massage techniques used in those days always fragmented the body; full body massage was unknown. If, say, a patient had a pain in his forearm, only that part was massaged. However, as Bülow-Hansen was an exceptionally sensitive person, and never worked "mechanically", her massage in fact succeeded in melting her patient's muscular armouring - despite the fact that she knew nothing of Reich's theories on the subject, and had no interest in them whatsoever. In some ways her massage was a parallel development to Wilhelm Reich's ideas, but it owes nothing to him. Her technique was her own entirely "new" invention. After massaging her patient for some time, Bülow-Hansen went back to see Braatöy and reported: "The patient began trembling all over and she felt a tingling sensation all round her lips. What do you make of that?" Braatöy replied: "Have confidence in the patient. She's the one who is suffering, after all." So she carried on working in this way, and unlocked anxieties, feelings and memories in the patient.

These effects of her treatment came as a complete surprise to Bülow-Hansen. She confided in me one day that she would never have reached that point without the warm support that she received from Dr Braatöy. They co-operated closely for years, during which time Bülow-Hansen developed her original and highly effective form of therapy. She also used her method to treat a number of doctors, who were glad to give her their support afterwards. By the time I arrived at the Institute, Aadel Bülow-Hansen had brought together a large staff and numerous students. As the first step in my training, she personally gave me some sessions of her massage.

I should mention here that when I stopped going to Ola Raknes, my therapy was by no means finished; but quite simply, he had gone as far as he could with the methods at his disposal. He finally said to me one day: "Either take a lover, or stop your therapy."

So Aadel Bülow-Hansen's massage sessions were like a continuation of my previous therapy. She demonstrated to me the function of the startle reflex in my own body. This concept of the startle reflex is fundamental to understanding the essence of the method. For example, when I was lying on my back my knees stayed somewhat bent, my back did not relax fully onto the mattress, my shoulders were raised and my arms could not stretch out completely. I needed a cushion under my head because the muscles of my neck were so contracted. And I was most surprised to discover that as Bülow-Hansen worked on my back, my knees bent even more; while when my knees straightened out, my back contracted again. My body was like a see-saw! But by the end of two sessions she had succeeded in making both my knees and my back rest flat on the mattress. I was astonished: this was the first time I had encountered the concept of postural change. This concept became very important to me, although it had never been so much as mentioned during my therapy with Raknes. At the same time, new energies were moving in my body. I had never felt anything like them before, even during my sessions with Raknes. One day a violent pain ripped through my back. Soon afterwards my whole body began trembling and I felt intense currents of energy rising within me. It was an extraordinary experience. I received a massage session once a week, but it produced results to marvel over throughout the whole of the intervening week!

Aadel Bülow-Hansen's approach opened up a whole new way of looking at things, even from a Reichian perspective. It is interesting to note that Reich arrived at the body by way of psychoanalysis, while Bülow-Hansen arrived at psychology by way of physio-therapy. Two totally different points of departure that together form a clear polarity. Psychoanalysts enjoy high social status and command large fees; physiotherapists are at the bottom of the ladder and are paid modestly. But even though she charged very little for the treatments given at her Institute, Bülow-Hansen's therapeutic successes had earned her a high reputation.

So now I was undergoing the second phase of my therapy, which had been interrupted when I went to study physiotherapy. I was constantly amazed by everything that came up, especially by the unfamiliar emotions. All of a sudden I found myself reacting spontaneously. Words shot out of my mouth before I even had time to think about them - and until then, I had always been such a quiet, reserved person! While Aadel Bülow-Hansen was massaging someone, she always kept a close watch on their diaphragm. Her massage covered the entire body, but her aim was to release the energy blockage in the diaphragm. She never explicitly mentioned breathing as part of the therapeutic process, but her massage produced spontaneous, unconscious breathing. Eventually we arrived at a point where my hips began to tremble. However, my breathing remained firmly under my conscious control. Aadel Bülow-Hansen was baffled by the failure of the unconscious breathing to appear, and finally told me that she could not continue working with me on her own. Instead, she felt that I should begin seeing a psychiatrist trained by her: Dr Houge. This way, I would have two treatments in parallel: she would carry on working on my body, while Dr Houge would give me psychotherapy. So I underwent a new and very complete training programme.

Indeed, anyone who wanted to work at the Bülow-Hansen Institute had to undergo extensive preparatory training. First there were three months of individual massage treatment, twice a week in the beginning and once a week after that. After this the trainee was allowed to treat six cases under supervision, and finally he became a fully-fledged masseur. The six patients whom I treated under supervision reacted so remarkably that I found myself becoming more and more fascinated by this method of treatment. I became so passionate about my work that I completely forgot about Nic Waal. Each time I went to tell Bülow-Hansen about my patients' reactions she would smile and say something that confirmed my "discoveries", then explain to me what I should do in the following session. I came to realise that this treatment demanded everything that the therapist had to give; it was an even more active way of working on the body than the methods developed by Wilhelm Reich.

Meanwhile, I was also going to Dr Houge for psychotherapy once a week. For many weeks I told him all about my family situation and my relationship with my in-laws. Then one day he said: "We can carry on talking about your family like this until the end of your life. But now we're going to pay attention to your breathing instead." So I lay down on the couch. He touched my head very lightly, then laid his hands under my body, on my back. As I lay there breathing freely, all of a sudden my body spontaneously began writhing like a snake. We were both astonished, for Dr Houge himself did not have much experience of this kind of treatment. He had told me that I would be an "experimental" case for him. Now, as my body continued to move sinuously, I remembered reading a description of something similar in a book by Braatöy, which he identified as the orgasm reflex. But I felt neither shame nor pleasure in these spontaneous movements. Finally, after several minutes of this, I asked my therapist: "May I take a rest now?" and he exploded with laughter.

From that session onwards, Dr Houge and Aadel Bülow-Hansen began co-operating in a remarkably effective way. Her massage would bring me to a point just prior to abreaction, but she would not allow me to abreact or let the serpent-like movements appear. Each time she would stop the massage before my tears began to flow. She always knew when to stop because she kept in complete contact with me and my breathing; when the trembling surfaced she would stop and let it subside. At that point I was ripe to go to my psychotherapist. The massage gradually dissolved my muscular armour, and a dynamic pulsating pressure grew up inside me. The material released by Bülow-Hansen's massage was so strong that I remained in intensive psychotherapy for more than three years. I dug deeper and deeper to uncover alternating layers of aggression and sexual desire. The method used by my therapist was most unorthodox. He was a psychiatrist, but he had been trained in body techniques by Bülow-Hansen and had himself undergone her massage treatment.

The revelation that astonished me most during my therapy was the moment when I remembered how my parents had forced me to eat. The memory was accompanied by very intense sensations: they had pinched my nose shut and held my chin to make me swallow. I relived the feeling of terror: "They're going to kill me!" I already knew that I had experienced several traumas related to food in my childhood. For example, my father wanted me to have beautiful teeth, and so during my early childhood I was only allowed to eat black bread - then believed to be very good for dental health - until my large intestine rebelled and I developed acute colic. My father also insisted that I eat everything put in front of me. If I left a dish he made sure it was served to me again at each meal, and nothing else, until I had finally managed to gulp it down.

In those days my father was very interested in oriental philosophy. One of his favourite sayings came from a Tibetan monk: "Give me a child from its birth to the age of two, and I will shape it for life." And now it was as if Raknes, Bülow-Hansen and Dr. Houge were together doing everything in their power to refute the monk's claim and my father's wish. But they virtually had to use a pickaxe to dig me out; so much had been imposed on me ever since early childhood that now it was embedded not only in my character, but in the very substance of my body. My father had insisted that his daughter should be in excellent physical condition, insensitive and functional, well educated and well behaved, never opposing his ideals or his authority. Defenceless in my own structure, I fought against any change that the massage therapy might bring; or rather, my body fought it. I was so heavily "armoured" that my conscious desire to change was barely strong enough to overcome the changes my father had brought about in me.

In the end the therapy won the battle. The results it produced were marvellous, and the experience left me with a much deeper understanding of everything that my patients went through. It was through daily practise of this form of massage that biodynamic theory came into being. Aadel Bülow-Hansen asked me to write up the theory of her treatment, as she did not enjoy that side of the work: she preferred expression and exploration. I first collected her theories on the startle reflex and postural change, and then I began to develop my own theories.

Note: The Startle Reflex Pattern

The best illustration of the startle reflex is the involuntary reaction to a pistol shot: the whole body flinches, there is a predominant contraction of the flexor muscles, and the breath is sucked in sharply and held.

This reaction typically occurs in all situations of acute danger in which we are exposed to a sudden shock bringing with it physical, emotional or mental stress. It represents an essential protective mechanism for the organism, since any action must be preceded by contraction. This is particularly clear when we look at animals' reactions; when they receive a shock, they instantly ready themselves to fight or flee. Their energy is concentrated to the maximum in their contracted muscles. Virtually the same process goes on in human beings in all situations that they perceive as life- threatening in some way: and the stronger the contraction of the whole muscular system, the more potential energy is available for taking appropriate action.

Once the situation has been neutralised, the body reverts to its original state of balance between contraction and expansion, and the functional harmony of the muscular reactions and the rhythm of breathing is restored.

However, this cannot happen until the emotional expression needed to create an outlet for the action of the antagonists (a reaction of the extensor muscles and a corresponding out-breath) has also taken place. If this release is somehow prevented from occurring, the natural biological rhythm is interrupted. The organism then develops weaker startle reflex reactions accompanied by muscle tension, restricted breathing, and finally postural changes. Now the flexors and the respiratory muscles - especially the diaphragm - become permanently stuck in a state of slight contraction, as if the cause of the shock were still present. Since the startle reflex cannot be sustained for long periods, the body attempts to relax and regain its equilibrium. But this equilibrium will give way to tension again if the normally adequate reaction of the antagonists cannot produce an equivalent degree of relaxation.

And so unresolved situations of this kind can lead to a state of repression with the following physical symptoms:

- A slight tendency to breathe in
- A slight disturbance to the muscle tone
- A slight postural change
- A slight "anxiety tension" in the diaphragm.

Together, these symptoms represent the "somatic compromise". In chronic cases, this compromise generally takes one of two contrasting forms: there is the hypertonic type, characterised by a loss of flexibility and rigidity of the flexor muscles, and there is the hypotonic type, in whom the extensors have become over-stretched and soft. The neurotic organism often displays a combination of both these types in a mixed structure.

MASSAGE AS A FORM OF PSYCHOANALYSIS

The vegetotherapy I had undergone with Ola Raknes involved no massage. It could best be described as analytical psychotherapy coupled with body and breathing exercises, if one could call them exercises at all. I would rather say that the experience of the body and the inner process was put into focus, and that at times suggestions were given to surrender to certain movements or breathing impulses. Raknes concentrated on an essential part of Reich's therapy, called "orgonomy", the purpose of which is to free orgone energy from psychological repression. I was not familiar with orgone therapy at that time, but, in retrospect, I feel that a major part of Raknes's work was that of an orgone therapist. Orgone energy (which I now call "bioenergy") can be transmitted to the client by the therapist's consciousness of it, and to a larger extent by the touch of the therapist's hands. Raknes had this touch and this consciousness, and he was able to convert Reich's theories into practice in a very simple and direct way. I know now, as a Reichian analyst myself, what an incredible dimension direct work with life energy gives to therapy and healing. As my understanding of therapy grew, I came to appreciate Raknes's approach more and more. His work was close to psychoanalysis in spirit; its essence was the liberation of life energy from psycho-sexual repression. To him I owe the re-awakening of my feelings and my spontaneity. But it was the massage work of Aadel Bülow-Hansen that reached inside my muscular armour and changed my character pattern once and for all. She helped me to recover my sensuality and my sense of myself. My experiences during my training with her were completely new to me. I had never previously thought of human beings in terms of muscular tension, breathing and postural change. On the other hand, nor had I read Wilhelm Reich and his theory on muscular armouring, for Ola Raknes had said to me: "You must not read, only explore and experience."

The fact that it is possible to influence the unconscious and the emotions by massage was a great revelation to me. So too was the discovery that the human organism is capable of repressing emotions and conflicts by muscular tension and by chronic contrac-tion of the diaphragm. I came to understand that the body carries out its process of repression from the top downwards, from the surface towards the depths of the body, towards the pelvis and the legs. When I massaged a patient's legs, often my work would produce reactions in his face and emotions would rise up in his throat. Then the patient would need to speak about his feelings; often he would cry or sob, and so release the feelings boiling up from within him. Specific problems might be dealt with, such as difficult life situations, marriage problems, the loss of family members or close friends. During the sessions, patients often remembered painful - and at times traumatic - experiences from childhood. They would then abreact the emotions the original situation had generated, as if it had just happened.

I greatly valued my patients' trust in me and the help and understanding I could give them. I was a trained psychologist and had myself experienced abreactions while undergoing analysis. In this respect I was different from my colleagues at the Bülow-Hansen Institute, where physiotherapy was strictly segregated from psychotherapy. In the clinic I worked solely with massage; if emotions came up during the session, we were instructed to stop the physical treatment immediately and refer the patient to the psychiatrist. But in my independent work at home I dealt with both aspects. In this way I had a great opportunity over the years to see how close a relationship there is between the muscles, breathing and emotions.

One of the first things that struck me was that the body literally "encapsulates" [1] emotions and stressful experiences by making the muscles so rigid that the contractions become chronic; the repressed emotion is held intact by the muscular tension itself. But by working methodically on these areas of permanent tension, the encapsulation dissolved and the repressed emotions of the stressful experiences "came back to life", so to speak.

The process of emotional encapsulation is a fascinating and complex phenomenon, and one that played a central part in my research for many years. Not only does it explain the physical and vegetative process of repression, but it also helps to explain the associated psychodynamic process when repression is re-awakened during therapy. It provides the key to understanding the success of Bülow-Hansen's treatment. Yet neither she nor my other colleagues were interested in discussing what actually took place in the body depths during and between the massage sessions. We learned the method, we followed the rules we were given, we got excellent results - and that was that. I was alone in asking these questions, exploring the method and theorising about the answers.

What surprised me was that it was possible in many cases to cure really neurotic people without psychotherapy. Doctors and psychiatrists sent their neurotic patients to the Bülow-Hansen Institute, and after treatment we sent them back for re-examination. And the doctors and psychiatrists were surprised by the results, but very satisfied with them. They became more and more interested in the Bülow-Hansen treatment, so that our waiting list kept getting longer and longer. The institute preferred to take people suffering from a chronic neurosis with numerous psychosomatic symptoms that no one had previously succeeded in relieving. Some of the patients who came to us had spent fifteen or twenty years going just about everywhere and trying treatments of every kind, all in vain. So it was tremendously gratifying to work at the Bülow-Hansen Institute, because we cured people whom no one else had been

1 We use the term "encapsulation" to designate the process of armouring or enclosing which keeps the energy static, as though encapsulated.

able to help! The clinic operated on an out-patient basis: patients came to us for one treatment session a week. Aadel Bülow-Hansen had originally envisaged giving them one session a day, but experience proved that, far from being more effective, more frequent treatments interfered with the dynamic process. It appeared that a certain lapse of time was necessary for a physical dynamic to emerge from the depths of the soma.

I was fired with enthusiasm during this period. More and more I was coming to understand what Freud meant when he said: "There is a frontier between the soma and the psyche that no one has explored yet, and it will be up to those who continue my work to embark upon this exploration." As I saw it, we were working on the soma and so setting in motion a dynamic process that transformed the psyche. The Bülow-Hansen treatment was truly a voyage of discovery through regions as yet unmapped. Bülow-Hansen was mainly interested in refining her new techniques, and left the development of the theory to me. As I did so I felt, both then and for years to come, all the excitement I imagine Stanley and Livingstone must have felt as they hunted for the source of the Nile. I was so passionately involved in my work that, immersed in it, I forgot Nic Waal, Ola Raknes and Wilhelm Reich almost completely. The discoveries I made in my therapy with Aadel Bülow-Hansen and the things that happened to my patients each day overwhelmed me with a flood of theories which I had no idea how to relate to the theories in force at the time. Only gradually, over the course of years, was I able to sift all this information to develop the theory of Biodynamic Psychology.

There seemed to be no bounds to my enthusiasm. Every day I gave between twelve and fourteen hour-long massages, yet every evening I was so full of vitality I longed to go out dancing! I did not feel tired in the least: my work was so absorbing that it energised me. But in fact I went home, took a bath and then sat quietly, dressed all in silk, keeping my husband company; for he loved to have a "Dresden doll" by his side. But as I meekly sat there, I was actually busy incubating my ideas: questions, answers, observations, hypotheses, proofs. My husband rarely spoke, so I had plenty of time and leisure for thinking, writing down my impressions and working out my theories.

One observation I had made was that people encapsulated their conflicts by changing their posture. Postural change was a fundamental concept in the vocabulary of the Bülow-Hansen Institute. The aim of our treatment was not only to make muscular tensions disappear, but also to transform the patient's neurotic posture (chronically contracted due to a loss of elasticity in the muscular tissues) into a normal, harmonious posture. Dr Braatöy had written: "Every postural change engenders a revolution", and we saw his assertion confirmed every day in our work. The goal of our treatment was to dissolve the patient's neurotic tendency to hold his muscles constantly flexed and restore his capacity to extend them completely. The massage worked on the posture and the personality at the same time. Aadel Bülow-Hansen explained this in the following way: originally the flexor and extensor muscles are in equilibrium. However, as the individual experiences conflicts where he is unable to abreact or to breathe freely, the resulting process of repression in the body causes his muscles to get shorter and shorter. This process of muscular shortening gradually leads to a change in the skeletal muscular structure and the connecting tendons, with the flexors starting to overrule the extensors. Over the years the body adapts to the flexion pattern, and the pain and discomfort caused by this contraction of the flexors (and by the repression of emotions) actually bring about a change in the position of the bones themselves. The entire skeletal structure is forced to deform itself to follow the chronic contractions of the muscles. This is how postural changes are produced in our civilisation. Stress, coupled with the inability to react and abreact, produces muscular contractions to hold back the free flow of emotional energy; the contracted muscles then bring about postural deformation.

This permanent flexion pattern is the person‘s "neurosis". Within the muscular tension lie emotional conflicts, encapsulated in an inactive form. The person no longer feels the emotional pressure, nor even remembers the conflict or the stressful situation, but he unconsciously avoids any reminders of the painful experiences of the past. So he builds up a corresponding character behaviour pattern which works together with the flexion pattern to keep both the memory of the situation and the corresponding emotions far removed from consciousness. Gradually the person‘s emotional energy becomes static, held in place by the muscles we call "suppressors", and so no mental energy is needed to maintain the pattern of physical repression. This is an unfortunate, if ingenious, way to neutralise conflicts. With similar ingenuity, the emotional charge that was aroused in the original stress situation and then repressed retreats back into the depths of the body, where it is neutralised.

It seems to me that this process of encapsulating emotional conflicts is analogous to the process by which the body tissues encapsulate harmful bacteria in a sheath of calcium in tuberculosis. Just as the tuberculoid encapsulation may dissolve by itself and the bacteria become active again, so memories, feelings and inhibited impulses may emerge from the body depths as the muscular armour encapsulating them dissolves. We can therefore talk about "latent psychodynamics" in much the same way as we talk about "latent tuberculosis" or any other latent illness involving the encapsulation of bacterial and toxic substances in the body tissues. During the process of encapsulation and rigidification the muscles change in consistency: they lose their elasticity and harden like cement. A person can live his whole life with encapsulated bacteria in his tissues without them ever becoming "alive" and active, providing his immune system is strong enough. Likewise, a neurotic person can live his whole life without ever coming into contact with his anxieties, fears, repressed feelings and memories. He is effectively "solidified" in his flexion pattern, and unless he actively seeks to "get in touch with himself" and his "real personality", or some situation in his life robs him of his "neurotic equilibrium", he may never feel what we call "psychodynamic pressure". As with tuberculoid encapsulation, it is when the body's defences fail that the repressed material becomes active and the latent symptoms manifest themselves. This can happen as a result of severe stress in everyday life; exposure to trauma or physical exhaustion can break down a person's neurotic equilibrium and muscular armour, so that the encapsulated emotions start to emerge from the body depths. Once the muscular contractions have relaxed and the energy encapsulation has disappeared, the process is identical to the one described by Freud: when repression fails and the defences fall, the neurosis or psychosis makes its appearance.

As a psychologist I was fascinated each time I could combine Freudian theories with my experiences of Aadel Bülow-Hansen's muscular treatments. I realised there is an inner dynamic - a psychodynamic - in the body that can force suppressed feelings to the surface (into consciousness). Until this happens, however, the feelings are held intact by the suppressor muscles and encapsulated in the muscular and postural structure. This encapsulation takes the form of infiltrations of biochemical by-products in the muscle tissue which, together with the chronic tension of the suppressors, change the muscle consistency and make it increasingly hard and insensitive over the years. This forces the whole bone structure to slowly adopt a more bent and contracted posture. In this way the person literally "embodies" his neurosis. And so we can see how emotional repression and muscular armour are closely interrelated in the neurotic posture, and how the character forms according to the neurotic changes in the body itself. The goal of our massage work was to loosen the encapsulation held in the muscle tensions gradually and carefully, without releasing too much of the psychodynamic material underlying the repression.

I developed these theories, which are the foundations of biodynamic psychology, while working daily as a masseuse at the Bülow-Hansen Institute. During this time I was working neither as a psychologist nor as a psychotherapist, and I used none of what I had learned at the University and with Ola Raknes. In my thoughts, however, I was making the synthesis all the time.

At the Bülow-Hansen Institute we constantly transformed postures. And the effects of our work went far beyond simple, mechanical postural changes alone: for the neurotic reflex of contraction was dissolved and replaced by the capacity for complete extension. As a result of this transformation, the neurotic tendency to hold back everything on the psychological level gave way to spontaneity. Indeed, our patients were often astounded by the spontaneity of their own reactions.

I myself changed more psychologically as a result of the Bülow-Hansen massage treatment than I did during my Reichian therapy with Ola Raknes. The postural change which the massage produced liberated my diaphragm, and my emotions surged up. I surprised myself constantly by saying things even before I was aware of thinking them, like a child. All of this had a dramatic and lasting effect on my relationship with my husband. He was an authoritarian character and I had always been submissive. But now I spontaneously started acting differently, and the familiar patterns of our relationship changed as well. For example, one well-worn drama that we played out over and over again was the battle of the cinema. I adored films, but my husband did not share my enthusiasm. So I would suggest hopefully: "Let's go to the cinema!" and now and again he would agree, but only on condition that we went to see a particular film. If his choice was not being shown that day, he would refuse to see anything else. "Can't we see another one?" I would plead. "No", he would reply flatly. "We are not going to the cinema today." The argument never continued for long, and I always gave in - before my therapy with Aadel Bülow-Hansen. But during the therapy, my will, which had been so thoroughly crushed in my childhood, started to reassert itself. I could not be obedient any longer, I could not go on restraining myself, and I rebelled: I went through a phase of voicing my feelings freely and holding nothing back. Every little issue became a big drama in this process of liberation, and each battle ended with my saying that I wanted a divorce.

After some time, the violence of my reactions subsided somewhat. Now, when our familiar conflict commenced, I could simply say calmly to my husband: "If you don't want to go to the cinema, I'll go by myself." I had changed so much that I no longer played my role of the submissive wife, and in turn he was able to stop playing his authoritarian role. Our relationship became much easier. The difference was extraordinary! Previously I had had to fight for everything, and in consequence he treated me as a hysteric; but now I simply said to him: "I'm doing this or that", and the very tone of my voice left no room for discussion. By liberating my body, the massage treatment had also given me much greater freedom in my relationships. Its psychological effects were fantastic. For me it was very important to have gone through this experience, because it enabled me to understand my patients better.

Sometimes we received the strangest telephone calls at the Bülow-Hansen Institute. One morning the husband of one of my patients called to complain that his wife seemed to be undergoing a complete personality change. "She was always so submissive, so gentle, so easy-going, and she always did whatever I wanted", he told me. "Now she has turned into an absolute fury!" Each day, as soon as he got home, his wife had taken to expressing all the resentment that she had been storing up over the years. It must be said that this woman had been suffering from severe anxiety for a very long time. Now her anxiety had disappeared, but instead the anger behind it was flooding to the surface.

Another patient was married to a policeman. When she first came to the Bülow-Hansen Institute, her anxiety was so great that she could not leave her house without being accompanied. During the course of the treatment she, too, experienced a dramatic personality change. But when people asked her: "Whatever is Mrs Boyesen doing to you?" she could only reply: "She just does that" (gesturing with her fingers). She was unable to explain the treatment more clearly. And indeed, I did simply do "that", making a certain movement with my fingers while touching the muscle. One day, the policeman telephoned in bewilderment to ask me: "Whatever have you done to my wife? She has always been the most loveable and sweetest person on earth. She never protests, and she always agrees with me no matter what I say or do. But this morning, she disagreed violently with me. I became terribly angry, and as I left the house she opened the window and shouted at me: "If you want to understand, telephone Mrs Boyesen!" What on earth is going on?" I explained to him that his wife had been suffering from nervous anxiety for years; now that symptom had disappeared, and her repressed emotions were making their presence felt.

Patients suffering from anxiety neuroses got better particularly rapidly, and the process through which they went was always identical. First came the often explosive chain reactions, the emotions, the memories... and then the illness simply vanished. I was amazed to find that even the very first patients whom I treated under supervision made an excellent recovery, despite my inexperience. And every day I continued to marvel as I saw, over and over again, the living proof that neurosis really could be cured with the hands alone! But when I tried to talk about the Bülow-Hansen treatment to psychologists, doctors or psychiatrists, to physiotherapist colleagues, or even to my brother-in-law, who was a surgeon, none of them was willing so much as to listen, for they simply could not believe what I had to say. Every time it was the same story: I would begin talking about the massage treatment that cured neurosis, and they would hurriedly change the subject.

During this period, I attended psychology conferences quite often. Aadel Bülow-Hansen once said to me: "It must be strange for you to take part in discussions with your colleagues, knowing that you have knowledge and experience that the others do not have and do not want to know about!" In fact, I found myself becoming more and more isolated. In the beginning I could still talk to my colleagues at the Bülow-Hansen Institute, or enjoy fruitful exchanges of ideas with Aadel herself, with whom I was on excellent terms. But even here I soon learned that some subjects were taboo. Aadel was happy to discuss practical aspects of the treatment and her own theories. But she disliked "psychologising", so neither she, nor anyone else for that matter, was willing to hear, understand or recognise the theories that were slowly maturing within me.

And so the theory of biodynamic psychology developed in silence and solitude.

Many people came to the Bülow-Hansen Institute when their neurotic defence mechanism (the muscular armour) suddenly broke down because of emotional stress, physical overload or traumatic experiences. In such cases, where the "suppressor" muscles (which form the defences) no longer hold the emotional encapsulation intact, the freed energy may cause nervous tension, inner pressure, breathing difficulties, and other psychosomatic symptoms. To treat these symptoms we first had to re-establish the functions of the suppressors, so that the flexors could resume their control over the encapsulation for the time being. Once the patient had regained a state of equilibrium, we then worked to establish a natural tonus and balance between the flexors and the extensors.

Another category of patient also came to the Institute. These people had psychosomatic pains, but in their case the psychodynamic did not impinge upon the nervous system. Although their muscular armour had lost its equilibrium and was causing them physical pain, their emotional encapsulation had not failed. To treat these patients we had to loosen the chronic grip of the suppressors. So the treatment would affect the encapsulation process and nervous symptoms or strong vegetative reactions would appear, which we quickly learned to welcome. As we slowly unlocked the neurotic encapsulation, the underlying psychodynamic was able to emerge with minimal force from the body depths and rid itself of the pathological repression. As a psychologist, I saw this emergence as one of the main goals of the psychotherapeutic process; while as a physiotherapist, I saw it as a psychotherapeutic consequence of the physical treatment. My colleagues saw their task as one of carefully removing the patient's postural defences while changing the consistency of his muscles. The psychological and vegetative reactions that accompanied the treatment were phenomena that were accepted, but not discussed further at the Institute.

It was not clear to us students, nor probably even to the staff, what we actually did and why it was so effective. I do not think Mrs Bülow-Hansen ever understood, or felt the urge to understand, the medical and psychotherapeutic significance of her method. As long as we followed the rules that she gave us, the massage worked. To me, the most marvellous part of the treatment was the moment when a patient's diaphragm relaxed, his breathing rose up into the chest, and his whole body extended to its fullest limits. The contrast was startling; in place of chronic contractions and a bent posture the whole organism sent a flood of energy rushing towards the extremities of the body, and the patient stretched and yawned pleasurably. It was fascinating to watch this dynamic begin of its own accord, from the innermost depths of the body, and set the process of expansion in motion.

One of the most important elements of our work was massage of the facial muscles. Shock, fear and feelings of all kinds are always expressed in the face. If, instead of experiencing these feelings, a person represses them, his facial muscles will stiffen to suppress the outburst. Because of this there are many "hidden" tensions in the face, and we sometimes need to go very deep into the muscles there to release the startle re-flexes. Sometimes, though, a very light touch, such as gentle stroking of the forehead, would succeed in deepening the patient's breathing and produce the wave of extension. It was a principle that Trygve Braatöy had discovered by chance: as he was stroking a horse's muzzle, the animal not only stretched out its neck, but also stretched all four legs, as if in a reflex of well-being. So the aim of our work was to induce this extension reflex. The expansion of energy in the organism automatically reversed the repression - the contraction - on the psychological level. This was the reason why we spent so much time working on our patients' facial tensions.

Another of Braatöy's discoveries also influenced us greatly. He watched a very young baby lying on its stomach and holding its head up; when the baby smiled, its head dropped down again. It was unable to smile and hold its head erect at the same time. Braatöy concluded: "The smile bends the posture", by which he meant that an emotional expression changes the way in which the body is held. Later, when the child was bigger, Braatöy noticed that it could now hold its head up whilst smiling; its neck muscles had become stronger to compensate for the movement. This discovery was a great help to us in recognising the relationship between energy and posture.

We worked constantly to provoke the extension reflex. To achieve this, we needed to dissolve the chronic contraction of the flexor muscles caused by repeated startle reflexes. So we paid particular attention to these shortened muscles, using a special massage technique developed by Aadel Bülow-Hansen. Whenever the patient felt pain during the massage, she encouraged him to breathe and stretch instead of following his habitual pattern of contracting his muscles and holding his breath.

She also used another technique which I developed further, and which I later named the "shock-impulse". This technique has an extremely powerful effect and produces excellent results. Muscular tensions are eliminated. However, the treatment sets off a chain reaction of postural and psychological changes, and it is essential to continue giving the massage regularly each week; otherwise the patient can become seriously blocked. Since the method has clear limitations, Doctor Braatöy drew up a set of guidelines for its use. He insisted that it should not be used to treat hysterics, pre-psychotics, psychotics, anyone whose ego was weak, and most notably depressives. In short, it was a technique to be used very prudently, since it could provoke reactions so strong - pains, high fevers and sudden changes in muscular tension, for example - that they sometimes amounted to healing crises. The process was fascinating. We unwound the case histories of our different patients in reverse, from the present back into the past, like a film projected backwards. Old symptoms reappeared, and the patients went through veritable cathartic crises. Often Aadel Bülow-Hansen would make encouraging comments, such as: "Aha! This patient's old headaches (or acute colic, etc.) have come back again, and that's where everything began! So we're on the right track." We took our patients back to their childhood illnesses, and by doing so we eventually eliminated the source of the illness. Patients came from all over Norway, and even from Sweden and Denmark... It became ridiculous at times: they paid so much to travel so far for a treatment that cost so little!

Aadel Bülow-Hansen was a psychologist in her own way. She taught her students not to interpret and not to psychologise. Aadel was detached, professional, but also very warm. We loved her very much. During that period, as I have mentioned, I spent all my evenings reflecting and meditating on theories. As a psychologist I had learned to view repression as a mental process, and I paid no attention to the body. But while practising the Bülow-Hansen treatment, I discovered not only the repressive function of the organism that was the source of neurosis, but also the therapeutic process that could eliminate the neurosis- a fascinating experience for a psychologist like me. During my therapy with Ola Raknes this process was already very clear to see; but it was still largely psychological, focusing on my feelings of resentment towards my parents, etc. But the Bülow-Hansen treatment approached the problem from an entirely different angle. It consisted solely of muscular massages - a treatment more vegetotherapeutic than vegetotherapy! Yet in fifty minutes of massage, each little tension in the body was touched and treated. It was as if we gradually and methodically "seduced" the resistances on each level: first the physical, then the psychological. We were shaking the emotional encapsulation by gradually undoing the muscular defences. The psychodynamic revealed itself either in the form of psychological processes or of vegetative discharges, or both. Sometimes this happened during the session itself or in the days immediately following it. For many patients, though, it took a certain amount of time to come into contact with the unconscious and the deepest layers of the body.

THE VEGETATIVE DISCHARGE

The most fascinating thing for me was to see that patients could be cured by massage, that their neuroses could be cleared simply by working on the body, in many cases without any psychotherapy at all. Some patients did need psychotherapy to deal with conflict material that surfaced during the muscular treatment. The majority, though, apparently had no need to work out their conflicts emotionally. They seemed to resolve their nervous conditions in an inner, physiological way. From my point of view as a clinical psychologist and a Freudian and Reichian analyst, this was astonishing. I asked myself constantly: how is it possible? Where do the feelings go?

Finally the answer came to me: the key to the mystery is the vegetative discharge. Somewhere in the depths of the body, there evidently exists a mechanism that dissolves neuroses, psychological conflicts and emotions that have not been abreacted. This means that it is not even necessary for an emotional discharge to take place; instead, a biological mechanism completes the emotional cycles on an organic and unconscious level. This idea made absolute sense to me. After all, we all sometimes find ourselves in situations where we are obliged to suppress our emotions; but we are not compelled, robot-like, to discharge and abreact all those unexpressed feelings as soon as we get home!

However, many people are left with residual stress in their system, and this can give rise to nervous or psychosomatic conditions. I was amazed to find that some people, when exposed to similar situations, did not experience any long-lasting effects. In one way or another they managed to discharge the nervous tension organically and so maintain their mental and physical equilibrium. So somewhere, somehow, there had to be a mechanism for eliminating emotional residues. I started searching for this regulatory mechanism, tracking it down like a hunter stalking his prey.

It took me several years to locate it precisely. I only knew that the mechanism I was looking for had two complementary functions: dissolving the impact organically, and resolving the emotional conflicts. I also knew that this mechanism operated in a subtle, silent way, and was more active in some people than in others. The power of the Bülow-Hansen massage methods led me to pose many questions. For example: What is the physical equivalent of psychological repression? What happens inside the organism when you repress emotional energy? What becomes of this emotional charge? Finally, why is it that, when faced with the same situation, one person will become neurotic or experience intense conflicts while another will remain quite undisturbed? This question was an extremely important one, and neither Aadel Bülow-Hansen's theory on startle reflexes nor Reich's theory on muscular armouring, although essential, could provide a satisfactory answer. We were accustomed to thinking only in terms of muscular armouring, but now I started to wonder what other, less visible forms of armouring might be concealed beneath it. I felt I was really doing pioneering work, mapping the frontier between the psyche and the soma that Freud had left to his successors to explore.

From that time on, the link between the psyche and the soma occupied my entire life. One of the answers I discovered was the theory of the vegetative discharge. It became increasingly clear to me that of the patients with severe neurotic symptoms, the ones who recovered best and most rapidly were those who experienced dramatic vegetative discharges. Not emotional, but vegetative discharges were the key. I realised that neurosis in fact developed as a solution to the conflict that arose when a psychological or emotional cycle was not completed with a vegetative discharge, but remained latent in the organism. So the vegetative reaction was the bodily equivalent of the emotion. As I had been very interested in Cannon, James and Lange's physiological theories of emotion when I was a psychology student, I began to analyse the vegetative reactions in terms of the sympathetic and parasympathetic nervous systems, and to see in them the bodily counterpart of the emotions. In therapy it is possible to make repressed emotions reappear; but if the vegetative conflict is not dissolved, the core of the neurosis remains intact. The eminent psychiatrist, the late Dr Trygve Braatöy, said that if by working upon the muscles and the tendons one could influence the inner organs of the body, this would have a radical effect upon neuroses. That was precisely what we did every day at the Bülow-Hansen Institute. We succeeded in curing patients who had tried all sorts of other therapies in vain. So the key clearly seemed to be the vegetative discharge.

For example, I treated an actress who had collapsed on stage. Since that time, she had suffered from a severe anxiety neurosis and was unable to go out of her house. The first treatment I gave her was in the neck and shoulder region, on the upper part of the trapezius muscle, which was particularly hard. When I applied the shock-impulse method, the tense muscle fibres melted like butter under my fingers. My patient suddenly started trembling and shuddering, and shades of green and yellow appeared in her face: all clear signs of a vegetative reaction. During the following week she frequently had feelings of nausea and she vomited. All my patients who suffered from anxiety neurosis had very strong vegetative reactions: trembling, perspiring, stomach pains, nausea, vomiting and diarrhoea. Unpleasant though they were, I was delighted to see these symptoms appear because they meant that the patients were on the road to recovery. These treatments opened up vast perspectives for me across a new terrain as yet unexplored.

I now began to look upon the vegetative discharge as not merely a positive reaction to the treatment, but an actual vegetative abreaction. It was actively involved in the process of dissolving the emotional encapsulation, an essential part of an interrelated dynamic of mental, physical and vegetative processes. Yet whenever I discussed the subject with my colleagues or with psychoanalysts, I was always astonished to find that they were completely unaware of the importance of the vegetative discharge. I remember how one evening, after listening to a lecture by a Jungian analyst, I asked her what she thought about her patients' vegetative reactions. She looked surprised: she had never noticed anything of the kind. My question made no sense to her. Nor did I meet anyone else who was aware of these phenomena and their importance, apart of course from Aadel Bülow-Hansen, who simply used to say: "If nausea develops, stop the treatment, and if the patient starts trembling all over, just ask him to lie on his side." Or: "That's a good reaction, the treatment is progressing well!"

This attitude was fundamental to my daily practice. While I massaged my patients I was now always alert to their vegetative reactions, waiting for the symptoms of a vegetative abreaction to appear. At the beginning of each session, I encouraged the patients to welcome these reactions as evidence of progress in their therapy. We therapists were full of enthusiasm during this period. Whenever the patients complained about their physical discomforts, we were always ready to reassure them: "Oh, has that happened? That's excellent!" Their reactions were an integral part of the "de-neuroticisation" process, and our patients learned to value them as part of their cure.

Many signs of physical change appeared in our patients as their therapy progressed; some, for example, showed a noticeable expansion of the chest. One woman had a dress to which she added different coloured pieces of material to show how much her chest was expanding. Indeed, most of the patients had to buy new clothes during the course of the treatment.

Another particularly noticeable area where many of our patients experienced a postural change was in the shoulders. When someone is afraid, he raises his shoulders and the contraction causes his trapezius muscle to shorten. If the fear persists or is re- experienced frequently, this new way of holding the muscles can gradually become solidified into a neurotic postural deformity, which remains in place even long after the original source of danger has disappeared. And the person himself is not even conscious of his deformity. There is no feeling left in that part of the body. Now the contraction of the muscles and the postural deformity are no longer produced in response to an influx of nervous impulses; instead, the inelasticity of the tissues and the presence of chemostasis cause this part of the body to become so solidified, so rigid. The consistency of the muscles changes: hypertonus or hypotonus develops, depending on the case. So my task as a masseur was to use my hands to change the consistency of these solidified areas, to restore the muscular tissues to their original state of elasticity. And whenever the treatment succeeded, it always filled me with wonder and delight to see a patient's contracted muscles fall back into their original position after a massage. On one occasion I had to work very intensively on a patient in whom one shoulder had dropped, but not the other, because her dressmaker had complained that it was impossible to make her a well-fitting dress. Finally the second shoulder dropped too... and the dressmaker was satisfied!

Another phenomenon that I found particularly interesting was the exhaustion that often overwhelmed patients during the treatment. By observing this phenomenon closely, I gradually came to realise that the organism effectively stores up tiredness in the muscles. The muscles attempt to neutralise this tiredness by making themselves stiff, and so a considerable amount of energy is used to keep the muscles contracted before they eventually solidify. The effort involved in repressing the muscular impulse and suppressing the related emotional charge puts a tremendous strain on the muscles and the whole vegetative system. During the encapsulation process the muscles also change consistency as the emotional residues - the biochemical components involved in the emotional charge - infiltrate them. During massage treatment we change the muscle consistency back to normal, so dissolving the solidification. At this point the stored biochemical residues and muscular fatigue erupt out of the muscular tissues, and the patient experiences vegetative abreactions and overwhelming tiredness throughout the whole body. We call this the "100 years tiredness", because the muscles have been holding on for years and years. As soon as the muscular contraction gives way, the patient immediately - though fortunately only briefly - feels the full weight of the exhaustion to which he has been exposed. The hypothesis that I developed at the time to explain this process was that a factor must exist, a kind of "tiredness hormone", that was immobilised in the organism by the muscular tension but eventually released into the circulatory system during the treatment. (I later gave this mystery factor the name of chemostasis). I compared these phenomena to the findings of the following well-known psychological experiment: when a little blood is taken from a tired dog and injected into the veins of another dog which is not tired, that second dog then also becomes tired. So the blood must contain some kind of "fatigue factor", which is eliminated from the organism via the kidneys and the natural excretory processes. This pattern of exhaustion was particularly likely to appear during "shoulder falls" or other major postural changes.

Sometimes the patients also experienced dramatic vegetative reactions such as diarrhoea. In other cases there were no visible symptoms of change at all, but something was clearly happening in the depths of the body. I was not yet sure of the exact nature of that "something", but it had to be a vegetative reaction that was not dramatic; a gentler, more subtle process.

Another important postural transformation that we often witnessed during the treatment came when the upper part of the body in the region of the collarbones opened up to allow the breath to pass through more freely. We noticed that many people hold their shoulders forwards, with a hollow space - quite deep in some people, shallower in others - under the collarbones. The thorax is flat instead of being "full". But when a patient's respiration succeeded in rising into the chest, this hollow space was filled from the inside, and the thrust of the energy caused the shoulders to open out into the correct position of their own accord. I found it very interesting to observe children, wondering as I did so: "Where does postural change start? How does it work?" I discovered that the starting point of the process was a very slight respiratory block, which created a kind of shadow in the hollow in front of the shoulders. This shadow gradually deepened until it became a cavity. Very intense emotional conflicts or even traumas were always to be found at the root of respiratory blocks of this kind.

During my own therapy, Aadel Bülow-Hansen brought me to a point that went even beyond free and complete thoracic respiration: my back straightened up completely and the position of my head changed. That was when I understood that there was no need to tense my muscles in order to "hold" my back upright; the unrestricted flow of breathing itself holds the back in its correct straight position. So it is possible to "stand up straight" and yet remain relaxed. But the child-rearing practices popular in our Western cultures produce tensions, one of the most common being a contraction of the pectoral muscles. As a result, parents and teachers spend much of their time urging children: "Don't hunch up like that! Stand up straight!" But now, when the children try to straighten up, the effort puts a strain on their spinal muscles, neck and shoulders. And so the body's attempt to counterbalance the original contraction of the muscles at the front actually leads to the development of additional tensions in the back. A painful and chronic pattern of tension is established. The "military" posture appears, together with all its associated psycho-somatic complaints. The body is not free.

The Bülow-Hansen massage treatment reversed this chronic pattern of tensions. The patients' shoulders opened, their backs straightened and their bodies were able to revert to their original, natural condition. The procedure was not complicated: we simply observed where the breathing was blocked and felt the contracted muscles with our fingers. Then, by massaging the blocked areas, little by little we removed all the obstacles that prevented the breath from expanding and moving freely, until the full natural respiratory flow was restored. (I want to emphasise that this method is fundamentally different from bodywork techniques such as the Postural Integration system developed in America. Such techniques often proceed too quickly, without allowing enough time for the vegetative discharge to come into operation and dissolve any blocked energies.)

Once the vegetative discharge process begins to function, the tensions are dissolved automatically at their source. Now the body no longer feels any need to revert to its former tense state. When the therapist follows the pleasure principle a true process of transformation can take place. There are two fundamental aspects to the pleasure principle: the pursuit of pleasure and the avoidance of its opposite, which we refer to as unpleasure. We possess psychological defence mechanisms which help us to avoid the unpleasure the vegetative discharges bring with them. For example, all of us would do almost anything to avoid feeling nausea, trembling, or suffering from diarrhoea or stomach aches. So in fact the main function of the psychological defences is to prevent the cycle of vegetative charge-discharge from being completed. When we repress an emotion, we also inhibit the vegetative discharge; and so we prevent the unpleasant vegetative phenomena from occurring. If the emotion is fear, though, the vegetative symptoms are generally stronger than the defences. An accelerated heartbeat, a feeling of faintness, hot or cold sweats, stomach pains - all these are natural manifestations of the vegetative system that actually endanger us, because they cause us to lose control. But if there were no vegetative charge we would experience no emotion.

What happens during a conflict? A vegetative charge develops, but no corresponding vegetative discharge takes place: the "gestalt" is left incomplete in the vegetative system. The charge is repressed and a neurotic equilibrium is then established. Once this has happened, the therapist treating the neurosis must first provoke the hidden vegetative charge, allowing it to come to the surface, and then encourage it to leave the system in the form of a vegetative discharge. And so the emotional-vegetative cycle is completed.

The vegetative discharge is an essential part of the therapeutic process. If, whilst working to dissolve a patient's muscular armour, the therapist forces the muscles to relax, they will indeed decontract and lengthen; but if the therapist is in too much of a hurry and allows too little time for the vegetative discharge to take place, the muscles will simply revert to their previous state of contraction after the treatment. This was the great secret that I discovered during my voyage of exploration through the borderland between the psyche and the soma: the all-important VEGETATIVE DISCHARGE. Without this abreaction of the biochemical residues of repressed emotions, we can achieve nothing. Unless a genuine vegetative discharge takes place, the therapy produces only an emotional reaction which may be nothing more than a momentary response to the therapist's provocation. No truly therapeutic effect results from this. I personally had very distinctive vegetative reactions. While I was being massaged by Aadel Bülow-Hansen, my body gave off smells so strong that, after my session, the room had to be aired for at least two hours before it could possibly be used again. Bülow-Hansen described these terrible smells as a mixture of fear and aggression. Although I was not conscious of these feelings, they were aroused in the depths of my body. I also sweated so heavily during this period that I had to take several showers a day, and still my "id" continued to smell in spite of everything.

A fourth key figure now joined Raknes, Braatöy and Bülow-Hansen in influencing me deeply: Sigmund Freud, whose works became my favourite reading matter. I was also very interested in Pavlov's work, particularly his experiments in inducing neurosis. In these experiments a dog's behaviour was conditioned as follows: the experimenter showed the dog a circle when he gave it food and an ellipse when it was not fed. Before long the dog began to salivate as soon as it saw a circle, but did not react when it saw an ellipse. Pavlov then progressively made the circle more elliptical and the ellipse more circular until the dog could no longer distinguish between them. The animal then became neurotic. I concluded from this that the dog's vegetative system lapsed into a state of confusion, which was the cause of the neurosis. The interpretation given to Pavlov's experiment by Professor Schelderup in his book, "Neurosis and the Neurotic Character", also supported my views. He argued: "The dog only developed a neurotic reaction because its head was restrained, forcing it to pay attention to the image. If it could have turned its head away, the neurosis would not have developed." So in his opinion it was not the difficulty of the problem that made the dog neurotic, but the fact that it was forced to look at the screen and so develop conflicting vegetative reactions. In another, similar series of experiments in which sheep were presented with maze problems, the sheep did not develop any signs of neurosis. This was because they could move freely.

I received further confirmation of my theories one day, when a psychiatrist who was visiting the Institute after a very long absence remarked to me: "How strange, you don't hear anyone shouting or crying here any more." Her comment puzzled me, because I had never encountered anything of the kind at the Institute. I questioned Aadel Bülow-Hansen, who told me that when she first began her practice she encouraged her patients to discharge emotionally. All the patients - and all the students too - used to shout and sob all the time! But she later decided that the massages should be stopped before the emotional discharge could occur, because she had realised that there was no need for it. Only the vegetative discharge was necessary. Her views confirmed the theory I was developing: that the vegetative discharge preceded the emotional abreaction. It seemed very clear to me that it was possible to dissolve neurosis right to its core, without encouraging crying or emotional release during the treatment. This is not to say that emotional discharge is not important, but it is not always necessary. The physiotherapists at the Bülow-Hansen Institute became very skilled in adjusting and even stopping the treatment if emotions rose to the surface. We also noticed that emotions and mental insights could appear spontaneously during the intervals between treatments (in dreams and in ordinary situations at home or work). In a few cases, where patients had suffered very serious traumas in early childhood, Aadel Bülow-Hansen sent them to Dr. Houge for psychotherapy. There they could abreact their emotions. But the majority did not need this emotional discharge, nor was it appropriate for them.

As Aadel Bülow-Hansen had recognised, the seat of the blockage, the point at which the problem really needed to be tackled, was the muscle. The muscular tension which eventually gives rise to the blockage starts out as a normal emotional and organic reaction to a conflict situation, and should disappear once the situation changes. But, if the conflict continues for long enough, the muscular tensions are maintained and develop into a chronic, permanent startle reflex. Then, because the tensions are not released, no vegetative discharge can occur. So a permanent startle reflex gives rise to a permanent vegetative startle reflex, and all of this must be repressed. "Repression" here refers to the individual's attempt to avoid the unpleasure that the conflict arouses. He tries to fend off the uncomfortable vegetative reaction he fears by bringing into play his psychological defences, which use muscular contraction to keep the psychic energy intact. Unwelcome thoughts, feelings and emotions alike are repressed by a powerful combination of psychological, muscular and vegetative defences, and new behaviour patterns develop. Once the individual's primary aim has shifted from the pursuit of pleasure to the avoidance of unpleasure, his original personality becomes submerged as a secondary personality, with its characteristic armouring, makes its appearance.

In the light of this theory, it was clear to me that the startle reflexes are maintained by the psychological defences until the muscles solidify. Once this has happened, the muscular tension no longer bears any relationship to external or internal conflicts; for now the blockage is established, and all the preliminary stages have hardened into chronic rigidity. Psychic energy is no longer needed to maintain the defences. This process of solidification has very important consequences: the person now begins to display "neutral" energy, but this is accompanied by a tremendous loss of sensitivity. Only when the individual's ability to function well as an integrated whole begins to break down, when the defences cease to operate and some kind of provocation occurs, is the repressed material reactivated. The encapsulation is no longer able to dam the flood of energy and the latent dynamic surges up, accompanied by its retinue of psychosomatic symptoms which produce the "nervous condition". This process fascinated me: I became increasingly eager to understand the relationship between the muscular armouring and the vegetative system.

I now turned my attention to the question of residual tension. At that point I had still read nothing by Reich. Although I was familiar with Ola Raknes's therapeutic methods and was now amassing experience with Aadel Bülow-Hansen's approach, my mind was still divided into compartments and I had not yet succeeded in making the synthesis between the two. It took me a long time to work out exactly how Pavlov and Freud's theories could be reconciled with Aadel Bülow-Hansen's massage methods. Yet I was very certain that when we massaged a patient, we were in very close contact at all times with the Freudian unconscious and the Pavlovian physiological reflexes. However, the task of integrating these different approaches was a particularly difficult one because in Norwegian hospitals, in terms of prestige, the physiotherapist languishes in the basement while the psychiatrist occupies the penthouse suite!

Little by little I came to understand the mechanism by which an incomplete vegetative cycle - which functions in the same way as Freud's pleasure-unpleasure cycle - is maintained in that state of non-completion by a very slight contraction of the muscles. At the outset, when the individual is in a situation of conflict, his muscular tension becomes very pronounced. By the time the situation ends, everything has been repressed. The tension cannot be seen, and the person no longer feels it. All the same, a tiny, invisible contraction - a residual tension - persists in the muscles. It is this minimal residual contraction of the muscles that maintains the repression of feeling and prevents the vegetative discharge from occurring. So whenever emotions are repressed, there is nothing to be seen; the mechanism at work is simply the slight residual tension in the muscles. Only the skilled touch of the masseur can detect these invisible tensions, but they are the key to understanding how repression anchors the emotional energy in the muscles.

I then developed a layer model to describe the structure of the muscular armour. My massage system today is still founded on this theory, which states that it is necessary to dissolve the layers one after another, and so gradually undo the different stages of the startle reflex pattern.

II THE FIRST BIODYNAMIC THEORIES

THE THEORY OF THE VEGETATIVE DISCHARGE

As soon as I understood that this massage technique worked on the body in much the same way as psychoanalysis, I became more and more eager to find out exactly what happens in physiological, organic terms when a conflict is repressed, and when a conflict is dissolved during therapy. This question occupied my thoughts constantly. The main focus of Freud's theory of repression is psychological; but at the Bülow-Hansen Institute I had come to recognise that neurosis could be cured simply and solely by treating the body. I had witnessed countless cures that involved no psychotherapy whatsoever.

All these patients had suffered for years from severe neuro-physiological and neuro-vegetative disorders, and the majority of them had previously undergone some form of psychotherapy or psychoanalysis, but nothing had worked. So now, in an attempt to ans-wer my question, I formulated the following hypothesis: If it is possible to influence the vegetative system, then it is also possible to dissolve neuroses. After all, I had observed over and over again that patients who had vegetative reactions got better very quickly. So my theory accounted for the powerful effect of massaging muscular tensions in the following way: first the massage affected the vegetative system, then the vegetative discharge took place (in the form of stomach-aches, nausea, diarrhoea, etc.), and finally equilibrium was re-established.

At that time I had not yet begun to make any connections between my theories, the Bülow-Hansen massage technique, and Reich's vegetotherapy approach. That may seem rather strange, but I had not yet read Reich's works; while my understanding of vegeto-therapy was strictly limited to the things I had experienced during my therapy with Ola Raknes. But, as I mentioned earlier, Raknes did not massage me at all. His therapeutic approach focused mainly on psychological work combined with breathing practice.

During this period at the Bülow-Hansen Institute we worked exclusively on areas of muscular tension. Our approach was based on the theory that once the neurotic tensions were dissolved, the patient was cured. But while working in this way, I ran into a delicate problem. Three of my patients, whose neurotic muscular tensions I had succeeded in dissolving, fell into such a deep state of depression that they had to break off the treatment. Faced once again with a host of unanswered questions, I was truly perplexed by this development. But as I studied the circumstances more closely, I soon realised that these patients had not had any of the usual vegetative reactions. I concluded from this that if tensions are dissolved without a vegetative discharge, the nervous encapsulation remains intact despite the improvement in muscle consistency. So in certain cases, where all the muscular defences fell but no vegetative discharge occurred, patients would lapse into depression. That was when I really recognised that we were working blindly on the body. I had become extremely skilled at detecting muscular tensions with my fingers, but now a whole new domain emerged about which I knew nothing: the different qualities of muscular consistency. At that point another of Aadel Bülow-Hansen's pupils entered my life: a woman called Lillemor Johnson.

HYPERTONUS AND HYPOTONUS

Lillemor Johnson had done a great deal of work in psychiatric hospitals. Her experiences there had led her to focus on what she called "the absence of tonus" - that is, hypotonus. Her very interesting observations helped me to formulate a number of theories to explain this problem of depression. She had discovered that many patients in psychiatric hospitals suffered from varying degrees of hypotonus. In contrast, though, our patients at the Bülow-Hansen Institute tended to have too much nervous tonus. I became increasingly aware of the complexity of this problem.

One day, as Lillemor Johnson, Aadel Bülow-Hansen and I were sitting together in a hotel bar, Lillemor began to talk about hypotonus. I can clearly remember how hostile both Aadel and I were to her theory about hypotonus, for her views were diametrically opposed to our habitual way of thinking. All the same, I could not ignore the things she was saying, for suddenly it struck me: this was exactly what had happened to my three patients! They had lost their muscular tonus! Hidden beneath the layers of hypertonus there was hypotonus, and it was this hypotonus that triggered their depression. I became completely fascinated by this approach.

Lillemor Johnson's explanation helped me to recognise that beneath a superficial layer of hypotonus there could equally well be layers of hypertonus in the depths of the muscles. All kinds of combinations were possible: for example, there might be hypotonus on the surface, hypertonus underneath it and another layer of hypotonus at an even deeper level, close to the bone; or vice versa. Lillemor Johnson had developed a very interesting method of diagnosis.

My own experience confirmed her theories. As I have already mentioned, I loved to play tennis and was also an avid skier. All this sport had given me very beautiful, shapely legs, of which I was tremendously proud. Once, while I was still a physiotherapy student, one of my fellow-students gave me a vigorous ankle massage. It was extremely painful. But when the teacher asked me whether it hurt, I replied: "Yes, but that's because Miss X is doing a very good job!" He retorted: "No. It's because of a lack of exercise and your age!" I did not understand what he meant. At that time I was only thirty-two years old, and I was convinced that I had excellent legs, solid and strong. But as Aadel Bülow-Hansen massaged my legs and eventually removed the outer layer of chronic hypertonus, she did indeed reveal layers of hypotonus underneath it. My legs lost their beautiful shape, the graceful curve of the muscles. I was very unhappy about this change, but I could understand that a sense of resignation had caused hypotonus to develop in my feet and ankles at a very early age. Later, thanks to all the exercise and sports in which I engaged, a layer of powerful tensions was formed on the surface of the muscles. Once these secondary tensions had disappeared, the hypotonus was uncovered.

More and more, I could now understand Lillemor Johnson's theory of hypotonus in the mentally ill. She said that these patients had almost no tonus, except at one particular spot in the body where there was extreme hypertonus: the area at the base of the skull and the nape of the neck. She called that area "the ring of psychosis": it seemed to be one of the last defences against the unconscious rising up and invading the patient's consciousness to the point where it could overwhelm his ego.

I found this theory extremely valuable, and paid more and more attention to the underlying layers of hypotonus when giving my patients treatment. I had not been aware until then of the importance of hypotonus, because I had never had the opportunity to use massage in my work with psychiatric patients. Now I realised that neurosis is associated with a great number of tensions, whereas in psychosis most of the chronic muscular tensions have disappeared. I was also able to see the analogy between this view and Freud's theories, which state that neurotic and psychotic symptoms originate from the collapse of the individual's defences. But Freud, of course, was referring to the psychological defences; while I was concerned with their bodily counterpart, the physiological defences.

BLOOD CIRCULATION IN THE NEUROTIC ORGANISM

My work at the Bülow-Hansen Institute offered me an extraordinary opportunity to study and learn. Whilst massaging patients for ten hours a day, I was able to make more observations than any doctor, psychologist or vegetotherapist could hope to do, because I worked systematically on all the parts of the body. My sensitivity and my experience grew steadily as the years went by, until eventually I could sense even the tiniest changes in the consistency of the muscles under my fingers and spot even the subtlest changes in posture and breathing.

But now my own personal experiences confronted me with a whole new series of unanswered questions. As I said, I had been very proud of my legs, and my pride had suffered a severe blow as they lost their elegant shape. What was more, the disappearance of the superficial hypertonus from my leg muscles was accompanied by another disagreeable change. Due to the long hours that I spent on my feet each day, massaging patients in an almost static position, the veins in my legs - which had never been visible before - began to protrude. Now, looking back, I can see that this development was the natural consequence of my failure to follow my natural, spontaneous impulse to move: for when the day's work was over, my only desire was to go out dancing. But my husband did not share my enthusiasm, so I suppressed my longing and went quietly home to sit beside him. In doing so, I actually inhibited my natural impulse towards self-healing: for if I had satisfied my urge to dance, my blood and energy circulation would have been restored.

This phenomenon, and one other, finally helped me to understand the role of the blood circulation in neurosis. The second phenomenon was the very intense sensation of combined "pleasure-anxiety" that I experienced while receiving massage treatment from Aadel Bülow-Hansen. The sensations were focused around my mouth: in Freudian terms, I had an oral fixation. At first I felt energy all around my mouth, in the form of tingling. It was neither pleasant nor unpleasant, just a neutral sensation. All the same, it was marvellous for me to feel that something was happening in my body, that energy was moving in me. This energetic tingling was accompanied by swelling in the area around my mouth as a mass of fluid accumulated there. I also felt the same tingling sensations in my chest, which was a revelation for me: normally I had very little sensation in my breasts. I puzzled over these phenomena for some time.

After some months had passed, I finally began to experience the feelings around my mouth and in my breasts as pleasurable. I became aware that I had discovered the sensation of the libido. Pleasure now began to invade my whole body: but at the same time I was also shaken by intense anxiety. The anxiety came welling up from my legs, where deep-rooted conflicts were held in the muscles. Rapidly changing sensations shot through them: one moment they felt as cold as ice, the next red hot. My energy circulation was trying to establish itself, but during this process I had to go through a number of seriously disturbed states as the conflicts anchored in my legs played themselves out. The internal pressure of the libido caused my legs to swell up as it fought its way through the deep layers of resistance, and it also caused the ice-cold feeling. Whenever I went skiing during this period, no matter how much warm clothing I wore my legs stayed as cold as ice.

I was extremely unhappy about the continuing deterioration in my physical appearance. By now, not only had my legs lost their tonus and their shape, but they were swollen and the veins were bulging out. I decided to wear support stockings; but Aadel Bülow-Hansen, who at times could be very authoritarian, forbade me to do so. At first I defied her prohibition, but then the other students warned me that Aadel had said she would not treat anyone who wore elastic stockings, because they restricted the blood circulation. This put me in an awkward situation, because I was right in the middle of the series of massages Aadel was giving me, and needed her help: nobody else could treat me at this stage of my dynamic process and my postural transformation. So there was nothing for it but to swallow my pride and throw away my stockings. Aadel continued to treat me, and the deep process of change continued to unfold; but in my legs I could see no signs of change at all. I was in despair. Whatever should I do? It was then that I heard of a certain Dr Olesen.

A friend who was a doctor specialising in rheumatism talked to me at length about this remarkable man, who lived in Copenhagen and was about eighty years old. I was very interested by what she told me, so without saying a word to anyone at the Bülow-Hansen Institute I set off for Copenhagen to consult him. I had to keep my visit secret, because Aadel Bülow-Hansen had a very strict rule that no one was to receive any treatment other than her massage. My rheumatologist friend had some scruples about referring me to Dr Olesen; she was concerned that if I told him I was a physiotherapist, he would probably refuse to accept any payment from me. So instead we decided that I should present myself to him simply as a wife and mother.

John Olesen was a medical doctor, but he was regarded as a homeopath because he did not use the usual allopathic treatments. "Homeopath" at that time had something of a pejorative sense. I knew little about his method of treatment, except that he worked with a technique that he described as a "pump massage", which mainly affected the circulation of the blood. His treatment acted on the various bodily fluids, on oedema, on cellulite, and above all on what he called the "vein pump". Dr Olesen's experience had taught him that the chief cause of circulatory problems was in fact the vein pump. He said that the level of fluid pressure in the body and the presence or absence of tension could lead to problems with the return flow of the blood and the lymph fluid from the cells. He was convinced that the muscles themselves "pumped" these fluids back into the veins and the lymph circulatory system. So the object of his massage technique was to activate the vein pump and so help the blood to return to the heart and the lymph to circulate, rather than stagnating in various parts of the body. At the same time, his treatment also affected the vegetative nervous system by bringing the sympathetic and parasympathetic systems back into equilibrium.

Dr Olesen's approach interested me greatly, because I could see a connection between his theories and my own. So he gave me a pump massage; and as he did so, I suddenly found myself blurting out something that Trygve Braatöy had said on the subject: "If we can affect the viscera and the intestines through the agency of the muscles and tendons, then we can also cure neuroses in the most direct way". At once Dr Olesen stopped massaging me, stepped back, and asked me in a very serious tone who I was, since clearly I was not simply a housewife and mother. So I confessed my true profession, and my confession marked the beginning of an extraordinarily rich relationship between us. He explained his theories to me, and especially his ideas about cancer. I asked him whether he attached much significance to the breath, whether he watched the patient's diaphragm as he massaged. He said no, the breath was unimportant. He was only interested in the circulation of the blood.

Dr Olesen also spoke about another phenomenon, whose full significance I did not appreciate until two years later: the "transudation pressure" (see page 54), which is produced by an accumulation of fluid in the tissues, and which he identified as the source of nervous disorders and psychopathological symptoms. He was interested in the chemical composition of this fluid, and carried out intensive research into psychosomatic pains. In one experiment he injected a sodium solution into muscular tissue. According to the logic of physiology, this injection should have produced a painful contraction; while according to his own theory psychosomatic pains were the result of tissue contraction. But the injection did not produce any contractions or cause any pain, so he was forced to conclude that another factor, "something else", must be involved in producing these symptoms. He was unable to explain the nature of this "something else", but I realised that the missing factor must be the energetic charge of the fluid. Dr Olesen's sodium solution was energetically neutral, unlike the fluids circulating in the body, which are charged with energy.

At this point my voyage of discovery converged to some extent with the theories of Wilhelm Reich, who described stasis as an energetic phenomenon: energy stasis is a well-established concept in Reichian terminology. So now I also turned my attention to bodily fluids. My interest in this subject had already been aroused while I was working at the Dikemark hospital, because it seemed to me that the bodily fluids are the closest thing to consciousness; that is, the different ways in which the blood circulates or accumulates correspond very directly to the emotional charge in the person. For example, when someone becomes emotional his blood rises to the head; while if an emotional outlet is denied, his face becomes pale. These blood and fluid reactions are more closely related to the ego than the contractions of the muscles, because they are the "carrier" of the emotions. The contractions of the muscular defences have many layers, which may only be uncovered after much therapy, whereas the blood and bodily fluids come straight to the surface with the emotional charge. I found these concepts very useful as I attempted to develop a definition of "ripe" material: that is to say, the phenomena closest to the ego, because they can be discharged and integrated the most easily. While massaging patients I had noticed that two specific phenomena always appeared together and seemed to be related: as soon as a repressed emotional state was ripe (that is, ready to be discharged), an accumulation of fluid appeared in the part of the body associated with the emotion concerned. Where there was oral frustration and aggression, for example, the area around the mouth became swollen.

As time went by my observations continued to confirm this relationship; once emotional energy held in the body had begun to move and had become ripe, it was accompanied by a movement of fluid in the body, particularly in the membranes of the charged area. Now, when I massaged, I concentrated on these subtle changes in the fluid pressure in the membranes. For example, I might focus on a very small, specific point in a muscle that was distended with fluid, which I came to recognise as the product of an uncompleted emotional cycle. As the emotion was repressed, the blood circulation was also restricted and biochemical deposits were laid down. I gave the name of "tissue armour" to the metabolic residues deposited in the body in this way. As the process of repression continues the trapped fluid is eventually reabsorbed, but the tissue armour remains in place. So when the energy begins to move again the process of repression is reversed, but now the tissue armour prevents the energy from flowing freely, and fluid again builds up at the blocked points. In this way the accumulation of energy causes a related accumulation of fluid.

This relationship between fluid and emotional energy means that when the masseur is working on these points where the fluid pressure is high, he is actually working directly with the physical counterpart of the material closest to the ego. I also discovered that these fluid pressure points are not necessarily confined to the muscles: for example, I often worked on very small bumps on the cranium, which has hardly any muscles. Yet very intense vegetative reactions could be provoked simply by massaging these tiny points.

Some patients developed skin complaints, such as inflamed blotches and pimples. Their symptoms were vegetative reactions that were provoked by massaging the pockets of fluid; they were not solely reactions to the work on the muscles. So during this period I was far more interested in the pockets of fluid than in the muscles.

My encounter with Dr Olesen raised a host of new questions in need of answers. At first I was quite unable to integrate the things I had learned from Ola Raknes and Aadel Bülow-Hansen into his theories. The biggest problem was the role of the diaphragm. Raknes and Bülow-Hansen attached great importance to the diaphragm and to muscular tensions, while Dr Olesen had no interest in them at all. When I asked him about this, he replied: "The breath has no particular significance in my opinion."

It was some time before I succeeded in making a synthesis between these differing points of view. Only after I had incorporated the theory of blood circulation (the vaso-motoric cycle, as it is known today) into the model of the neurotic process did Dr Olesen's approach begin to make sense to me. I concluded that the physiological mechanism by which repression operates is an incomplete vaso-motoric cycle: the blockage of a natural impulse. The neurotic organism is unable to eliminate the tissue armour and the various metabolic waste products completely (especially adrenaline and lactic acid).

As I continued to try to discover what was closest to the ego in the body, I observed how, when children get angry, their faces swell a little and turn red. If the process that has been set in motion is then interrupted and repressed before it has reached completion, the fluids that have risen into the face and the metabolic waste products cannot be completely reabsorbed into the circulatory system. Some residues remain in the face, where they stagnate. I likened this phenomenon to breathing: when a person is prevented from expressing an emotion, he holds his breath on the in-breath so that no discharge takes place with the out-breath. No tears, no sounds are released. And so the non-completion of the respiratory cycle means that the vaso-motoric cycle also remains incomplete.

My research now took another direction as I began to develop an electrolytic theory of neurosis. I left the Bülow-Hansen Institute because there was nothing more for me to learn there, and went back to the Dikemark hospital to work as a clinical psychologist. I was eager to work with mentally ill patients. The medical staff of the department in which I worked were excellent: they were true researchers. As soon as I took up my post, the doctor in charge took me to visit a ward for the chronically ill.

My first emotion was one of shock at the sight of these patients' deformed bodies. The doctor explained to me that schizophrenics were now treated with psychopharmaceutical drugs which calmed them, rather than the harsh regime of cold showers and straitjackets that had been necessary in the past. At first I was very impressed by this apparent therapeutic revolution; but I found that I could not ignore the physical deformities shown by so many of the patients. Upon reflection, I realised that the drugs used to control these patients' schizophrenic symptoms created an artificial tissue armour. In mentally ill people most of the muscular defences have been removed (the encapsulation is broken) and the energy has started to flood up from the depths of the body, but no vegetative discharge has taken place. So the artificial tissue armour produced by the drugs creates a dynamic pressure which blocks the upsurge of nervous energy. The result of this drug-induced repression is that the patient becomes calm, but his body becomes deformed. This deformation is evidently caused by the presence of the artificial tissue armour.

I became very interested in the psychological and physical dynamics of energy, which I named "force". At that time I had not yet encountered the concept of bioenergy, so I could not apply it to my observations. But I knew that the schizophrenic patients' deformities were nothing but a severe oedemic condition caused by the mystery X-factor in Dr Olesen's research, and that "force" played a role in this pathology.

Although I was then a clinical psychologist, the doctor with whom I worked knew me very well: he had sent me patients while I was working at the Bülow-Hansen Institute. So he allowed me to try out the Bülow-Hansen massage techniques on some of his psychotic patients. One patient had been autistic for two years. Contact with her was very difficult, as she could not express herself at all. I set to work massaging her, and began to dissolve the muscular tensions. She was a typical psychotic patient: her whole body was hypotonic with the exception of an area of marked tension at the base of the skull, the "ring of psychosis". As I worked I paid very close attention to her breathing, and saw how as soon as she started to breathe freely the blood began to pulse in her neck - especially in the region of the sternocleidomastoid muscles. Each time I stopped the session at that point. But one day, immediately after her treatment, she suddenly began speaking - and she had so much to say that I could only sit down and listen to her. She talked non- stop for two hours about the history of her illness. It was clear that the tensions in her neck had completely prevented her from expressing her emotions, which were now all flooding back at once.

This patient's case opened up tremendous new horizons to me. I asked myself how such a young and beautiful girl could have become so psychologically ill and so physically deformed. Since my meeting with Dr Olesen, I had become even more intrigued by deformities. Dr Olesen had told me: "I sculpt bodies to give them back their beauty." The concept of accumulation helped me to understand what he meant. Muscular tensions cause energy to "accumulate", and the energy then becomes static. I was able to observe for myself how "force" causes fluids to accumulate. When the muscular tensions are dissolved by massage, the energy begins to move; but as soon as it encounters a new area of muscular tension it accumulates there and fluids begin accumulating at the same spot, causing swelling, oedema and deformities. By viewing these phenomena in this way, I was able to make the connection between Dr Olesen's theories and my own. I remembered that according to physiological theory, the vegetative system was activated by simple changes in pressure. That meant that distension pressure, or fluid pressure, could influence the vegetative system and create a neurovegetative imbalance. When the energy was blocked and the area concerned became swollen with fluid, the vegetative system became imbalanced and this in turn caused a nervous disturbance.

These observations were very important for me. I was eager to use massage to treat these physical deformities, the oedema, the stasis and the cellulite; but I was not sure how to go about it. So I only massaged the muscular tissues, and the result was that I aroused too much emotion and liberated too much energy in my patients. Indeed, the next time I massaged the patient who had been autistic, she entered into a psychotic phase and developed paranoid delusions that she was being poisoned. This was because when I succeeded in dissolving the "ring of psychosis" in her neck muscles, the released energy shot up into her head and agitated the nervous tissues.

Although now I understand perfectly well what happened to my patient, at the time I was quite unable to explain it. I learned a great deal from this woman. Her experiences confirmed the theory that muscular tensions develop on top of an underlying layer of resignation, or hypotonus. In her case, the muscular armour acted as a gigantic encapsulation that held all her emotional energy in stasis. Some people are able to live this way for their whole life, without any visible neurotic or psychotic symptoms, because all their energy is very well encapsulated. But I realised that exhaustion, emotional conflicts or simply overwork could cause this encapsulation to dissolve.

My patient's story illustrated this fact clearly. She told me that she had had five children, one after another, that the family had very little money, and that her husband spent what little they had on luxury cars. All of this had driven her to desperation many times. The family lived in a dismal basement and the children suffered constantly from pneumonia. Gradually my patient sank into a state of total exhaustion. Finally, one summer, the family went to an island for their holidays. When they arrived, they found that the house where they were to stay was on the opposite side of the island. But, despite my patient's pleas, her husband refused to take a boat to their destination, so she was forced to walk all the way across the island carrying heavy luggage. Her husband strode on ahead, and she had to keep calling out to him to wait for her. He would stop for a few moments, but whenever she caught up with him he began striding ahead again. When, utterly exhausted, she finally reached the house, an agonising pain shot through her back and she began crying and shouting. She felt as if a burst of energy had been injected into her head, from outside. And that was the beginning of her psychosis.

I was very interested in these case histories at that time, because I was trying to confirm my hypothesis that both psychoses and neuroses often begin with muscular pains. I already knew that the encapsulation and the muscular armour gradually lost their capacity to control energy, until the defences were maintained by a few muscles only. And if ever the tension in these last few muscles was released, then there was nothing left to prevent the upsurge of emotional energy. While working as a student on the women's psychiatric ward of the Ullevaal general hospital, I heard about a research study that confirmed my hypothesis that the onset of a bout of depression or psychotic crisis was often associated with a physiotherapeutic massage. This study revealed that the majority of the patients had received a massage of this kind shortly before being admitted to hospital. My theory of emotional energy contained by the restraining armour of just a few muscles developed during this period. For people whose armour had reached this state, a simple massage could be sufficient to dissolve the few remaining tensions and release the latent neurotic or psychotic process. The psychodynamic thus instantly set in motion was an organic, biological process that pushed its way outwards from the depths of the body. I felt that it was important to recognise that mental illness comes from the depths of the body. It originates from a psychological conflict that has been repressed and encapsulated in the body by a number of somatic defence mechanisms.

An invisible barrier separated the men from the women at the Dikemark hospital. I worked mainly with the women. The senior doctor responsible for the female patients was interested in the psychological approach, whereas the doctors who worked with the men were only prepared to look at their patients' illness in physiological and biochemical terms. They were forever talking about electrolytes, while for our part we talked about psychotherapy all the time. As a result, different therapeutic regimes were used to treat the two groups of patients: while the women were given psychotherapy, the men received only drugs. On the anniversary of Norway's independence from Sweden the whole clinic got together to celebrate, and I had a chance to observe the groups of patients of both sexes that had formed outside.

I could clearly see that it was mainly the men who showed signs of the physical deformities that were the hallmark of chronic psychological illness; there was visibly less fluid accumulation in the women. At the time I was interested in the relationship between electrolytic theory and physical deformities. And now, suddenly, I understood this relationship! Right there and then I discovered the bridge linking psychopathology and nervous fluid. It was the bridge between the psyche and the soma; between the body and the spirit.

During this period the Dikemark hospital was engaged in research into catatonia. This involved carrying out biochemical analysis to determine the protein content of catatonic patients' cerebrospinal fluid immediately after a catatonic crisis. A special dietary regime was then devised for these patients, based on the findings of the analysis. I developed my own theory of catatonia as follows: when a catatonic patient had an emotional abreaction, the powerful exhalation produced caused a certain quantity of protein to be released, as spinal fluid samples taken from the male patients revealed. The cathartic process could also release large quantities of adrenaline, which is an essential component of the tissue armour. Unfortunately, though, I was unable to talk to anyone about these aspects of the theory, because according to the unwritten law of competence that prevailed in academic circles then, and still does today, a psychologist had no business to make pronouncements about biochemical questions. All the same, I understood the importance of the phenomena that took place between the anion and the cation. But before going on to explain my theories in greater detail, I first want to report on my observations of people suffering from schizophrenia.

SCHIZOPHRENIA

I was particularly interested in schizophrenia, which I understood in the following way: the "split" that we associate with schizophrenia is actually a split between the patient's primary and secondary personalities. This split manifests itself in a forceful battle by the genuine and healthy part of the person against the neurotic part of the personality. The origin of schizophrenia lies in the collapse of the sufferer's defences and the re-emergence of repressed emotions and conflicts, causing the personality to change markedly. I discovered that the schizophrenic process was characterised by a dynamic pressure that emerged from the deeper-lying layers to push against the superficial layers of the muscular and tissue armour. This dynamic was unable to pass through the surface layers, so it could be neither expressed nor discharged. But despite this it continued to operate, because by its nature it was a healing process, a movement towards a cure that had suddenly become blocked and was now stagnating.

The problem was that the impermeable upper layers of the muscular and tissue armour in these patients had not been dissolved and unblocked; while at the same time a deep-lying dynamic had been set in motion, releasing repressed emotional material which could not be integrated by the ego. Instead, the energy of this repressed material kept on battering against the armoured surface layers. To put it another way, the primary energy had come into motion, but was unable to pass through the more recent layers of repressed material lying nearer the surface of the body. This way of looking at it also helped me to see why schizophrenics often refuse to get up in the morning. The dynamic process operates more powerfully during the night, when the functional body/mind is at rest and there is time for the unconscious (the id) to go to work. On awakening, the person is still in contact with the deep knowledge that a healing process is going on, and may feel that the id is actively searching for the road to liberation. But the superficial layers of the tissue armour prevent the energy from flowing freely and being discharged.

We classified schizophrenic patients into three main categories. The hebephrenics were resigned and did not want to do anything at all. The paranoiacs had a strong concentration of energy in the head; through a mechanism of projection and false in-ter-pretation they were convinced that they were being "sent" this energy from outside. The third type, the catatonics, had succeeded in maintaining a certain integrity of consciousness. Because their minds remained reasonably clear I concluded that, relatively speaking, the catatonics were the healthiest type of schizophrenics. They were how-ever also blocked, trapped in a very distinctive kind of "stubbornness". Let me relate a little anecdote to illustrate this catatonic structure. A catatonic patient had been lying immobile in bed in the foetal position for months on end. One day, while on his rounds, the consultant psychiatrist - followed by a retinue of medical students - entered this patient's room and announced: "Here we have Mr Karlsen, who has been lying in bed in the foetal position and refusing to get up for months." All of a sudden Mr Karlsen raised his head and loudly declared: "That's not true!" This example clearly illustrates my theory about the deep layers that are activated in the catatonic, and about his rigidity and stubbornness. A certain integrity is still present in the background.

Another example of catatonia was presented by a patient sitting on a chamber pot, repeating incessantly: "Don't make ca-ca! Don't make ca-ca!" This patient was experiencing a very intense anal conflict: between letting go and holding back. A third example was a catatonic patient who had been in hospital for an extremely long time. Finally he appeared to have recovered, and was discharged. But no sooner had he arrived at the door of his home and put his arms around his mother than he relapsed into a catatonic state.

Ola Raknes had once pointed out to me that catatonics basically have very clear minds. This led me to wonder about the phenomenon of their "stubbornness", and I developed a theory to explain it: in catatonic states the person becomes stubborn in order to protect his primary personality and his free will. The "force" itself keeps the muscles stiff, and can sustain the catatonic state well beyond the person's normal physical capacity.

In this respect the catatonics are the total opposite of the hebephrenics, who resign themselves and yield to their secondary personality. They have given up the fight for their primary personality and, in doing so, they have relinquished their willpower. Remember, though, the primary personality is the one that has the bioenergy and the libido. Hebephrenic patients are blocked, but at the mental level. My main interest was in the paranoiacs, whose energetic conflict was situated in the head. I myself had an oral fixation, and had thoroughly explored this aspect of my character structure. In doing so, I found that I could feel most of the symptoms of schizophrenia without actually becoming schizophrenic myself. For example, in the morning I could often feel the pressure of energy in the interior of my body and in the area around my mouth, and I was also reluctant to get out of bed because I sensed that this energetic process was a healing impulse. The moving energy was working to release my neuroses, my repressions and inhibitions, but it was unable to pass through the blocked layers of muscle and tissue. I had not yet developed the concept of psychoperistalsis. But I felt a clear sensation of pressure inside my head, pushing its way towards my mouth. Gradually, as my kinaesthetic sensitivity increased, I realised that what I was feeling was the pressure of energy; I understood that the schizophrenic is familiar with this pressure of the descending energy currents, and that it is associated with an oral fixation.

I was lucky to have the opportunity to experience these movements of energy in my own body. Little by little they helped me to understand that when a profound dynamic process of this kind was unleashed without the help of a therapist, it could easily lead to confusion and severe organic deterioration as a result of poor energy circulation. I realised why so many schizophrenics lose their teeth and why their organs deteriorate: it was because their energy circulation was blocked, and so their cells received too little nourishment from oxygenated blood. Because of these patients' severe oral fixation (caused by oral deprivation in infancy), their jaw and gums are particularly tense and energy accumulates there. This energetic stasis causes the roots of the teeth to deteriorate, and eventually the teeth fall out. The concept of tissue armour is fundamental for understanding these phenomena. Stasis acts like a sponge that absorbs stale energy and toxic fluids; since these layers of stasis are not eliminated, fresh blood is unable to penetrate into the zones concerned. With the aid of this concept of stasis zones I was able to explain the progressive physiological deterioration that takes place in schizophrenics; stagnation of their bodily fluids caused a host of disorders.

At this point I must explain in more detail the meaning of the word "stasis" at that time. I understood it to mean a fluid pressure. But on one occasion when I started talking about it to a Reichian analyst, he remarked, "That's strange. When you use the concept of stasis, you mean fluid. Wilhelm Reich thought of energy." I replied that there was no conflict, since what we were dealing with was energetic fluid!

I had actually discovered this phenomenon of stasis by observing the behaviour of fluid within the body, and it took me some time to understand that the fluid had an energetic charge. It was this energetic charge that gave the fluid its power, and now I realised that this must also be the mystery Factor X that Dr Olesen had referred to in his experiments with fluid. I remembered how, when he failed to get the result he expected after injecting a sodium solution into muscle membranes, he concluded that something else in the fluid - Factor X - must be causing the pressure; a factor that I now knew was energy. The psychosomatic pain that Dr Olesen was investigating was caused by energetically charged fluid pressing against the membranes. But his injections failed to evoke this pain, because the sodium solution he used had no energetic charge.

I now come to what, in biodynamic theory, we call the plasmo-faradic principle. A series of case studies led me to develop the following theory: Energy can provoke contraction. Where bodily fluid is highly charged with energy - that is, where an area of static energy has attracted fluid, which has also stagnated and taken on the energetic charge - the fluid has a powerful ability to cause contraction. The pressure of the energetic fluid pushing against the membranes from the inside produces a spastic counter-pressure in the membranes, pushing back towards the interior of the body. The result is an intolerable psychosomatic pain. At the same time, since it is confined by the tissue armour, this fluid pressure irritates the nervous tissue. Little by little I was able to build up a clear picture of the various factors underlying psychosomatic pains, and especially those responsible for irritating the nervous tissue of the brain. Now I understood how, by irritating the membranes of the cerebral cells, the energetic fluid could provoke hallucinations. If someone's central nervous system and motor system are irritated in this way, his limbs begin to move of their own accord; while if the energetic fluid puts pressure on his auditory or visual systems, hallucinations are activated internally. So the irritant components of the tissue armour have a powerful effect on the perceptual nervous system; an effect produced whenever emotions are released, since energetic fluid then rushes up into the head.

FROM THE LIBIDO TO COSMIC ENERGY

Understanding the relationship between the tissue armour and "force" (which nowadays we call "bioenergy") helped me to understand all sorts of phenomena. The dynamic force arising from the depths of the organism put pressure on the membranes of the armoured layers and so caused painful psychosomatic and neurotic symptoms as well as disturbing the balance of the neuro-vegetative system. This imbalance took the form of feelings of anxiety, emotional stress and sensations of horror. I observed this "force" in my patients and I felt it in myself: it was an overwhelming flood of energy that was impossible to resist. Psychopharmaceutical drugs were the only thing capable of halting and neutralising these powerful energetic phenomena, which they did by creating an artificial tissue armour that reinforced the armour already present. In my work as a physiotherapist at the Bülow-Hansen Institute I had already noticed that we unleashed a very powerful dynamic force in our patients as soon as we dissolved their muscular armour. Once unleashed, this force set off a chain reaction, so it was important for us to carry on treating the patients right through to the end of this process. So the therapeutic relationship imposed constraints on both sides: because of the chain reaction and the constant need to release more and more of the "force", the patient could not cope without his therapist; while the therapist was obliged to carry the treatment through to the very end, which could cause problems if he himself became ill.

As I pondered on the nature of the energetic fluid, I found myself forced to consider some very fundamental questions: "What is energy? Is it positive or negative, or both? What role do anions and cations play?" Everything I had observed led me to conclude that there must be two kinds of energies: one going upwards and the other downwards. The upgoing energy had an emotional quality, and originated from the depths of the body, while the downgoing energy seemed to come from the top of the head. I myself, as I mentioned earlier, had experienced this ascending energy as a sensation of pressure towards my mouth. I was fascinated by the great power and intensity of this energy. It is the same extraordinary strength that infants develop in their mouths while suckling: a strength so great that I could not imagine how such a tiny body could produce it unaided. But if this energy did not simply come from the body, where did it come from? Many people said that they experienced it as a flow of energy from the top of the head down to the mouth, and that was what I had also felt. Suddenly I recognised that this energy must indeed come "from above"; that it was cosmic energy.

Now I could also understand why, when a schizophrenic feels this extra-ordinary sensation in his head, he imagines that "someone" has sent him the energy "from outside". Schizophrenics, who also feel these energetic phenomena in the head much more strongly than most other people, simply give a paranoid interpretation to their sensations. I too had felt this strong pressure of energy in my head, which I thought of as "force" since I had not yet read Reich or encountered his concept of "cosmic energy". It felt as though there was a constant force pressing downwards from my skull, which seemed more than my body could contain. At times when it dissolved and spread throughout my body, it always brought a deep sense of relief and a feeling of universal well-being and confidence. I could not relate this experience to any part of my own personality, but was simply conscious of it. I was part of it, rather than it coming from me.

When I later realised that what I had experienced was Reich's "cosmic energy", it was easy to understand its effect on schizophrenics. This force, which felt like a spinning tension pressing relentlessly on the skull without any release, was bound to be wrongly interpreted and seen as an evil force or external entity attacking their sanity. It was equally clear to me that, just as cosmic energy is a reality, so the distortions and hallucinations it caused would be perceived by the schizophrenic as reality. So the basic conflict in schizophrenia was twofold. First the defences and encapsulation failed in their efforts to simultaneously block not only the upgoing stream of emotional energy emerging from the depths of the body, but also the downgoing stream of cosmic energy. Once they had failed, a veritable "emotional salad" was produced; a mixture of repressed material, hatred, psychotic elements and feelings of persecution resulting from the re-emergence of their unacknowledged hatred and murderous rage. I also understood why "rational therapy" was bound to be useless in these cases, since the schizophrenic fiercely defends the reality of his sensations and refuses to believe that what he is feeling does not exist, is "just a figment of his imagination". And he is right to do so, because he really is feeling the existence of this force, this pressure of energy in his head. But when it builds up in the head, this same libidinal force that deformed my "beautiful legs" can also have a very harmful effect on the head itself if the energy is unable to pass through the layers of stasis and circulate freely. The fluid pressure and poor blood circulation that result can produce severe physiological deformities, and can even end up by destroying the cerebral nerve tissue.

Once I had recognised the cosmic origins of this energy, I again found myself confronted with all kinds of questions about its exact nature. Did it originate from the anions or from the cations, I wondered? Was it positive or negative, alkaline or acid? Eventually I concluded that it must come from the cations and have alkaline properties. I deduced this from the fact that, provided it was able to circulate freely on the surface of the skin, the descending cosmic energy did not exert an uncomfortable pressure, but instead produced feelings of pleasure and euphoria. This led me to take an interest in euphoria-inducing drugs, which I predicted must be alkaline or cationic substances; predictions that were subsequently confirmed by physiology researchers. So it was clear that the libido was a "euphoria drug" for the body: cosmic energy that caressed the tissues and the erogenous zones and produced feelings of pleasure when it circulated freely in the body. It was only when this downgoing energy encountered blocks, and so was prevented from circulating normally, that its pressure could become too strong; if this happened, though, the energy was likely to be interpreted as a hostile force sent from outside. Most healthy people feel this energy, but since it meets no resistance and circulates freely, they experience it as a pleasurable "streaming" sensation. But in schizophrenics the tissue armour resists the downgoing energy so strongly that it cannot pass through, but instead accumulates and causes all kinds of problems. So these patients very naturally experience it as something unpleasant and threatening. I went to see Ola Raknes to tell him about my theory. "You mustn't think that I'm schizophrenic myself", I hastened to reassure him, "but I have come to the conclusion that the libido consists of cosmic energy." Without saying a word, Raknes got up and left the room. Immediately I was seized by a fear both irrational and rational: "Oh no!" I thought to myself, "now he thinks I've gone completely mad and doesn't want to have anything more to do with me!" But in a few moments Raknes returned, and presented me with an article by Wilhelm Reich entitled: "From the theory of the libido to the theory of cosmic energy". My first reaction was one of dismay and sore disappointment. I felt as if my whole world had collapsed around me: I had been so sure that I was the only person to discover this fantastic theory! But before long I forgot my disappointment as I was gripped by Reich's article, in which he presented a precise theory of the origins of life that confirmed my own hypotheses.

Reich's theory ran as follows: Since cosmic energy is "negative" (-) and is carried by the cations, while a physiological sodium solution is slightly acid (+), this produces a particular ratio of positive to negative charges. This ratio can for example be found in sea water, which contains a huge amount of cosmic energy. But this is not in itself sufficient to create life. Proteins must also be present, since they carry a negative charge and perform much the same function as the resistance in an electric heating element.

Electrical energy has to accumulate up to a certain point before it can be transformed into visible light or perceptible heat; without resistance the energy simply passes through and nothing can be felt or seen. Similarly, the tissue armour of schizophrenic patients resists the passage of cosmic energy; and without this resistance, which causes the cosmic energy to accumulate, it would be impossible to detect the energy's existence. So, returning to Reich's theory of the origins of life, a source of resistance (in the form of sulphur or proteins) is needed in order to accumulate a certain critical mass of cosmic energy, which then triggers a contraction. I myself had noticed that the cosmic energy in proteins tended to produce a contraction response, and that the cosmic energy in muscle tissues did so too.

Dr Olesen had developed a particularly interesting concept that he called "exercise through rest". According to him, the muscles continue to work in a certain way even while we are resting. So an animal that does not use its muscles (such as a dog kept tied up) does not lose its muscle tonus. The energy itself produces contraction and tension in organic material such as muscle tissue. I had experienced this phenomenon myself: on several occasions when I was resting and relaxing deeply I could clearly feel the flow of energy running through my legs, which gradually regained their original shape and their natural tonus. Yet I did nothing at all except rest! So I developed a theory to account for this apparent miracle: energy itself produces a normal tonus and a contraction that allow life to exist. Since by its nature energy pulsates, it produces alternating phases of contraction and expansion (relaxation) in protoplasm. The proteins themselves have this capacity to contract and expand, this natural pulsation that is the essence of life. This was "my" theory of the origin of life, and I was most surprised to discover that Reich had also discovered it, even before I had! But once I had got over my disappointment, I found it wonderful that we were both thinking along the same lines about the nature of life.

At this point I want to briefly describe two alternative cases that one may encounter when studying fluid pressure in the membranes. In one case the fluid is charged with energy; in the other the energy has withdrawn, leaving only stagnant fluid. We use two concepts to describe these phenomena. The "distension pressure" is an active pressure that causes the proteins, membranes and muscle fibres to contract; while the "transudation pressure" is the mechanical pressure exerted on the membranes by the residual uncharged fluid left behind when the energy has withdrawn. Both types of pressure disturb the balance of the vegetative system.

SOLIDIFICATION

The physical deformities of the mentally ill are the result of a process that I call "secondary solidification". This process is preceded by encapsulation, the formation of muscular and tissue armour, the physiological defence mechanisms. The energy stagnates. Over the years the organism reaches a compromise state of equilibrium in which repressed material is held encapsulated and solidified. The person is functional, but neurotic. But as soon as the defences fall, the underlying energetic dynamic emerges in various forms and symptoms. The encapsulation dissolves, and the energy released pulsates its way towards the surface until its path is again blocked by the tissue armour. So once again the energy accumulates, attracting more fluid, and this fluid eventually causes physical deformities. These deformities are then locked into place by fatty deposits and infiltrations in the connective tissues (oedemas, cellulitis), and so a state of secondary solidification is reached. Two pathological phenomena can occur in this state: oedemas (too much energy in the tissues), or constrictions (too little energy). Both these conditions strongly affect the quality of the tissues, and can cause a wide variety of symptoms: deformations, congestion and malfunction of the organs; atrophy of the tissues; arteriosclerosis; neuritis; even cerebral haemorrhages. Looking at all these effects, we can see what an important role the dynamic force of energy plays in the genesis of problems treated by conventional medicine.

One of the phenomena that interested me greatly at that time was the process of ageing. During the massage treatment, which concentrated on working deeply on the muscles, we did everything in our power to release the latent dynamic force. But where the surface layers remained blocked while we worked on the deeper layers, our patients appeared to grow old before their time. Their faces became lined; some put on weight, all looked much older. We were very conscious of this phenomenon, which we called "the parasympathetic appearance". Nowadays we know how to prevent it, but at the time we could only watch as many of the people we were trying to help took on this distressing parasympathetic appearance. Some people's skin became grey and lifeless, with various degrees of oedema; others developed dry, sagging skin prone to wrinkling, with bags under the eyes and contracted pupils in red-rimmed, watery eyes, as if they had just been crying. Their faces all had a sad, old look, which was a typical reaction to over-stimulation of the parasympathetic system. I worried a good deal about this phenomenon, which I also observed in myself. It was triggered by the energy dynamic rising up from the depths of the body to the head and face, only to become blocked there because the surface armour prevented it from being discharged. If the person could not identify with the psychological and emotional pressure it caused, the energy stagnated as a neutralised conflict.

This discrepancy between the deep dynamic and the surface layer is very important. I myself felt it particularly strongly when I simply lay down and allowed the deep process to work. I have already described the movements that developed in my pelvis during my therapy with Dr Houge: they were not accompanied by any feelings, either of pleasure or of anxiety, but were purely muscular movements. I also experienced another, similar phenomenon, which I shall describe in more detail later, when an inner impulse caused my tongue to keep pushing its way out of my mouth. These movements, too, were emotionally neutral; they were purely motor impulses driven by a very powerful energetic dynamic coming from the deep layers of the organism. Between this dynamic from the unconscious depths and the surface layers with their close connection to the ego and the conscious mind there lay a discrepancy, a split.

These phenomena helped me to understand why, so often, schizophrenics are reluctant to get up in the morning: for immediately after waking they are most strongly in contact with the deep dynamic that is working to liberate them, but they are still imprisoned by the surface layers of armour. Gradually I came to understand more and more clearly that the origin of the schizophrenic process lay in this deep dynamic, whose purpose was to eliminate all repressions and free the primary personality completely. The schizophrenic's illness was caused by the conflict that developed, once this deep process of liberation had got under way, if it was not in fact possible for the person to become free.

One day, as I lay on the couch in Dr Houge's therapy room, he asked me when I would regard my therapy as complete. I told him: "When I can lie down completely quietly, without sudden jolts of energy in my body, without orgasm reflexes, without any interior pressure, simply relaxed; when there are no more uncontrolled motor movements, no discrepancies between the deeply mobilised energy and the blocked surface layers; in short, when my energy has been liberated and I have become conscious of it, then I will have finished my therapy."

At this point I shall say a few words about my therapy with Dr Houge, because it will help me to illustrate my theories. Dr Houge had explained that he had observed alternating layers of sexuality and aggression in me. He asked me to lie on the couch and simply breathe, and from time to time he would push my lower jaw forward to help liberate my breathing. At a certain point during this phase of the therapy, a strange phenomenon occurred which greatly surprised us both: such enormous quantities of liquid began flowing out of my vagina that at first we thought it must be urine. But the fluid was colourless and odourless, and we concluded that it must be coming from my uterus. For six months this liquid continued to flow at every session; there was so much of it that we had to cover the couch with a plastic sheet, and even then it often ran down onto the floor and had to be sponged up. I tried wearing a contraceptive diaphragm, but it was quite unable to hold back the liquid. So there was nothing to be done except allow the process to take its course.

During this period I became aware of many sexual sensations and desires that had to do with my father, as well as numerous sexual conflicts. My father, as I mentioned earlier, was strongly influenced by Oriental philosophy, and was determined that I should grow up in perfect health, and above all with immaculate teeth. So he decided that I should eat black bread - which I loathed - and was so strict about it that he ordered my mother, the governess and the nursemaid to stuff the bread into my mouth forcibly. I screamed and cried in protest every time, but they held my nose to make me swallow. The feeling of having both my nose and mouth blocked in this way was terrifying, and when I relived it years later in my therapy, I became intensely aware of the violence that can be inflicted on children under the pretext of bringing them up properly. My father also used to see to it that any food I did not eat was served up to me again and again at each subsequent meal, until I had finished it. It was his way of teaching me to be obedient. And indeed I did become an extremely well-behaved, obedient little girl who worked hard at school and was always polite: but I had no "force", no real life in me any more, and there was no sparkle in my face. All the bioenergy, all the life force in me had been repressed. Now, looking back, I can more easily understand my father's paradoxical feelings towards my sister, who had not allowed herself to be repressed and was very lively. Although my father was forever saying how proud he was of me, it was when he was watching my sister - who, far from being polite and obedient, was cheeky and independent - that a real expression of joy came into his face. It was much the same with our collie dog. My father had trained him so well that the poor animal would wait outside the door without moving a muscle for hours on end, even when the weather was ice cold (and in Norway it really does get cold!) My father certainly appreciated our dog; but when he looked at another dog that was less well- trained, but unruly and bursting with life, his face would light up with pleasure.

My father's approach to child-rearing had repressed my primary personality and created a secondary personality. It was not surprising that he then found me less appealing than my sister: for the secondary personality is an expression of defeat in the fight for life. The person's energy becomes encapsulated, and their contact with the bioenergy is lost. So the deliberate goal of all my successive therapies - with Ola Raknes, Aadel Bülow-Hansen and Dr Houge - was to make my father's plans fail. Indeed, the goal of all therapeutic work is to dismantle the tragic mechanics of an education that attempts to transform children into miniature adults instead of allowing them to be themselves. Unblocking my repressed life energy was an enormous undertaking; but once the energy began to move, nothing could hold it back. I was severely blocked to start with, but I received help and support in my process of liberation.

The problem for schizophrenics is that they do not receive any real support. The same process of energy liberation has started spontaneously in them, without the aid of therapy, and so they find themselves alone, without help or protection, desperate and not understood.

It was during this period that I began developing the concepts of the primary and secondary personalities. The secondary personality only possesses physiological energy, since the bioenergy has become encapsulated and the original personality has been scorned. I was particularly interested in the pre-pathological stage of schizophrenia. During the course of the schizophrenic process, the encapsulation collapses and all the repressed material comes flooding to the surface, together with all the rage that has built up over the years in which the personality has not been respected. The repressed hatred becomes a dynamic force that sets a process of purification and cleansing in motion; but this natural healing process is not completed, and ends as secondary solidification sets in. Psychiatric hospitals do not allow the process to reach its completion either: whenever outbreaks of rage and hatred occur, the doctors and nurses immediately take action to repress these unwelcome emotions again. I also noticed that in schizophrenics of the "simplex" type the energy was not strong enough, so they became resigned. Their conflicts were too powerful. The catatonics' strategy was to withdraw into a cocoon of stubbornness, while the hebephrenics were mainly blocked in a state of secondary solidification. They were trapped by stasis, by the irritant components of the tissue armour, and their energy rose up into the head, bringing with it a mass of toxins and a feeling of intense pressure.

I was particularly interested in children's temper tantrums at this time. As I observed them closely, I came to realise that this was how children learned to exercise their free will. During the tantrum, there is a look of freedom on the child's face. The issue that prompts the child's rebellion is not important; the important thing is the impulse to free himself from his parents' repressive interjections, from the superego, from the harsh words of adults. I cannot forget one little girl, who begged and pleaded incessantly with her mother for a fur coat on a boiling hot summer's day. The arguments her mother put forward had absolutely no effect; she wanted her fur coat, and that was that. Since the temperature was 35 degrees Celsius, she sweated terribly when her mother finally gave in; but she had exercised her will and won. Another example that comes to mind is a three-year-old girl who demanded a Coca-Cola. When her parents told her she could only have milk, she yelled at the top of her voice for an hour. Finally her father gave in and brought her a glass of Coca-Cola. But, far from being satisfied, she immediately began yelling again; now she wanted milk!

If this phase of self-assertion in children is repressed, their will is broken and a secondary personality becomes established. In the schizophrenic process, however, the defences collapse and the primary personality can no longer be suppressed. It comes bursting out with a loud cry - and then everything becomes totally blocked.

Very often, it was the things I experienced in my own therapy that taught me the most. For example, because of my oral fixation I had an unusually rigid mouth. My lips - especially the upper lip and the area just above it - were insensitive and rather hard, lacking in mobility. I was unable to pucker my lips, or to imitate the sound that children make by vibrating their lips when they play at being trains or cars. The annular muscle around my mouth had become so solidified and insensitive that I simply could not do so. It took a very long time during my treatment with Aadel Bülow-Hansen to relax these muscles and liberate the energy blocked there. But gradually, as my mouth became freer, I found that energy was also being released in my chest and sexual organs. At first this energy seemed to be neutral, and only produced movements; but after some time I began to experience a marvellous sensation of pleasure. It was extraordinary; after a long period during which I felt so exhausted all the time that I considered stopping the treatment, all of a sudden every single cell in my body was awash with a sensation as sweet as melting sugar. I melted away completely. Now, instead of complaining to my friends: "I'm so dreadfully tired!", I could hardly wait to describe my new sensations to them. "I feel myself melting like sugar! I feel so sweet!", I told them. They replied: "Yes, of course you do; you are very sweet!" but they could not understand that I really, literally felt like melting sugar in every single cell of my body! These sensations were what Reich had called "libidinal streamings": a pleasure so intense that at times it was almost unbearable. As I felt this sensation of the libido invading my entire body, I began to understand the difference between the local orgasm and the total orgasm. In a total orgasm all the cells vibrate and pulsate in complete harmony; but while the muscular and tissue armour remain solid, it is impossible to achieve. I was very pleasantly impressed: I was discovering how wonderfully gentle and sweet eroticism and sexuality could be, and finding that they existed in my arms, in my fingers, throughout my whole body. But to reach this point, I had first had to experience the deformation of my legs and feel the sensation of conflict throughout my body.

One day I discovered that the feeling of pressure inside my mouth diminished when I made little sounds, like a baby. As I did so, I felt a very pleasant energy that caressed my skin and flowed over my chin and down my throat. It was a marvellous, utterly pleasurable experience: I called it the zephyr's caress. The internal pressure disappeared, and suddenly a memory of my very early childhood came to me: I was in the cradle, making these little infant sounds with my mouth and enjoying the limitless sweet stream of pleasure in my body, when suddenly, abruptly, my father's face appeared above me. He shouted and slapped my face, and ordered me to be quiet immediately. At once everything stopped, and I lost the feeling of pleasure.

Some days after reliving this memory, I asked my mother about it. She hushed me and took me into another room, because she did not want my father - who was within earshot when I raised the subject - to hear what she had to say. Then she told me that at the time when I was still in the cradle, my father had been going through a process of bitter conflicts with his own father as he fought to establish his independence. My grandfather was an extremely authoritarian man who expected his son to succeed him as director of the family business. All this was very stressful for my father, and he developed psychosomatic symptoms from which he suffered terribly; he had painful headaches, and could not bear to hear my little sounds during the night. He often silenced me violently. He also strongly believed that children should be obedient. My mother explained to me that in the beginning he used to get out of bed and hit me; but before long he only had to call out: "No! Stop it!" in a loud voice, and I would be quiet at once. I was then only a few months old, and my father was very proud of his success in educating me. It was clear to me that I had lost my libido during this early period of my life.

Another interesting phenomenon caught my attention: during the period immediately before I rediscovered my libido and relived the memory of its loss, I felt cold all the time. This sensation of cold seemed to be a manifestation of anxiety. First I felt a mixture of pleasure and anxiety, then I felt as if my whole body was on fire, and finally the inner conflict in my tissues became so intense that my body became cold. Reich also speaks of "cold energy".

After going through all these experiences, culminating in the rediscovery of pleasure, I thought my neurosis must finally be coming to an end. I was wrong; there was more to come. I now entered a stage in which my oral fixation manifested itself in the form of an intense feeling of pleasure. This feeling became so intense that when I was lying down, I could no longer feel the limits of my body. I was nothing but an immense field of energy radiating around a single point that was a centre of extraordinary pleasure: my mouth. I called this phenomenon the "oral paradise". Now I understood what it was that children felt during this phase. Just as it is possible when making love to experience the genitals as the central point from which an extraordinary pleasure flows, so for orally fixated people this centre is the mouth. This is why many orally fixated people are frigid, or can only experience a local orgasm. But now I had reached the point at which everything within me was becoming unified. While this process went on, I needed to lie down for hours at a time without being disturbed. This also happens with schizophrenics who have a strong oral fixation: often they, too, cannot feel the limits of their own bodies, and can spend hour after hour simply lying still in a state that "normal" people find incomprehensible.

Meanwhile, my therapeutic adventures were still not over. As I lay there one day, the pleasurable sensation suddenly vanished and my mouth became rock hard. I wanted to cry; I had lost my oral paradise, my sweet pleasure. My mouth seemed to be searching for a nipple, as if the nipple had just been snatched away from me and I had to fight to get it back again and keep it. Again I asked my mother what this memory meant: when I was a baby, had I ever tried to cling on to her breast with all my might? She replied: "How stupid we adults are! Let me tell you what happened. I loved you so much, I found you so sweet and lively, that whenever I gave you the breast - and I breast fed you for nine months - I used to snatch it away from you again so that I could see how you fought to get it back. I only meant it as a game, and it gave me such satisfaction to watch you: your face went all red, and you were so alive and so beautiful in your strength that I felt tremendously proud of you." I asked her if she had done it often. "Yes", she replied, "three or four times a feeding." And she told me that she had played this game from just a few days after my birth, right up to when I was weaned at the age of nine months.

So that was how I had become so strongly orally fixated! Each time I was fed, I had learned to expect the pleasure to be interrupted and could not abandon myself to it fully; even when I found the nipple again, I still could not relax completely because I was expecting it to be snatched away again at any moment. So a startle reflex became established in my body, and my libido could no longer flow uninhibitedly. I had begun losing contact with my libido in the first few weeks of my life.

This was a very rich period for me, during which I developed the outlines of all my theories on schizophrenia; and in doing so I was greatly influenced and helped by the phenomena that I experienced during my own therapeutic process. I received one of my most important clues from the "stubbornness" that I had first encountered in myself after my meeting with Dr Havrevoll, and then in my therapy with Ola Raknes. This problem continued to accompany me all throughout my subsequent therapy. My stubbornness felt to me like a wild animal inside my head, tearing from side to side and spinning around so wildly that at times I thought my head would burst. It never reached the point where I actually exploded with rage, but the feeling was so intense that I called it "stubbornness itself". And it was this stubbornness that helped me to understand one of the key factors in schizophrenia. The schizophrenic becomes stubborn in a desperate effort to preserve his unity in spite of the deep split that has developed between his primary and secondary personalities.

Now I realised even more clearly just how fundamental the temper tantrum period is to the child's development. After the oral phase, this is the second most important stage; the tantrums are a powerful exercise in self-affirmation, and they also help to get the child's energy moving downwards from the pelvis, so that it does not stagnate in anal fixation.

During my therapy with Dr Houge, another very important change occurred: the "stubbornness itself", the wild animal raging inside my head, now became transformed into a ball of energy in the centre of my brain. I became aware of this ball every time a conflict arose between my primary and secondary personalities. It was a very clear indicator of the conflict going on within me: for whereas in the past I had always been so well-behaved and obedient, now I suddenly felt the urge to say "No!" again. I found this ball of energy in my head an astonishing experience. It made me think of the story I had heard from a woman patient who was admitted to hospital during a psychotic episode. She told me: "Everything began when I felt a ball of energy inside my head. One day, while I was knitting, it exploded. I got up and ran around the garden, screaming. I heard voices in my head, and then I was taken to the psychiatric hospital." I was amazed by the similarity between her experience and mine. The difference in my case was that the ball of energy in my head did not explode; instead it transformed itself into a motor impulse in my tongue, which began poking out of my mouth. This only happened when I relaxed and allowed the inner dynamic to take its course; while I was active nobody would ever have suspected the existence of such an odd phenomenon in me. I only had these experiences in the solitude of my own room (or during my sessions with Dr Houge). Another unusual, and disquieting, phenomenon occurred around the same time. Sometimes, when I relaxed deeply, my heart would start pounding so furiously that it sounded like a tractor engine.

Finally, one day, something of an explosion occurred, and an enormous rage came bursting out of me. It appeared that whenever I relaxed I let my defences fall, enabling the repressed rage to rise up and activate my heart so furiously. I could not help remembering the three patients who had died while undergoing autogenic training with Dr Schultz: they had relaxed so deeply and totally that they had died of heart attacks on the couch. It seems that when a certain point is passed in the relaxation process, it becomes a dynamic force operating primarily on the vegetative system - not on the emotions or the memory. As a result the heart can enter into a state of crisis, and if a vegetative discharge is not encouraged at this point - as, luckily for me, it was in my therapy - the situation can become dangerous.

The more I rediscovered my libido in my body, in my tongue, on the surface of my skin, the more my spontaneity re-emerged. My movements became completely unpredictable. One day the ball of energy in my head began spiralling down towards the root of my tongue, and suddenly I heard myself cry out: "Mama!" It was the energy itself that had moved my tongue and produced the sound "Mama". I was so startled that I asked Dr Houge if he had heard it too. "Yes", he reassured me. This experience enabled me to understand the origin of the sounds that animals, birds and babies make instinctively. Vital energy itself makes the vocal cords move and creates the sound. Libidinal energy accumulates, a tension develops, and the sound becomes a way out, a channel through which this energy can be liberated. The pleasure principle expresses itself in the form of surprise and delight. So I was tremendously proud that my instinctual force had finally become stronger than the repression holding it in check: the id had said "Mama!" And I understood clearly how the instincts work.

Instincts are bioenergy itself, which manifests itself in different ways according to the structure and influences the muscles. The energy puts pressure on the muscles, and as it does so the entire being tries with all its might to free itself from this tension and let the energy flow freely. This is how language originates in the body. First the tension builds up, then the energy is set free and is expressed in the form of sound.

FREUD'S THEORY OF THE LIBIDO

During this period I felt much closer to Freud in my ideas than to Reich. I still knew little about Reich, and had read none of his work except his articles about the cosmic energy he had discovered through his experiments in physics and astronomy. I myself had discovered cosmic energy independently, through my own experiences and through my therapeutic work with my patients. I was particularly interested in Freud's theory of the libido as the "energy of life". This theory aroused strong opposition in its day, and Freud finally bowed to the pressure brought to bear on him. He retracted his assertions, and subsequently treated this concept in such a theoretical way in his writings that his colleagues objected to his "metaphysical" understanding of the concept of vital energy. Freud had given up, while Reich had fought for these ideas. I also found myself in the position of fighting for these ideas; but because I was a woman - and what was more, one who looked very immature and "girlish" - nobody took me seriously. I was anonymous, I was a wife and mother. Nonetheless, during this period Freud's theory of children's psychosexual development became very important to me.

The things Freud talked about were not only real and true in psychological terms, but also real and true in physical terms, in the tissue itself. The oral fixation is a completely real, demonstrable accumulation of stagnant vital energy in the mouth, the tongue and the tissue around this whole area, right down to the root of the tongue deep in the throat. And the anal fixation is an equally real accumulation of energy and stiffening of tissue around the anus, accompanied by tension in the whole of the pelvis. A person can be completely imprisoned by this fixation, so that if the defences around the anus do eventually loosen, the energetic release in the tissue armour can produce unbearable itching.

Only when the tissue armour has been dissolved completely, so that the person regains his full libido circulation and his natural sensuality, can he really come to terms with the tremendous energetic change that takes place when a fixation is released. And to succeed in dissolving the armour, we must influence the vasomotoric cycle, the emotional circulatory system in the blood that I described on page 42. The concept of membrane permeability is also important here, since it is this permeability that permits the bioenergy to circulate in the body. Every time a vasomotoric cycle is not completed, every time an emotional cycle is interrupted, metabolic waste products and stocks of adrenaline accumulate in the tissues, where they build up into tissue armour. Only when the tissues are purified and all these deposits are flushed out can the energy pass through the membranes and circulate harmoniously. But each fresh repression counteracts this purification process, and contributes yet another layer to the tissue armour. These stratified layers of armour in the tissue explain the typical lack of radiance in the skin of people who have become locked within their secondary personality. The vital energy is "buried" far beneath the tissue armour. I did not then think of energy blocks in terms of the segments of Reichian muscular armour (I had not encountered his theory at the time), but in terms of the stratified layers of the tissue armour.

An experience that I had with one of my patients helped me to understand the essence of Freud's libido theory. One of Aadel Bülow-Hansen's fundamental rules was that her method should never be used to treat hysterics. This was because when hysterics received massage, their symptoms kept moving around during the treatment without reaching any resolution; like an inflated balloon, which can be bent and squeezed into all sorts of shapes, but cannot let out the pressure inside it. Finally, though, I had an opportunity to work with a hysterical patient, and I did give her some massage treatment. One afternoon, while I was working on this patient, I saw energy moving in her. It looked like a red wave rising up her chest; then, instead of going to the throat and vocal cords (to be expressed), it rose immediately to the top of her head. This woman suffered from hysterical headaches. I realised that these must be caused by libidinal energy, by bioenergy mounting directly into the brain. I found confirmation in psychiatric literature that hysterical symptoms did not move along the same pathways as the nerves. It seemed clear to me that they followed the course of the energy in the body. So I had actually seen the libidinal energy - which, in this case, had an aggressive quality. Freud's concept of the libido really did refer to a genuine, physical force that could be seen on the surface of the skin: vital energy. In my patient's case the energy was unable to move into the throat for expression; so instead it rose up into her head.

Not long afterwards, I attended a seminar on Freud's theory of the instincts and the libido. At one point the speaker said: "Nobody has ever seen the libido of which Freud speaks", and I wanted to leap up and shout for joy: "I've seen it! I've seen it! I see it every day!" Because indeed I did, and everything I had seen convinced me that the bioenergy flows through the skin and the muscle membranes, in much the same way as electricity flows through a cable. But when the energy becomes blocked and cannot be expressed, quantities of fluid are attracted to the area (in accordance with Reich's law that energy attracts fluid, which I shall describe later) and stasis develops. So when I worked on this excess fluid by lightly massaging the parts that were slightly swollen or distended, I was working on the symptom rather than on the underlying problem, and I could make it disappear without activating older layers of conflict.

I decided that from then on, I would work exclusively on the fluid in the membranes, concentrating on releasing only those areas of the body that were distended. Distended tissues pulsate more strongly with blood and bioenergy, and the masseur can feel this as slight vibrations and swollenness under his fingers. I concluded that it was in those areas that emotional conflicts were activated and circulating, looking for an opportunity to discharge, to abreact. I thought of these areas as "ripe" for treatment. By working on the membranes of these distended areas of tissue, I released the metabolic residues (the chemostasis) that had been deposited there as a result of incomplete vaso-motoric cycles. These waste products were then eliminated from the patient's body. I thought of what I was doing as a kind of "manual psychoanalysis" of the body; I was helping the patient to complete the emotional cycle that had been interrupted, but I was doing so at the level of the blood circulatory system. This was how I came to work exclusively with the membranes.

THE DISCOVERY OF PSYCHOPERISTALSIS

Around this time, I stopped working at the Dikemark hospital. My husband wanted me to be at home, nearer to him, so he promised to build an annexe onto our house for me to use as a therapy studio. But he was in no hurry to put this idea into practice, so I spent several months at home doing nothing. The children were at school or with their friends, my husband was at work, and I had two home helps who saw to the housework. I practised yoga, I went for long walks, I tried out all the latest skin treatments in the beauty magazines, I kept up to date with fashion, and so on. But as the months went by, I became more and more miserable and unhealthy-looking. None of these activities brought me any satisfaction, because I found no scope for self-realisation in them; I was only doing them to please my husband and because I had nothing else to do. Finally I stopped, and asked myself how I could best employ my abundant energies. There was still no sign of the promised annexe; my husband was not at all eager for me to start working again! In the end I dismissed my household helps and threw myself into looking after the house. I got up at the crack of dawn, I beat the carpets in the garden, I cleaned and tidied everywhere, I was forever making my children take vitamins, and so forth. One evening, my whole family got together and begged me: "Please, start working again!" For the first time in my life, my family not only wanted me to work, but they actively gave me their support. What was more, after a long discussion between us my husband finally acknowledged: "Yes, I understand. You have to work. I'm going to start building that annexe for your therapy studio right away."

Building the annexe took longer than we had expected. In the meantime, one of the physiotherapists at Aadel Bülow-Hansen's school asked me to take over her clientele, because she had just got married and was about to leave town. I had certainly not intended to work as a physiotherapist again; although I was keen to practise the Bülow-Hansen massage methods, I had only planned to use them to do "Reichian analyses".

After all, I was first and foremost a clinical psychologist! But in fact it was during this period when I was working as a physiotherapist and waiting for my therapy studio to be built that I made my discovery of "psychoperistalsis".

I very quickly realised that my style of treatment was too powerful, too dynamic for my new patients. They were used to the much gentler methods of the physiotherapist whom I had replaced. I saw that I would have to find a different way of working if I wanted to continue using these massage techniques. I kept thinking of Freud's words: "It is best to work on the part of the unconscious that is closest to the ego." So I made it my business to find out exactly what in the body was closest to the ego. The answer proved to be the emotional circulatory system in the blood - moreprecisely, the return flow to the heart through the veins - and the fluid and energy stasis and distension in the muscle tissue.

I now began working on the surface of the muscle membranes only. As I did so I noticed an intriguing phenomenon: quite loud gurgling noises - the sounds of peristalsis - could be heard from my patients' abdomens. I remembered that Aadel Bülow-Hansen had often said that these intestinal sounds were a good sign, so as time went on I began working only on those areas of the body that seemed to be associated with these sounds. After each session I asked my patients to describe their experience. Each time that I worked in this way, I now heard the same story: my patients told me how they clearly felt the inner pressure from which they were suffering diminishing during the massage, and, little by little, they felt their anxiety slipping away. Their psychosomatic ailments and muscular pains also disappeared, and they began to discover and delight in a new sensation: their bodies were filled with delicious feelings of pleasure and sweetness that seemed to flow through every single cell. They were enchanted, and I too was very pleased with my work, because I knew that, at last, I had discovered the physical counterpart of the part of the unconscious closest to the ego: the layer of repression that could be identified and resolved, the layer of emotional suppression that was ripe and circulating in the membranes, ready and waiting for my hands to reach it and release it. And every step forward in this process was accompanied by peristaltic sounds!

As I worked in this way, I gradually refined my massage technique. It became a synthesis of the methods developed by Aadel Bülow-Hansen, Dr Olesen, Reich, and conjunctive tissue massage, and it achieved quite remarkable effects. On many occasions, at the end of the session a patient would start to tell me about repressed memories that had come back into his mind during the treatment. This was a tremendously exciting period for me, for I realised that I had finally discovered what I had been seeking for so many years. Six years earlier, while I was studying with Aadel Bülow-Hansen, I had learned that in order to make anxiety neuroses disappear it was necessary to influence the vegetative system and so bring about a vegetative discharge (such as diarrhoea, from the anal system, or tears, which I regarded as a vegetative discharge from the oral system). I divided these forms of discharge into two categories, which I felt represented different degrees of intensity. Firstly there was the Reichian type of emotional discharge so familiar to me, which involved tears, sobbing and shouting. And secondly there were the words that patients used to express their problems, which were central to the psychoanalytical and gentle psychotherapy approaches. I was deeply convinced of the value of psychoanalytical therapy, in which the main cathartic process takes the form of verbal expression, of words that "soothe the patient's heart" and discharge the conflict.

I read an account of a research study carried out on pilots in the Royal Air Force (R.A.F.) during the war. This study found that pilots who spent a lot of their free time in bars, talking at length about the things they had lived through during sorties and bombing raids, showed fewer psychosomatic disorders and nervous symptoms in a medical examination than those who kept everything "bottled up" inside. The author of the article also described an experiment carried out under hypnosis on a former R.A.F. pilot who suffered from a stiff neck after the war. When, under hypnosis, he was finally able to let out the cries of terror and the painful emotions he had experienced but repressed during air raids, the stiffness in his neck also disappeared. Reading about these pilots' experiences helped me to understand the two different ways of discharging repressed emotional material. Both were upgoing, oral discharges; but one was strong, noisy and emotional, while the other was gentle and verbal.

I was determined to find out how this discharge process worked in physical terms. In the course of my therapeutic work, I had become more and more certain that the alimentary canal was the emotional channel: that the digestive tract transmitted the impulses of the id. This made sense to me, since in evolutionary terms the simplest type of animal is the single-celled amoeba, while the next step of development is a tubular organism that consists solely of endoderm. Now, as I massaged my patients, I often found myself wondering about the origin of the pulsating energy that corresponds to part of the unconscious. The answer emerged more and more clearly as time went by: emotional energy is an original, primitive form of energy that comes from the endoderm. As no part of a human being could be more primitive than the alimentary canal, it seemed to me natural that this should be the first place, the privileged centre in which instinctual energy circulated. I compared my hypothesis with Freud's theories, and I was struck by the fact that the oral and anal fixations - which are so central to his theories, and which I had found to be such real, physical phenomena - develop at the two extremities of this same alimentary canal. My belief in the key importance of this part of the body was confirmed: but the exact mechanism still eluded me.

I knew that emotional material could be discharged at two levels: from above, in an ascending motion through the oral system, and from below, descending through the anal system. Since there were also two forms of discharge from the oral system - the strong, tearful form, and the gentle, verbal form - it seemed to me that the anal system must work in much the same way. I was familiar with the strong form of descending, anal discharge - diarrhoea - but now I began to wonder what the corresponding gentle form of downward discharge might be.

It took me a long time to discover this fourth discharge mechanism; but as I continued to search for it, I became more and more convinced that it must exist. I kept thinking to myself: surely God or Nature cannot have created us as robots, as mechanical, powerless victims of our own emotions! If someone is having problems at work with his boss, surely he cannot simply let out all the rage he has been suppressing all day long, the moment he gets back home? Surely we do not necessarily even need to talk about our frustrations? I was particularly struck by the fact that individuals who have experienced similar traumas react in very different ways.

Some have a powerful emotional discharge; others develop blocks and psychosomatic symptoms; while still others seem to eliminate the effects of the shock on their organism in a mysterious, invisible way. I asked myself why some people became neurotic and others not, and I searched incessantly within myself for the answers to my questions. During this period I covered hundreds of pages with notes as I addressed these questions over and over again, in countless different ways. It was also a time in which I was living a rather difficult double life. At home I was still playing the part of a doll in a perfectly kept doll's house, surrounded by my husband and children; while during the day I often spent ten or twelve hours working with my patients. But I enjoyed coming home in the evenings to my "doll's house", and since my husband generally left me in peace - for he was not interested in my research, and we had little else to say to each other - I had plenty of time to reflect and to work out my hypotheses and theories.

This period of reflection brought me rich rewards. I was having some problems in my own therapy with Dr Houge at the time, because he had moved his practice to a new studio which he shared with two other doctors, and did not want them to be disturbed by the noise of screaming. But I had reached a point in my therapy where I had a tremendously strong need to scream: the "id" was screaming in me. Dr Houge tried putting a cushion next to my mouth to muffle the sound, and because it was not possible for me to scream at full volume as I wished, he kept on asking me to express what was happening in words. But, as I tried to explain, there were no words for what I was feeling. The dynamic pressure that was rising in me to scream was pre-verbal! There was nobody and nothing for me to scream at, there were no traumatic memories to abreact: there was simply an irrepressible urge arising from the depths of my body, compelling me to scream and yell to release the pressure in my throat. The process was not psychodynamic, for my psyche was not involved. It was more biodynamic, an urge without feelings that pushed mechanically for expression; it was the infant's instinctive wordless cry.

Finally I was forced to acknowledge that I could go no further with Dr Houge, although I was tremendously grateful to him for everything he had done for me. So I then went back to Ola Raknes, and spent a further year in therapy with him. But I found that he had changed dramatically since my first period of therapy-training with him. He seemed in some way to have "gone over" to the parents' side. Whenever I complained about my family, he would say in a sad tone: "Your poor parents! After all, they did everything they could for you!" He now also regarded crying as an escape, a defence mechanism. I continued to go to sessions with him, but I was left with the feeling that I must find some other place where I could be free to explore the extremely powerful dynamic process that was unfolding in me.

That was impossible at home, and I did not know of any other therapist to whom I could go. But my husband adored fishing and country walks, so I suggested that we should go for a caravan trip in the forests of northern Norway, close to the Swedish border. We duly set off, and I felt certain that out there in the wilds I would be able to scream all I wanted. All of this was long before the "primal scream" became fashionable! But I felt within myself a pressure so strong that screaming seemed the only thing that could relieve it. Dr Houge and Ola Raknes were not enthusiastic about this form of discharge, but I knew that I was in the process of releasing impulses from the pre-verbal phase of my childhood.

When we arrived at our remote forest destination, though, a dramatic event occurred that left me in a severe conflict. We had parked our caravan in a clearing and were just settling in, when suddenly a group of farmers brandishing shotguns appeared! My husband went to ask them why they were so heavily armed. To my horror, he learned that there were wolves in the forest and the farmers were going out hunting to protect their herds. I was appalled by the thought that I might be mistaken for a wolf and shot, or even attacked by a wolf myself. So, yet again, I had no choice but to keep quiet and swallow back my primal scream, but over and over again a single thought kept going through my mind: "I must, I absolutely must find an outlet for this energy!" I felt terribly disconcerted; but by now I was so used to functioning impeccably in my family circle that I simply sat quietly next to the caravan just as if I were at home, with all my theories, my papers, and above all my questions. Finally we drove back to town, and it was then that I discovered what I had been seeking for so long: the mechanisms of psychoperistalsis and self-regulation. After going such a long way to look for the solution, in the end I found it right there inside myself.

I have already mentioned the extraordinary sensation of pressure that I had been feeling around my mouth. This pressure was now stuck in my throat: the "id" wanted to scream. But one day, as I was lying down, the pressure suddenly began to melt away and a marvellous feeling of sweetness and inner peace swept through me: it was the soft movement of the libido. I understood that this was how nervous tension dissolved, and literally "sank" downwards from the throat into the depths of the body. First of all, this energy rose up through the emotional channel with an urge to find expression; when I was unable to express it, it went back down again, rippling down my body like a mild, warm breeze. While it was thrusting its way upwards, it could provoke screams and emotional discharges; but it could also reverse its direction into a harmonising, descending movement that dissolved the tension completely.

This was how I discovered what I call the "fountain", or the "melting principle". The moment when the ascending energy transformed itself into descending energy was extraordinary. I will try to describe it in detail: it was like a soft, calm breeze that emerged lightly from inside the tissue of my mouth to glide out through my lips and over the skin of my face. Like soft rings of smoke evaporating in the air, this breeze sifted down my chin and neck as tenderly as if it were showering kisses onto my skin. I had never imagined a relief like this, never dreamt that condensed tension could subside into these soft rings; it felt like being wrapped in a soothing fog, making my body so light it seemed weightless. Matter literally dissolved into air, turning flesh into spirit and carrying me from deepest despair to blissful well-being.

As I basked in this wonderful sensation of the libido circulation at work, I became aware of the immense power that it has to melt away internal pressure by gently caressing the tissue. I understood that the deep pulsations that had been repressed and later reactivated in me had finally managed to stream through me and reach the ego. This event was decisive: I realised that I would never again be the victim of the energetic movements that had tortured me for so many years. Now that I had found the melting fountain of the libido circulation, I would no longer have to submit to the strange forces that pushed my tongue out of my mouth or urged me to release a pre-verbal scream. This was a major breakthrough both in my professional career and in my private life, for I had discovered and been touched by the ultimate organic source of mental and physical self-regulation! From now on, the melting power of the libido circulation would enable me to handle the psychodynamic process at any point and to any degree in my body; I would never again be overwhelmed by the force from within, now that it had dissolved and begun to circulate.

I thought to myself: "First I was in the hands of my parents. Then I was in the hands of my neurosis. Then I was in the hands of my therapists. But now I have become my own healer. Life energy has cured me." It soon became clear to me that the peristaltic function and the melting fountain of the libido were closely connected in the process of organic self-regulation. I became determined to find a way to bring my patients into contact with these phenomena themselves, so they could become their own healers. With this intention foremost in my mind I continued to massage my patients, concentrating solely on the membranes that were swollen with energetic fluid. And over and over again, as I reduced the pressure in these membranes and my patients' symptoms gradually disappeared, I would hear the same loud gurgling sounds of peristalsis. I soon came to suspect that these sounds must be the key to the fourth, gentle form of vegetative discharge, especially now that I could see that they were somehow connected to the libidinal "fountain" and the melting principle.

One night when I was lying awake in bed, I heard these now familiar peristaltic sounds coming from my husband's abdomen. They were strong, aggressive gurgles, and soon he moved around in irritation until he found a more comfortable position. Then his breathing became even and deepened, and his belly produced some soft, long sounds as if in relief. As I listened to these changes, I became sure that peristalsis was indeed the gentle form of vegetative discharge. I realised that the organism does not necessarily have to undergo severe physical reactions such as diarrhoea in order to eliminate nervous tensions, for it has its own regulatory mechanism: psychoperistalsis. The channel for the instinctive, emotional energy - the "id" channel - is also the route followed by this same emotional energy on its downward journey, as the "fountain" melts tensions away.

This discovery made my work with my patients much easier: now I could regulate my massage to produce a more dynamic or more gentle effect. My technique became extremely precise, as I learned how I could lead my patients' awareness into deeper layers, or simply dissolve the layers that were "ripe" and closest to the ego. Working in this way, guided by the peristaltic sounds (to which I later gave the name of "psychoperistalsis"), I could also treat cases of depression and hysteria which we were not allowed to treat with Aadel Bülow-Hansen's methods. But with my new massage method I could simply choose how deep I wanted the effects of my work to go.

I was full of my discovery, and could hardly wait to communicate it to other people. The first person I told was Dr Houge, but to my disappointment he was so deeply involved in working with the Bülow-Hansen methods that he could not even understand what I was talking about. One day I asked him directly: "Dr Houge, don't you want to hear the truth?" He replied: "Gerda, you must not treat depressives or hysterics with massage!" I tried again to explain: "But can't you understand that I've found a method of treatment that lets me help the organism to eliminate nervous tensions? When I work with the peristaltic function, I can certainly treat cases of depression and hysteria!" My arguments were in vain; I was unable to interest Dr Houge in my discovery. I understood how Fleming must have felt when he discovered penicillin, and kept saying to his colleagues: "Look! Just look at what I've discovered", only to find that they saw nothing more than a speck of mould. Yet what Fleming saw in that grubby morsel was relief from suffering and healing for millions of people. I felt that I had discovered something analogous, but nobody wanted to recognise it.

I felt such a strong urge to talk about psychoperistalsis and its important function that I told all my colleagues about it. But nobody understood what I was saying. I felt as if I were standing in the middle of a bridge. On one side there were the clinical psychologists, whose refrain was: "You are too advanced for us. Go to see the behaviourists; experiments are their business." But when I ventured to the other side and tried to explain my discovery to the experimental psychologists, they would not even listen to me because I was "only a clinical psychologist"! So I was caught right in the middle of the cold war then raging in Oslo between the clinical and experimental branches of psychology; a war so bitter that the rival factions had taken up residence in separate faculties. Still, my psychologist colleagues' rebuff was no great disaster for me; after all I had a very pleasant life at home with my children, and my work still gave me endless satisfaction.

In a final attempt to get somebody to understand my theories, I explained them to my brother-in-law, who was a surgeon. I began explaining everything to him in detail, but his reply was: "For a theory to be worth anything, it must be capable of being explained in a few sentences." I told him that my theory could indeed be explained in a few sentences, as long as he was prepared to accept the fundamental premise: the function of vital energy. At that point he got up and left, saying: "That makes no sense whatsoever!" I kept on encountering this same problem: in order to explain my theories to somebody, I first had to persuade him to accept literally the concept of the libido as life energy in the organism. But as a clinical psychologist, it was scientifically unacceptable for me to talk of "energy". When I tried to describe the subject of my research work in a register kept by the university, I was asked to reconsider everything I had written and eliminate all references to the concept of energy. So I was obliged to keep quiet. However, my therapeutic results spoke for me; by then I had acquired an excellent reputation in Oslo as a therapist. Everything went splendidly - as long as I did not open my mouth. But as soon as I attempted to speak of my theories, not a soul was willing to listen to me. Such was the state of affairs in 1962.

THE PLASMO-FARADIC AND PLASMO-GALVANIC PRINCIPLES

I now began to focus my research work towards the "exact sciences", and I became intensely interested in electrolytic theory. One of the things I read was a treatise on electromagnetic currents in the fluids of the organism. This study helped me to confirm my ideas about the origin of life, and to develop them further. I based my concept of energy on the plasmo-faradic and plasmo-galvanic principles. The plasmo-faradic principle was already familiar to me from physiotherapy, where it was applied in the electrical treatment of muscles. When a motor nerve becomes damaged so that the muscle it controls can no longer be moved voluntarily, the muscle can be made to contract by passing an induced electric current (a faradic current) through it. So the energy in the muscles must have a similar effect to that of the electric current.

I have already described how my "beautiful legs" lost their shape and became hypotonic. When I lay down for a long time and relaxed completely, I could feel the energy slowly filtering into my muscles with tiny, rhythmical contractions, gradually giving my legs back their normal tonus and their original shape. From this experience I had concluded that it is vital energy itself that gives muscular tonus and causes muscular contraction. Cosmic energy in the human organism has a pulsating movement: it produces a contraction which is followed by an expansion.

Dr Olesen had also introduced me to the concept of "exercise through rest". He had discovered that muscles regained their tonus more readily when people were resting than when they were active. He had also noticed that animals that were kept tied up did not lose their muscle tonus. Based on these two observations, I developed the following theory: Hypotonus and resignation result from the withdrawal of energy. If the energy is allowed to move freely while the body is at rest, it will flow throughout the body and fill it completely - the process that I call the "libido circulation". The energy itself works to give a natural tonus to the whole organism, and it does so quite independently. I call this phenomenon the "plasmo-faradic principle".

This brings us to the second principle on which my concept of energy is based: the plasmo-galvanic principle. I had discovered that the cosmic energy within the organism has the ability to cleanse the tissue and dissolve the tissue armour; and now I found proof of this galvanic capacity. While I was a physiotherapy student, one of the doctors there - Dr Birger Tvedt, a specialist in relaxation and physician to the Norwegian Olympic team - had talked about the physiology of a sprain. He gave the following explanation for the swelling that develops around a sprained ankle: proteins come out of the bloodstream and create osmotic pressure by attracting large amounts of fluid to the spots where they have accumulated. If galvanic treatment is applied to the swollen area the proteins and colloidal substances are separated and transported back into the veins, and the osmotic pressure and the swelling disappear. I realised that, similarly, the tissue armour had an osmotic capacity, and I took this into account as I puzzled over the question of how to dissolve the tissue armour. I knew that the cosmic energy within the organism did indeed have the power to dissolve the armour and purify the tissue by breaking the metabolic residues (chemostasis) down into smaller particles that were then transported out of the body through the lymphatic system. So I concluded that the movement of this cosmic energy within the organism must be a galvanic cleansing process.

I later discovered that, in fact, things were even more complicated than I had supposed. All the same, these two principles are still helpful as an aid to understanding how massage works. Finally I realised that adrenaline and the sexual hormones act like cations in the body: in other words, they create a resistance that causes energy to accumulate and prepares the organism for powerful discharges. Adrenaline and the sexual hormones are central factors in the emotional processes, and this is one of the reasons why young people are particularly emotionally volatile during puberty.

It was during this period that I fully grasped the importance of the accumulation of repressed emotional layers that made up the tissue armour: for it is from this armour that psychosomatic symptoms and nervous pains originate. I also noticed that there was a very close link between the pressure of energetic fluid in the membranes and superficial tissues (the tissue armour), and the fluid pressure inside the intestinal walls (the visceral armour). During this period - a time that was rich in discoveries and theories for me - I also developed my theory of manic-depressive psychosis.

THE THEORY OF MANIC-DEPRESSIVE PSYCHOSIS

I discovered psychoperistalsis and developed the theory of manic-depressive psychosis virtually simultaneously, some months before I actually had a manic-depressive as a patient[2]. During this period, my thoughts kept revolving incessantly around everything I had seen at the Dikemark psychiatric hospital, and around the concept of cosmic energy. I had by then read "Character Analysis" by Wilhelm Reich, as well as several of his articles on cosmic energy. My enthusiasm was fired by his two basic theories of cosmic energy: Energy attracts fluid, and fluid attracts energy. Large concentrations of fluid attract smaller concentrations until the system reaches saturation point; then the stronger energy system begins to redistribute towards the weaker one. These two laws seemed to me to be fundamental, and I shall refer to them from here on as OR-I and OR-II respectively.

It was not until much later that I made the connection between all these different

2 See Appendix III, page 179

theories and my day-to-day massage practice. The majority of my patients suffered from headaches, and I found that there were two different types of headache. In one case the patients complained of a "force" inside their head, pressing outwards so that it felt as if their skull would explode; while in the other case they described the sensation as an "external force" pressing down on different areas of their head. Clearly two different types of "force" were at work: the first type, which began in the interior and pressed outwards, I called the centrifugal force, while the other type, which pressed inwards from outside, I called the centripetal force. There were also a few unfortunate patients who suffered from both types of headache.

Another theory that greatly interested me during this period was that of aggression-depression. According to this theory, aggression is the movement of energy towards the exterior, which the organism transmutes into hyperactivity of the sympathetic system. Depression is the opposite: the movement of energy towards the interior of the organism, which is characterised by hyperactivity of the parasympathetic system. These descriptions reminded me strongly of manic-depressive patients, whose behaviour alternates between a phase of aggressive activity and euphoria, and a phase of energy withdrawal and depression. I was also treating a cancer patient at this time, who had overall muscular hypotonus. Most of this patient's energy was static, stored in the intestinal walls. I found it very difficult to mobilise this deep stasis in order to make the energy go back into the muscles. So I was particularly interested in the direction in which energy moved. My experience had taught me that cosmic energy not only ascended and descended, but also moved towards the interior and towards the exterior.

This inward-outward movement in particular seemed to me to correspond with the psychiatric theory of the aggression-depression polarity. When somebody is unable to let out his aggression, he becomes depressive; and, as I have said, manic-depressives can swing from aggression and euphoria one day to deepest depression the next. It had often struck me how beautiful these patients were in their manic phase; they were full of energy, their faces glowed, and they looked extraordinarily young. This was because their energy, which was flowing outwards in this phase, attracted fluid and charged the surface membranes, producing their youthful appearance. But when their energy changed direction and retreated back into the interior of their bodies, their faces seemed to wrinkle like an old apple: the phenomenon that I called the "parasympathetic appearance".

The nature and function of these centripetal and centrifugal energy movements interested me greatly. By then, I was familiar with Reich's orgone experiments, and I tried to find the link between his observations and my own. "Energy attracts fluid and fluid attracts energy", says Reich's law (OR-I). For example, energy accumulates in the water of lakes. I focused particularly on his concept of saturation. As I have said, according to Reich's second law (OR-II), energy is drawn from smaller concentrations towards larger ones until saturation point is reached, when it returns to the smaller concentrations again. It seemed to me that manic-depressives displayed this same pattern, and that this theory of energy could account for the changes that occurred in the tension of their facial skin. With manic-depressives the muscular defences, the tensions and the tissue armour cease to work, either due to over-provocation or to accumulation, and the energy starts moving towards the outside. This process continues until the energy reaches saturation point and switches direction, which explains why the phases alternate so rapidly.

I vividly remembered two manic-depressive women I encountered in one psychiatric hospital. These patients organised gigantic parties at the hospital, and infected everyone with their delight. They were really very enterprising during their manic phase. Even the nursing staff declared that their work would be deadly dull without these patients. One day they left the hospital and went into town for a shopping spree. They visited a large department store, where they ordered a complete set of living-room, bedroom and kitchen furniture and fittings without arousing anyone's suspicions for an instant. It was only when each of them bought a dozen or more hats festooned with flowers and feathers that the store managers began to suspect something was amiss, and called the hospital. When I saw these two patients the following morning, they were unrecognisable. They looked years older, and their faces were wrinkled and shrunken. The previous afternoon they had been at the highest point of their manic phase, but now the energy had switched direction and become centripetal.

At the time of this episode, while I was working as a clinical psychologist, I had not yet discovered psychoperistalsis or developed any theories of my own about manic-depression. Indeed, as a psychologist I was not even entitled to treat these patients, since the view that this type of psychosis was constitutional, hereditary and endogenous was well established at that time. I was able to understand the energetic and emotional process of schizophrenia to some extent; but I could not yet see how manic- depressive psychosis was produced. In any case, I refused to allow manic-depressives to take part in my therapy groups during their pre-manic phase, as they were too disruptive; while in their depressive phase it seemed impossible to treat them.

WORKING WITH THE STETHOSCOPE

When I first started using my new massage technique to work on the fluid held in the muscle membranes, I followed the peristaltic sounds simply by ear. To begin with I had considerable success; but at a certain point some of my patients seemed to have reached an impasse. They complained that neither their anxiety nor their pains were diminishing. Why were they failing to respond to my treatment? When I examined my appointment book, I thought I had found the answer to this riddle. The patients who were making progress seemed to be the ones who came at the quietest times of the day. The resistant patients, on the other hand, usually came during rush hours when transport was difficult. I concluded that they probably had to hurry and arrived at the session under stress, and that this was undermining the effectiveness of the treatment.

But suddenly I realised that an entirely different factor was the main culprit. As I have said, I followed the peristaltic sounds with the naked ear, and now it occurred to me that the traffic noise during rush hours interfered with my hearing, so that my control lost its precision. But in order to release only the energy in the layers closest to the ego, it was essential to follow the peristaltic sounds precisely. The problem became even worse when I began working from home; my therapy room directly overlooked the street, and the traffic noise was always there. All my patients began to complain. I thought long and hard about what I could do in order to continue working effectively. Eventually I found the answer: since doctors use a stethoscope to listen to the heart and lungs, what was to stop me from using one to listen to the intestinal sounds, the "belly rumblings" from the abdomen?

The very next day I rushed out to buy a stethoscope. I spent a long time convincing the salesman in the medical equipment store that I needed a one-and-a-half metre long rubber tube rather than the length they normally sold to doctors! I was full of enthusiastic anticipation when my first patient arrived in my therapy room, and I was not disappointed. It worked wonderfully! Placing the "pick-up" on the patient's abdomen, for the first time I could really hear and follow the peristaltic sounds. I quickly learned to adjust my massage methods to respond precisely to the vegetative feedback that the sounds gave me. This little technical discovery opened up a new world to me. My treatment changed accordingly, and I began venturing into an area of research unexplored by me or by any other therapist. I called it "the ocean within", and it was not long before I was spending large parts of my days lying down with the stethoscope on my belly, discovering what psychoperistalsis was really about.

It was fascinating to listen to the sound registering the tiniest shifts in my feelings, every movement in my body, changes in breathing, and even changes in the stream of my thoughts. It was like exploring an entire new dimension of myself, the dimension of fluid. I compared it to Jacques Cousteau's undersea explorations, which he describes in "The Silent World". My inner ocean of intestinal waves and rhythmical fluids was also full of sounds, sensations and movements. It had its own laws and principles. To discern its mystery was a privilege and an insight into a remarkably sensitive and vulnerable part of nature. Exploring this new world was an exquisite experience, since I could only gain admittance to it when I was lying down and resting, free of obligations. But if I were expecting a visitor or I heard the telephone ringing, the waves would constrict. I did not feel this interruption as a constriction in my breathing or as tension in my belly. I could only sense that the process had stopped; the melting sensations disappeared and I felt empty, as if something was gone, taken away from me. There were no sounds in the stethoscope; there was no sense of the ocean within. Though the peristaltic waves were sensitive to interference, they only reacted to disturbances in my emotions. Demands, anticipation, insecurity, ambivalence - these all broke the flow of the waves, whereas neutral disturbances such as traffic noise, the radio, unfamiliar voices and so on did not.

The stethoscope became my most precious tool, a rubber necklace that hung around my neck from morning to night as I alternated between treating my patients and "treating" myself. Through the stethoscope I learned to listen to the language of the guts and explore the delicate relationship between psyche and soma. Usually the processes in the body appear in such subtlety they are invisible to the eye; they proceed so silently they are soundless to the ear. The physiological keys to change are usually only distinguishable by sensitive laboratory instruments. I often thought: how could I have missed this connection when I observed the explosive vegetative discharge of nervous fluid - diarrhoea? Should I not have realised that the answer was so simple, that in fact the same organs also provide for the gentler form of discharge? But natural laws are always logical and simple once we have discerned them. My work now took on new dimensions, and more than once I felt awed by the prospect of what this simple discovery would reveal. Slowly I began to see the connection between psychoperistalsis in the bowels and the libidinal streamings in the tissue. I had found a self-regulating method to release the libido circulation harmoniously. I watched my patients getting better...

Note: Using the stethoscope to control peristalsis

The purpose of this therapeutic technique is to activate intestinal peristalsis to encourage the elimination of stress by-products from the organism. To achieve this, we place a stethoscope on various areas of the abdomen, close to the navel. The stethoscope acts as an amplifier, so it enables us to hear even the tiniest intestinal sounds accurately. In this way the therapist can establish direct, intimate contact with the visceral tensions, and is constantly aware of the patient's immediate reaction to the treatment - whether massage or some other form of bodywork is being given. During the course of the therapy sessions the contraction in the patient's body is gradually loosened, and the muscular tonus improved. As progress is made in these areas, the body gradually reverts to its natural, spontaneous way of functioning; including the capacity for vegetative self-regulation, which is largely dependent on the general condition of the internal organs.

PSYCHOPERISTALTIC SELF-REGULATION

In discovering psychoperistalsis, I had found the body's own natural regulatory mechanism for eliminating nervous tension. Now I took to experimenting on myself with the stethoscope as often as I could. It seemed to me entirely natural that there must be a mechanism that would eliminate the by-products of stress automatically, even without massage. I wanted to discover the laws of this mechanism, because I felt sure that they would help me to understand what really happened in the organism when it was under stress.

The first thing I discovered was that when I was enjoying my work, my psychoperistalsis was open and active; but when my heart was not in whatever I was doing, the system remained closed. It seemed clear to me that psychoperistalsis followed the inner movement of pleasure, contentment, fulfilment and self-realisation. I found that two types of tension could interfere with this process: the first type had to do with the many repressed conflicts from earlier times, and the second with the effects of day-to-day stress on the organism. In my system of therapy the main purpose of massage is to unlock the psychoperistaltic process and so eliminate old, deep-rooted conflicts. Selfregulation is the daily practice of opening up this process to dissolve the tensions of the day.

I was also intensely interested in fluid at this time. To describe its behaviour I developed the concept of the "fluid tree" or "emotional tree", which I saw as being connected with the "tree" of the blood circulation, the vaso-motoric cycle. When I worked only on the little finger, for example, the psychoperistalsis opened and all the accumulated static energy of the "tree" flowed into the intestinal tract and was eliminated. By working on just one small part of the body, I could influence the stasis in the whole system and so regulate the excess of fluid in the whole body. So I reasoned that if massage could achieve all this, perhaps it could also be achieved without massage.

Once someone has rediscovered his self-regulation, all he needs to do is to sit or lie down, or embark on some activity that he enjoys; his psychoperistalsis will then open and the stasis, no matter where it has accumulated in the body, will be eliminated. This explains why, after a period of relaxation in which our psychoperistalsis has been activated, the old, weary-looking "parasympathetic appearance" disappears and is replaced by a natural beauty that is due to the radiance of tissues infused with cosmic energy.

During this period I submerged myself completely in the ocean of cosmic energy that I was discovering through psychoperistaltic self- regulation. At the same time, I was constantly searching for the key that would enable me to "open" the tree of peristalsis - that is, the complete system of fluid in the organism. And while I was treating Oscar, my first case of manic-depression who was so difficult to cure, I also started by hunting for this "key". It was as if, to begin with, the tree of peristalsis was closed; the organism was like a balloon, from which the energy could not escape. Instead, like the fluid, the trapped energy accumulated in the interior of the body. Only when I had found the "key" was it possible to eliminate the excess fluid from the body. My theory at that time was that, by eliminating the fluid, one could also eliminate the repression on the physical level.

As I continued to work with my patients, I was also busy writing down my theories. I had given up trying to talk about them to my colleagues or to psychiatrists, because they flatly refused to listen. Instead, I hunted avidly for scientific confirmation of the theory of psychoperistalsis. Finally I found what I was seeking in a Norwegian journal of medicine that I chanced upon in a psychiatrist's consulting room. It was an article by Professor Setekliev, a doctor who was very well known in Norway at the time. Professor Setekliev had directed a major research project on the intestine and its functions. The study showed that there were two kinds of peristalsis. The first, and best known, he described as the propulsive movement that carried food - the alimentary bolus - from the mouth to the anus. In this case the peristalsis was stimulated by the alimentary bolus itself. The second kind, whose function was unknown, he described as a process activated by the distension pressure of fluid inside the intestinal walls.

This article was the first scientific confirmation I had found for my theory of psychoperistalsis[3], as I was convinced the energetic fluid that triggered the psychoperistaltic response must be the source of the "distension pressure" Professor Setekliev had observed. But of course medical researchers could not confirm this theory while they continued to ignore the energy factor, so the second function of the intestines remained a mystery to them.

It was not until ten years later that I found further scientific evidence for my theory. I met a French doctor, also a researcher, to whom I talked about psychoperistalsis. He

3 See Appendix I , page 174

told me about a Japanese research study which had measured the electrical charge in the intestinal walls. The researchers had found that this charge was much, much higher than the charge measured in the hemispheres of the brain. He also explained to me that in Chinese medicine - as in alchemical medicine - each organ was believed to have both a physiological and an esoteric function. I realised that I had discovered the esoteric function of the intestines: the digestion of stress.

In the meantime, when I read Professor Setekliev's article I was so happy to have found confirmation of my theory that I tried yet again to talk about my discovery to psychiatrists and doctors whom I knew. Once again, though, I could find no-one to listen to me. Their standard answer was: "Unless the research has been carried out by a team of researchers and based on controlled experimental studies, it does not interest us."

FREUD'S THEORY OF HYSTERIA AND BIODYNAMIC THEORY

The word "hysteria" comes from the Greek word "hystera", meaning uterus. One day, in a lecture, Freud spoke of the hysterical male. All his colleagues burst out laughing because, since a man does not have a uterus, how can he possibly be hysterical? My contribution to the Freudian theory of hysteria throws some light on this question. We must start by going back to Hippocrates, who described hysteria as an illness caused by an excess of fluid in the uterus. If we regard this fluid first and foremost as an energetically charged substance, we can then explain the phenomenon of hysteria in energetic terms.

A polarity exists between the cranial and pelvic bones which causes energy to be drawn upwards from the pelvis and abdominal cavity, while energy from the cranial cavity is drawn downwards to the pelvis and legs. Ideally, there should be a pulsation between these two currents of energy, amplified by the solar (emotional) plexus and the sacral (sexual) plexus, which purifies the whole body according to the plasmo-galvanic and plasmo-faradic principles. The less interference there is with this pulsation, the greater the vitality, since the pulsation must penetrate through all the layers of the organism to purify and revitalise them. But where muscular and tissue armour is present, where psychological conflicts, defences and repressions are at work, a barrier is formed between the two poles. The energy then accumulates and stagnates on either side of this split, in the cranial and abdominal cavities.

In my view, this is the phenomenon of the schizoid split. With the schizoid character type, just as with the rigid, compulsive type, the energy does not seem to be connected to the emotional channel through the "plika[4]", and so it is unable to activate the emotional charge in the id (emotional) channel. Rather, the energy seems to have withdrawn and condensed at the base of the spinal column, in the sacrum (see Reich's theory on the accumulation of energy in the spongy bones). This energy pattern also corresponds directly with the oral and/or anal fixation of the schizoid or compulsive character type, and it inhibits the normal nervous dynamic, the dynamic pressure seeking an outlet. People with a schizoid character structure can talk for hours and hours without emotion, intellectualising, because their instinctual energy is not in contact with their emotional channel. With hysterical types the opposite is true: the emotional dynamic is always in the foreground.

Hippocrates' theory of excess fluid as the cause of hysteria makes complete sense when combined with the theory of the id channel and of energetic fluid. The force that we call the nervous dynamic is the outward symptom of this internal pressure, hunting for a way out. The pressure can be strong (finding expression through screaming, etc.), or gentle (verbal expression), but in either case it is the same force that manifests itself in dreams or in free association on the psychoanalyst's couch. In fact, in my view this dynamic pressure is the central element in the therapeutic process of psychoanalysis. It is a natural mechanism of self-regulation. Dynamic pressure develops in order to eliminate internal tensions and psychological conflicts.

While compulsive patients show extreme detachment from their feelings, hysterical patients lack this detachment altogether and are the victims of their emotions. This is due to their fixation in the genital region (Oedipus complex); the energy has reached the uterus and the sexual organs, but the nervous dynamic then creates a constant war between energetic expression (the id) and the psychological and muscular defences (the motor ego). This situation can cause permanent anxiety and the well-known psychosomatic symptoms of hysteria, because there is no proper "encapsulation". It is important to be aware that the nervous dynamic moves in an upward direction through the alimentary canal, which is connected to the whole emotional system. By contrast, the dissolving of tensions through psychoperistalsis - the process we call harmonisation - moves in a downward direction. Through its "melting principle", psychoperistalsis can help to saturate the ascending dynamic so that the emotional pressure dissolves. These upward and downward flows through the alimentary canal can work antagonistically or in harmony with each other, as if they use different channels within the same organ.

For a long time, this function of psychoperistalsis remained no more than a hypothesis. I needed to find confirmation from the outside world; and at the right moment, it came.

---

4 Plika: Danish concept, abbreviation of „parasympathetic rectal plexus"

When I moved to London, I began going to an acupuncturist. He was an excellent practitioner, and before long my mother and my family also began going to him. We all felt the same pleasant effects: a feeling of floating, of melting, etc. The treatment was really very similar to psychoperistalsis, which from then on I called "the natural acupuncture of the body". In fact I can actually feel the meridians the channels through which energy flows in acupuncture - when I give psychoperistaltic massages. And conversely, when the acupuncturist treated me with his golden needles, a delicious peristalsis opened up within me.

Everything went marvellously until the acupuncturist took a trip to America. Before he left, he recommended that I and my family should continue receiving treatment from his assistant: also an excellent practitioner. So we began going to the assistant for treatment, but something puzzling happened. He appeared to do more or less exactly the same things as his predecessor, he inserted the needles in the same places; and yet after each session I felt terribly upset and stressed. My psychoperistalsis vanished, and an unpleasant feeling filled my whole body. My family had much the same experience, so in the end we gave up the treatment. Not long afterwards, I met a woman who was also an acupuncturist and I told her what had happened. She gave me the answer to the riddle: "That's what happens when the needles are inserted too deeply." It was a moment of revelation for me. Here was confirmation of my theory that there are two channels between the membranes: an ascending channel through which the emotional, instinctive energy flows; and a descending channel carrying the spiritual, harmonising energy. The spiritual channel is closer to the surface, and contains more luminous energy; the emotional channel is the deeper of the two. The second acupuncturist had unintentionally inserted his needles in the emotional channel, whereas the first had been stimulating the spiritual channel.

Today, when I speak of psychoperistalsis, I am aware that instinctual energy rises up the emotional channel between the membranes until it reaches the "firing point", where it produces the movement of superimposition of which Reich spoke: like a flash of lightning, the energy is transformed and passes into the descending spiritual channel. I now also know that the heavenly feeling of sweetness I described earlier springs from cosmic light flowing through the spiritual channel: this is the first form of cosmic superimposition. Emotional energy is transformed by a second form of superimposition and then passes into the spiritual channel. The second form of superimposition is of course facilitated by the first form. This transformation of emotional energy into spiritual energy, which I call harmonisation, brings with it a sense of lightness; it dissolves feelings of hatred and gives release from the tyrannical demands of the instincts; and it opens up access to higher levels of spiritual consciousness (transcendence).

But let us go back to the case of hysteria. When the medical profession speaks of nervous fluid, to me this means that the energy is rising from the depths, bringing with it new layers of uncompleted cycles from the emotional circulatory system in the blood and so creating stasis in the whole body. The internal pressure then becomes so intense that it produces crying and movement. Because of the hysteric's profound anxiety there is no possible way out, no "fountain": the hysteric is unable to "melt" and let the energy harmonise and descend. In many hysterics there is a strong pulsation in the middle of the diaphragm muscle, due to excitation of the aorta. This large artery passes through a gap in the diaphragm, and its pulsation can easily be felt by putting a hand on the "emotional centre" of the body (roughly where the solar plexus is located). This pulsation again shows how the emotions and the reactivation of repressed feelings are closely connected to the increase in the energetic charge and blood flow. Hysterics are effectively the victims of their emotional and psychosexual feelings. But when the therapist succeeds, through massage, in enabling harmonisation to occur, the hysteric enters into a state of intense happiness. When treating hysterics it is important not to provoke too much ascending energy, because it will very quickly become blocked. It is better to use a very light, gentle harmonising approach.

I remember a young woman in one of my training groups in Paris whom I regarded as a typical case of hysteria. At a certain point in her "process" she discovered harmonisation, the "fountain". When I came back into the group room after a break I found her stretched out on the floor, her stethoscope on her abdomen and her face glowing with delight. She said to me: "Gerda, you have discovered the key to happiness!"

In fact the most striking characteristic of hysterics is their "permeability". They are less blocked than people with a character neurosis, who are much too rigid. Because of this, the "hysterical energy" circulates extremely rapidly, and so the symptoms keep moving around all the time. Hysterics' bioenergy is held back more by a form of psychic energy than by psychological defences. They have succeeded in constructing a very real tissue armour rather than muscle armour. This armour is however much more permeable to energy and so the hysteric comes under greater pressure from a strong energy field. Because the psychosexual pressure cannot be released, very powerful and painful bodily contractions are produced. The energy, which is blocked in the uterus, rises up the emotional channel towards the throat. As it passes through the opening in the diaphragm on the way to the heart, a feeling of acute anxiety or even panic arises. Hysterics fear this inflow of sexual energy to the heart, as it reactivates their original desire for their father and his subsequent rejection of their psychosexual feelings (i.e. the Oedipal complex and the genital phase).

When the energy enters the chest, there is also an organic reason for feelings of anxiety and panic. The plasmo-faradic (contractive) effect is exceptionally strong here, as the energy draws large quantities of fluid with it. This causes the distension pressure to change, producing intense pains. Hysterics try to release this inner pressure by becoming "hysterical": shouting, panic attacks, excessive crying. They can also experience intense pains or cramps in the uterus, diaphragm or elsewhere in the body, which orthodox medicine cannot explain and does not even take seriously. But these "hysterical pains" and "hysteriform symptoms" are all due to the plasmo-faradic principle of muscle contraction and the effect of changes in distension pressure on the nerves (OR-I).

Here it is worth noting that women who have had a hysterectomy can still be hysterics, for hysteria is an energetic mechanism anchored in the character structure (which can also be found in men). This explains why Freud had so much difficulty in validating his theories about hysteria.

ENERGETIC REGRESSION

Regression, in the Freudian sense of the term, reflects a genuine energetic regression, a withdrawal of energy, at a deeper level. For someone who is anally fixated, for example, the process can be described as follows: The organism experiences a conflict. It must find a way to escape from the pressure caused by this conflict, and it does so by withdrawing its energy, since without energy there can be no dynamic pressure. So the conflict is "buried". The organism constructs a solid tissue and muscle armour, and as a result the energy becomes static; it is encapsulated. An anally-fixated person withdraws his energy and stores it in the sacrum. His psychological defences - which reinforce the effect of the physiological defences work to ensure that no energetic pressure can build up in the anal region. So the person no longer feels any sensation of pressure on the anus at all. A similar phenomenon takes place in orally fixated people, as in the case I described earlier (where the person felt a ball of energy in the head that eventually moved down to the root of the tongue). Here the energy retreats from the mouth into the interior of the head, but the same mechanisms of solidification and encapsulation work to anchor it in place.

This withdrawal of energy also occurs in people fixated at a much earlier age, in the eye (ocular) segment. Their energy retreats into the skull, where again it accumulates and becomes encapsulated. No matter where the energy has become encapsulated, if the encapsulation subsequently loosens, the dynamic pressure will reappear. Schizophrenics, for example, who are fixated at the ocular and oral segments, feel a sensation of pressure from the top of the skull towards the interior of the brain, while with anally-fixated people the pressure originates from the sacrum and pushes towards the anus. This pressure reactivates the old conflict pattern.

Much the same happens with hysterics, but they are less strongly anally fixated and the energy is less firmly encapsulated. There is also a powerful attraction between the anus and the clitoris: they behave like two magnetic poles, so that the energy constantly attempts to flow from the anus to the clitoris. However, hysterics are clitorally fixated; they do not accept their sexuality, so the energy exercises an unrelenting pressure which keeps their conflict activated. This causes them to suffer from a constant feeling of longing. Hysterics may feel sensations at the level of the "plika" (see footnote on page 88), or fluid pressures may build up in the solar plexus and aggravate the normal pattern of stomach contractions. Pressure also builds up against the diaphragm when the energy passes from the abdominal cavity into the chest region. Hysterics are scarcely able to contain this energy, which ends by rising up through the emotional channel, bringing with it the familiar hysterical symptoms such as vomiting.

PSYCHOPERISTALSIS AND FREUDIAN DREAM THEORY

When I was a young clinical psychologist practising for the first time at the university clinic, I had a memorable dream. I dreamt that the director of the clinic was giving a party for all the staff, and had invited everyone except me. I woke up, feeling so tense that I could not get back to sleep; I had no peristalsis. When I finally managed to fall asleep again, the dream continued. The director of the clinic explained to me that there had been a secretarial error and he was terribly sorry, for he regarded me as one of the most important guests. He organised another party in my honour. When I awoke from this second dream I felt delicious currents of energy streaming down my body, and this time there was plenty of peristalsis.

I understood then that an essential function of dreams is to regulate psychoperistalsis. Freud described "good dreams" as the guardians of sleep. In biodynamic theory, these gratifying dreams have the function of opening up peristalsis. The dream acts as a kind of natural psychotherapy. The purpose of sleep and dreaming is to eliminate conflicts and accumulations of energy or emotions from the preceding day.

The simple fact of lying down on the bed is enough to trigger the stretching reflex. I have already talked about the importance of the startle reflex, which brings the flexor muscles into a state of chronic contraction. The flexors then become shorter than the extensor muscles, and the natural equilibrium between them is disturbed. This inhibits the stretching reflex, and as a result, the tensions trapped in the depths of the organism cannot be released. Luckily, the body also has a natural way to counteract this pattern. Thanks to the force of gravity, the simple act of lying down sets a process of dynamic relaxation in motion. The position of all the skeletal muscles changes, and little by little the equilibrium between the flexors and extensors is re-established. The residual tension in the muscles changes, the deep internal tension gradually dissolves, and the psychoperistalsis opens.

Sleep thus has an important effect on psychoperistalsis: an effect that, as I mentioned earlier, I call the natural acupuncture of the body. During sleep, peristalsis restores balance in the meridians and replenishes energy wherever it is lacking, so that the energy can flow freely and completely. Indeed, sleep should ideally eliminate all neurotic accumulations of energy. However, a certain amount of provocation is in fact needed in order to fully resolve conflicts and inner pressure. We have discovered that the most effective approach in "deep therapy" is to provoke first, and then to "melt" and harmonise. The repressed material is below a certain biological threshold and cannot be activated until it has been raised above this threshold. Provocation is needed to achieve this.

As a rule, when conflicts appear in everyday life the person concerned tries to reach a compromise or avoid the conflict as far as possible, which involves neutralising and repressing it. The diaphragm is used for this process of suppression. When we lie down on the bed, the contractions of the diaphragm cease and we begin reviewing our mental "audio and video tape" of the day's events. All the most intense and conflict-provoking experiences return to consciousness. So, as the first step in the process of stress elimination, we may first experience provocation in the shape of "bad" dreams. But if the provocation is too strong and "bad" dreams turn into nightmares, the distension pressure in the intestinal walls becomes too great and the closure principle comes into effect. To understand this, consider what happens when a cinema catches fire: everyone races to the fire exit at the same time, so it becomes blocked. The crowd must move back a little way from the exit and let people out gradually. The situation in the intestinal walls is much the same when the distension pressure is too high: although there is a need to discharge, the psychoperistalsis cannot function until the distension pressure is reduced. In order for the downgoing, harmonising energetic flow - the open principle - to come into play, the person must feel good, at ease with himself and free from any disturbing thoughts. If the psychoperistaltic closure is too uncomfortable the person usually wakes up, seemingly without having dreamt; just a moment of wakefulness "for no reason". Sometimes he may feel restless, or may be preoccupied with thoughts about his problems, his situation, etc. These nocturnal anxieties and images help to open up his psychoperistalsis, enabling him to fall asleep again, which in turn intensifies the psychoperistaltic reaction.

Nocturnal self-regulation is one of the main functions of sleep and dreams, and it explains why the regularity of night and day rhythms is so important: not only for physiological recuperation, but also for emotional and mental stabilisation. During sleep harmonisation occurs in the vegetative system, as a "dialogue" between the psyche and the soma resolves the conflicts and stresses of the preceding day. The unconscious is occupied with the psychological content, and brings it up in images and dreams. The more material it wants to resolve, the more vivid the dreams become. So psychoperistalsis is at its peak during the night, when the person is physically at rest and psychological barriers imposed by the conscious mind are at their minimum. This is one reason why we feel refreshed in the morning; this is why the previous day's problems may seem less gloomy, or a solution may even have occurred to us. Hence the common expression: "I'll sleep on it". This is also the reason why some of the most brilliant ideas produced by scientists and artists are conceived energetically at night, and become conscious thoughts, discoveries, or the key to a new invention in the morning. Provided the sleeper's dreams are pleasant and bring a solution, the open principle is able to operate. This gratification, this completion sets the psychoperistalsis in motion, enabling the vegetative system to dissolve surplus nervous tension and resolve mental problems. This, in brief, is the biodynamic approach's contribution to Freudian dream theory.

An example from my own family will help to illustrate this principle. My mother got into the habit of using the stethoscope when she was having difficulty in sleeping. As soon as the first sounds appeared, she felt able to relax more and more deeply until she experienced heavenly floating sensations, and finally fell asleep. My sister, on the other hand, did not believe in my theories. One day, though, her curiosity led her to put the stethoscope on her abdomen as she was lying down for a nap after lunch. She heard nothing, and eventually drifted off to sleep. When she woke up, she was startled by strange, loud sounds that seemed to come from outside. She took fright, thinking the children must have climbed onto the corrugated iron roof of the garage and were jumping around on it. It was only when she woke up completely that she realised the stethoscope was still in her ears, and the sounds she was hearing were coming from her own belly. My sister was a very natural, spontaneous person. When she was awake she had no peristalsis, but when she relaxed and rested, the psychoperistalsis began working.

I must mention one more example, coming from my time at the Bülow-Hansen Institute. One of the patients who was undergoing massage treatment there had problems with her three-year-old daughter. Since the age of six months, the child had needed an enema each day to evacuate her bowels. She was extraordinarily passive, and never played. She would sit for hours in the same position, not moving a muscle, apparently very calm: behaviour that was deeply abnormal in a child of that age. Her mother was very worried about her. Aadel Bülow-Hansen asked me to take this child into treatment. Just as I was about to start the first massage, I was called to the telephone. When I came back after about ten minutes, the little girl was still sitting in exactly the same place, in exactly the same position. Aadel Bülow-Hansen had warned me: "She can sit for an hour without moving while I massage her mother. It's truly astonishing!" The little girl was not catatonic, however; she was simply extremely passive. When the child was lying on the massage table, I noticed that she had no diaphragmatic breathing. I began to massage her very gently with the aim of freeing her diaphragm. After a few minutes of this slow, light massage, a respiratory wave passed through the diaphragm and completely filled the little girl's chest. I stopped the treatment at once and went to look for Aadel Bülow-Hansen. She told me: "Now, everything will start!" We never continued massaging our patients once their breathing "pattern" had been released, so that was the end of the treatment for that day.

Three days later, the little girl's mother telephoned in great excitement: "I must tell you what has happened! It's incredible! For the last three days my daughter has had diarrhoea! And she has become so restless, she's almost uncontrollable. There's no sign of the well-behaved, calm child she used to be; now she runs around the whole house! The second night after the treatment she refused point- blank to go to bed, and kept on asking for a bicycle. It was midnight before we finally persuaded her to go to bed by promising to buy her a bicycle the next morning. I can hardly believe the change in her: now she is natural, cheerful and playful, just like other children of her age!" The little girl never returned for treatment - a single massage was enough. Aadel Bülow-Hansen explained that children are very easy to treat because, unlike adults, they are not yet encased in a rigid layer of armour. Their armour is very "young", and their life-force and primary drive are still strong.

L.S.D.

For several years I worked in a variety of clinics and hospitals; developing my own methods, accumulating experience and knowledge, and integrating physiological and psychological factors into a single, unified theory that would enable firm diagnoses to be made. I felt on top form during this period: enthusiastic, strong, and very cheerful. I practised a great deal of psychoperistaltic self- regulation and dynamic relaxation, and I learned much from observing my own bodily sensations.

At this point I should like to talk about my collaboration with a psychiatrist who was carrying out research into the effects of lysergic acid, better known as L.S.D.. He prescribed the drug to some of his patients as part of their treatment, and also proposed that I should take it as a subject in one of his experiments. I refused, for two reasons: firstly, I am opposed in principle to all forms of chemotherapy, and secondly, I knew from my own experience and that of my patients that when one enters deeply into oneself, it is possible to have experiences just as intense and marvellous as those induced artificially by L.S.D., and without the risk of psychotic side-effects.

L.S.D. has, in fact, two faces: the "bad trip", which results when the Freudian unconscious is activated, and the "good trip", which is the discovery of the essential creativity of which Jung speaks; the oceanic feeling of being at one with the universe. Once the descending energy currents appear, they transport the body on an oceanic wave to merge with the universe. This profound feeling is one of absolute unity; there is no sense of separation, no individual identity at that moment.

The deepest cause of human unhappiness is the loss of our original sense of relationship with the universe, and our unceasing efforts to rediscover this unity. We have lost the rhythm, the oceanic wave, the divine descending currents that were our birthright; we have become isolated, mechanical and unhappy, and no longer have a sense of deeper meaning in our lives. Most people now have to content themselves with giving their lives some kind of artificial meaning, some neurotic significance such as ambition, the obsessive desire to possess material things, or power over other people. All these neurotic constructions disappear as soon as a person makes contact once more with the oceanic wave in the innermost core of his being. I myself felt such joy, such unending happiness in these states of profound dynamic relaxation, that I entered into timeless spaces, into eternity itself. I believe that the way of being adopted by the hippies of the "flower power" movement in the ‚sixties sprang from a genuine effort to rediscover the meaning of life. On the other hand, the use of drugs to re-experience the natural "narcotic" of the body - the harmonising force of the descending vegetative currents - actually destroys this hope. This is because the nervous system is made up of two antagonistic parts: the sympathetic and the parasympathetic systems. When one of them is activated artificially, this quickly triggers a reaction of over-excitement in the other. So the sweet, pleasurable sensations of the libido are soon replaced by agitation, fears, aggression and adrenaline effects, all of which produce the "bad trip". The problem with young people who want to "drop out" of society, as the hippies did in the ‚sixties and many still do today, is that they know very well what they do not want, but they have no idea what they do want. Because of this, they cannot enter into durable contact with the meaning of life.

Our world must find a way for people to escape from the states in which most become caught: weakness, neurosis, resignation, discontent, psychopathy, aggression and resentment. We need people who are full of compassion, strength and heart, and in contact with their innermost self. When a person regains contact with his descending vegetative currents, with the force of harmonisation, he is able to free himself from his state of dissatisfaction, transform his repressed feelings of hatred and manifest the "qualities of eternity".

The thing that struck me while I was working with patients who had taken L.S.D. was that deep dynamic processes had been activated in these people, deep energies awakened, but there had been no harmonisation, no completion of the emotional vaso-motoric cycle. As a result, repressed emotional and psychosexual layers had risen towards the surface, but had not been "digested". No psychotherapeutic work had been done to integrate them, nor had the organism's natural process of stress digestion taken place, so they remained in the organism. I learned that massage must be used cautiously with people who have taken L.S.D., because the energy moves around extremely rapidly. A combination of psychotherapy and massage is more appropriate.

MY MOVE FROM NORWAY TO ENGLAND

I had no idea what destiny had in store for me. By this time I had divorced with few problems. My elder daughter had gone to America to get married, my younger daughter was pursuing her studies in Copenhagen, and my son was at college in England. I was living happily in Oslo, content with my excellent position as a clinical psychologist and supervisor at the Vinderen Student Clinic. As my colleagues kept telling me, I was heading for a bright professional future in Norway. At home, after my work at the clinic, I was also giving psychoperistaltic treatment to a large number of clients suffering from all kinds of nervous tensions and psychosomatic complaints. I loved my life and my work, but all the same I could not find a single soul among my colleagues who would accept my research and discoveries. Even Ola Raknes, who appreciated the discussions I had with him, did not understand what I was doing with my massages. It was very frustrating; one day, at a psychology lecture, I heard the lecturer sigh: "Life is not easy for us as psychologists. Unlike doctors, we have no stethoscope to help us." And I longed to cry out: "But we do have a stethoscope!" But whenever I tried to speak of my work, people always replied: "You're too advanced for me!"

On one occasion I was invited to give a lecture at a conference organised by the Faculty of Psychology, which was attended by both clinical and experimental psychologists. I had hoped that at least the experimental psychologists would be interested in my research. They were not.

Then I met a psychiatrist who specialised in manic- depressive psychosis, and told him about the case of my patient Oscar (see Appendices). As I spoke, I saw his face taking on the expression that I so often encountered when I mentioned my work. It was as though I were telling him that I had plucked the moon from the heavens and brought it with me in my pocket. The only psychologist who was interested in my work was Professor Ursin. He invited me to use the experimental laboratory facilities at the

University of Bergen; however, to do so I had to get approval from another psychologist, Professor Christiansen. Although this professor was one of my friends, he did not accept the concept of energy at all. He refused my request with the words: "Gerda, give up psychology! Go to London and write novels instead!" (I had once confided in him that I wanted to be a writer.) Today I thank Professor Christiansen from the depths of my heart for his words. The idea of moving to London actually began to take shape in my imagination, and I began to speak about my departure. All my colleagues and psychiatrist friends advised me not to try to become an avantgarde therapist in London, but to work at the Tavistock Clinic, which was renowned for its advanced research. So I decided to apply for a job there as a clinical psychologist.

One day, in my waiting room, I found a professor from the Tavistock Clinic who wanted to try out my massage treatment. I told him of my desire to move to London, and without further ado he offered me a job at the clinic. He wrote to me twice, but I forgot to reply; I had not yet really made my decision. Finally, though, I telephoned the director of the clinic. She was rather short with me (my call had interrupted her at a meeting), and I abandoned the plan. Instead, I telephoned my professor of child psychology and confided to her my latest plan, which was to apply for a post at the Anna Freud Clinic. Her reply galvanised me into action; she said: "Fine, let's meet in London on Tuesday at the Norwegian Embassy." It was Friday! For me this was a gigantic step forward; I had never travelled on my own before.

I went outside to get my car, and there I met Ola Raknes. In all the years that I had known him, I had never before bumped into him in the street! He said to me: "I've heard that you want to leave for London. Would you be willing to take over my London patients? I have been going there regularly, but I've decided to stop. Here are the address and telephone number of my secretary in London; she will arrange everything." According to plan, I arrived in London the following Tuesday. I made contact with Raknes's secretary, and made all the necessary arrangements to take over his practice. Next I visited Ronald Laing, who promised me his fullest support. I settled in London and immediately had all the patients I could handle. Everything fell into place as if by magic. Ola Raknes, who came to visit me, complimented me on my work and said he was very proud of me. And so my new life in London began, in February 1969.

III NEW TECHNIQUES AND NEW THEORIES

EARLY DAYS IN LONDON

Ronald Laing and Cooper gave me a very warm welcome, recognising me as a Reichian analyst. Laing was particularly interested in my theories about psychoperistalsis. He offered to send me some patients and invited me to become a member of the Philadelphia Association. So I contacted the Association's legal representative, but he suggested that rather than becoming a member I should apply to the Ministry of Health for permission to open my own clinic. I went to live in the home of one of Laing's patients in Kensington High Street, where my children came to join me. I was working ten hours a day during this period. I also got in touch with the director of the Tavistock Clinic again, and she told me that I would be welcome to work there whenever I liked. However, given the nature of my research work and my theories she personally advised me to hold onto my independence and stay in the avantgarde. She felt that working at the Tavistock Clinic would be more likely to inhibit my research.

Next I began holding seminars for psychotherapists, after David Boadella - an experienced Reichian and the author of several books about Reich - kindly organised the first seminar for me. I also presented my work in a lecture to the Jungian Association of Depth Psychology. At this point I want to describe a particularly interesting case.

The patient in question had undergone L.S.D. therapy before coming to me for treatment. As I mentioned earlier, L.S.D. has a strongly provocative effect but does not resolve anything, so the material that has been provoked remains stirred up and undigested at different levels in the organism. This particular patient came to me with just such a mass of undigested material, and during the course of his therapy a harrowing story gradually emerged. His father was a criminal, an out-and-out gangster, who was determined that his son should grow up to be a "tough guy" and did everything in his power to achieve this aim. So, from the age of three onwards, the little boy was subjected to the most unspeakable horrors. During vegetotherapy my patient relived these dreadful scenes from his childhood. He had been forced to witness murders, tortures, mutilations... Having opened my heart to universal love and suffering, I found it almost unbearably painful to listen to this man's screams and sobs as he told his terrible story.

On one occasion his father took him to a canal, where he and his accomplices threw hand grenades at members of a rival gang who were aboard a boat. When the massacre was over, the father forced his little boy to gather the scraps of human flesh and bone up into plastic bags. There seemed to be no limits to what my patient's father and his henchmen were willing to do to "toughen him up"; they also tortured the child and forced him to take part in the orgies they held in an old cotton factory. But the little boy loved his father very much, and learned to dull his senses. One day his father even took him up in a light aircraft and flew low over the family home, where, before his mother's horrified eyes, he dangled the child by his ankle, head downwards, outside the cockpit of the plane. These were the events that made up the daily life of that little boy. The adult man seemed normal, but as soon as I led him to deeper levels with my method of dynamic relaxation (following the impulse from within), he became truly terrifying. More than once, when the urge to kill arose in him, I had reason to fear for my life.

Eventually, my patient remembered the final episode in his distressing story. He was four years old, and yet again his father and the gang were torturing him - for the fun of it, and to make him "tough". He remembered them plunging him into a bath of icy water, over and over again, and holding his head under the water. And suddenly he died. He told me how he left his body through the crown of his head, and saw the light of God. He had no desire to return to his body. But his father was deeply shocked by what he had done, and fought desperately to revive his son. And suddenly the little boy felt himself sliding back into his body; through the crown of his head, then through the neck, and then he was back completely, in a state of total shock. Beside him was his father, in tears, down on his knees, praying to God for forgiveness. The little boy caught severe pneumonia, and his father kept him close for weeks, cradling him in his arms, showering him with all his love, warmth and repentance. Eventually the little boy recovered, and his father gave up his criminal career. He became a Jesuit.

VEGETOTHERAPY

During my first years in London I worked much less with massage as a means of obtaining vegetative abreactions. Instead I concentrated on my patients' breathing and practised a deep, regressive, intensive form of vegetotherapy whose effects - long before Janov - were very much like those of primary therapy. Some of my patients wanted no massage at all; they only wanted vegetotherapy. During the therapy I gave them verbal instructions to guide their breathing. For example, one classic method was to have the patient lying on the couch and simply say to him: "Try to feel if there is anything you want to say or do." This method is now called "following the impulse-from-within". It is a subtle combination of psychoanalysis and advanced Reichian techniques. My personal therapy with Ola Raknes had given me the fundamental strengths I needed to work in this way: an open heart, tolerance, understanding. With these qualities to support me

I was able to let my patients express their feelings physically; and that is the essential difference between this type of therapy and psychoanalysis, which is purely verbal.

I experimented with various elements of the therapeutic situation. Freud used to sit behind the patient, at the head of the couch. Reich took a revolutionary step by sitting next to the patient, so that the patient could look at him upon opening his eyes. Now it was my turn to decide where to sit. I chose a very flexible approach: I might sit some distance away from the patient or beside him, behind him, in front of him, very close to him, or even touching him. My therapy room, though, was always laid out in the same way: there were two chairs facing one another, a psychoanalytical couch and a massage table. To this day, I still arrange my therapy rooms in this way. At the beginning of the session the patient and I sit on the chairs and have a brief talk, to help us decide which part of the "therapeutic furniture" we shall use: staying face to face on the chairs, or moving to the couch for verbal therapy or the table for massage.

During the first few sessions I usually let the patient talk as much as he feels the need to do. This gives him time to get to know me, and I have time to get to know him too. Then, when the time is ripe, he lies down either on the massage table, or on the couch for vegetotherapy. The basic instruction I give to the patient in vegetotherapy is: "You can say or do whatever you like, but you don't have to say or do anything at all. Just try not to hold back anything, any words or movements, and if there is anything you want me to say or do, just tell me." I call this the "midwife approach". It requires the therapist to let go of his own need to be active, to talk etc., so that he can be receptive, passive and patient, and can allow the dynamic healing process to develop of its own accord. The therapist's job is simply to offer total love and acceptance so that the patient's "impulse- from-within" can develop fully and transform his whole being.

Massage is the very best way for the therapist to discover the love that lies within himself; in fact it is quite impossible to give a massage without love. The atmosphere that develops is the most important factor of all in therapy: the therapist's empathy, tolerance and understanding create this atmosphere. "Dry" intellectualism is not merely insufficient, but it actually destroys the movement of life, the biodynamic process itself. So the arrangement of the therapy room is not an unimportant detail; it is one of the factors that creates an atmosphere in which the therapy can go really deep. The smaller details are also important; my patients' strong abreactions taught me to keep plenty of paper tissues in the room, and a plastic bucket in case they needed to spit or vomit. Deep vegetotherapy provokes all kinds of abreactions as the body struggles to rid itself of its impurities.

THE PSYCHODYNAMIC PROCESS

While I was working in Norway, our present two fields of activity were still separate: psychoanalytically-oriented psychotherapy, and physiotherapeutic massage. In London, however, I discovered how to bring these two forms of therapy together, and I also began really using vegetotherapy and the method of the "impulse-from-within". I was constantly astonished by all that could happen while I simply sat there on my chair, facing the patient. But thanks to my flow of descending energies, my inner harmony, my contact with the ocean of cosmic energies, I gradually came to develop my own "therapeutic wisdom"; the ability to ask the right questions, to give the right answers, to intervene and to be silent at the right times. It was as if my contact with cosmic energies had opened the door to an inner therapeutic skill: my intuition. I remember one amazing example of this ability: during a session with one female patient I thought I glimpsed the outline of a penis on her stomach. When I looked more closely, the image vanished. I made an encouraging noise: "Mmm hmm?", and my patient at once replied: "Yes, now I'm beginning to understand that I've always believed I have a penis!"

So the time passed, and I was intensely happy in my work. As I worked with my patients, the deep contact I experienced there opened up my psychoperistalsis and en-couraged my own process of purification and self-healing as well as theirs. Nowadays I often say that the best therapy is to be a therapist.

My attitude towards my patients is always to believe what they say, even if it seems extraordinary to me. Some of them have greater psychic abilities than I do, and so I let them guide me. Because I am not a "superego type" of person, new questions and new theories are forever springing up in my mind.

The people who came to me for therapy in London were a very different type from my patients in Norway. They were what I called "people in transition". Most of them had taken drugs which had opened them up to a higher consciousness of universal truths, but had also made them more difficult to treat because their energy was so "loose". I had to be very careful when massaging these people, especially those who had taken L.S.D., because their synapses were over-activated and so their energy moved around extremely quickly at the slightest provocation. This was all the more true of hysterics who had tried L.S.D.

The thing that fascinated me most of all was seeing how much could happen to a patient when I was doing nothing at all. I remember one man who had suffered terribly at school, where he had been bullied and treated as a scapegoat by the older boys for several years. He had lived with his grandmother, and everything in his life had been too small for him: his home, his room, his school uniform. When I tried the impulse-from-within method with this patient, some quite extraordinary sessions resulted; yet all I did was sit on my chair, accepting and open to all his discharges, his gasps and cries, his vomiting, as he struggled to break loose from his neurosis. His inner healing forces rejected and expelled everything that prevented him from living fully, and opened him up to experience inner happiness. A powerful personality appeared, set free by his outbursts and screams. So when the first of Janov's primal scream therapy patients began arriving in London, my patients were able to tell them: "But Gerda has been using the primal scream with us for years!"

Not everyone was equally responsive to the impulse-from-within method. When I suggested to some patients: "Feel your body... what does your body want to do?", they simply answered: "I don't feel anything. All I can feel are tensions... here, there..." They experienced their bodies as "wooden", and so what they needed was a much more physical technique. For them I used the method I now call "deep draining", which is a peristaltic variant of Aadel Bülow-Hansen's massage technique. Other patients again had their energy so strongly encapsulated that I had to use more powerful methods than the "impulse-from-within".

I made a distinction between patients who had a dynamic process going on within them, and the more "wooden" or "rigid" patients who needed my intervention. With the first group of patients it was simply a matter of speaking directly to their unconscious, their id, their body - not to their conscious mind. For example, I would say: "Feel your body... let it breathe..." and then simply allow the unconscious to rise into consciousness. Nothing more was needed. The therapist's voice and his choice of words are extremely effective therapeutic tools, and can be used to speak either to the conscious or to the unconscious mind. With the second group of patients, I would begin by speaking to their conscious mind: "Try to feel your chest sink down into you when you breathe out." If they moved into a dynamic process, I would then speak to their unconscious: "Just allow it to happen..." This method is very powerful. In vegetotherapy it is important for the therapist to be clear which part of the patient he is addressing. When I say: "Feel your body and breathe deeply", for example, I am talking to the ego, the voluntary part. But when I say in a soft voice: "Let it breathe", it is the unconscious, the id, that responds. Sometimes I ask my patients to put their hands on the upper part of their chest, for in many cases this is where the whole process begins.

Of course, this technique is based on Reich's theory of respiration. Most Reichian analysts touch their patients, but I developed this technique so that it could also be used in classical psychoanalysis, where touching patients is forbidden. Neo-Reichian therapy, on the other hand, tends to go too far in the opposite direction and touch patients too readily. Ola Raknes, who regularly visited Reich at Orgonon after the war, explained to me that Reich attached great importance to theoretical criteria in relation to touch: when the patient should or should not be touched.

This reminds me of an anecdote Raknes told me about one of his visits to Reich. During a supervision session in which Raknes discussed his patients with Reich, Reich said of one patient: "Do not touch him under any circumstances." Not long afterwards, however, Raknes had an intuition that it would be right to touch that patient, and he did so. At the next supervision session he told Reich about the incident, and confided his fear that Reich would now reject him because he had not obeyed Reich's instructions. And Reich replied: "I will never reject you for disobeying me; but I might reject you if you were too obedient."

Of course I touched my patients as well, and I also used Reich's techniques of massaging the masseter (jaw) muscles, the cheeks and the nape of the neck, and dissolving the different segments of the muscular armour. But my interventions were never rough or hard; my way of dealing with bioenergy is a profound, regressive, yet gentle therapy. To be sure, it is not difficult to make patients cry or scream using physical techniques, and certain Reichian therapists make full use of these techniques. But if the scream is a simple discharge of physical pain caused by stress in the muscular armour, it has no therapeutic effect; on the contrary, it is anti-therapeutic. The manipulation techniques in Reichian vegetotherapy should only be used to help the patient express an emotion that is already present; never to provoke emotions artificially.

There is great confusion in neo-Reichian and bioenergetic circles about the role of manipulative intervention by the therapist. For my part, I had learned the art of light touch from Aadel Bülow-Hansen, and I knew that this gentle approach was far more effective than heavy pressure on the muscles. After all, what does a muscle do when another muscle puts pressure on it? It becomes hard and resistant. In any case, the therapist should not try to use force against the patient's resistance; on the contrary, it is better to befriend and "seduce" the resistance, without losing respect for it. When that resistance originally came into being it was important; it was needed for protection. When the therapist works with a light touch, the patient is less on his guard and can surrender to the authentic emotion. One of the methods I often used is known as "dynamic relaxation".

What happens when someone relaxes? First of all there is a feeling of well-being; tensions are felt less, and they loosen a little. But as someone goes further into deep relaxation, the muscular tensions begin to dissolve and the dynamic process overcomes his resistances. This is the true secret of biodynamic therapy; it is a matter of letting the psychodynamic process emerge from the depths of the body so the emotions rise up of their own accord and are discharged, accompanied by vegetative abreactions. This produces an authentic transformation. Dynamic relaxation can be induced by massage, by psychotherapy, or by simply lying down. It works on a simple principle: the patient feels so secure that he no longer needs his defences. The defences can then dissolve and the repressed emotions return to consciousness, where they can be abreacted.

I constantly worked to unify my methods, and I introduced many of the techniques that I had learned from Aadel Bülow-Hansen or developed myself into Reichian vegetotherapy. I had begun trying to integrate the techniques and theories of Bülow-Hansen, Raknes and Reich - both in theory and in practice - while I was still in Norway. But at that time psychoanalysis and physiotherapy were like night and day, with no conceivable link between them. In London, however, these techniques blended into a single approach, and it was as if I were playing different melodies on the same piano. This was how I developed my own approach of "biodynamic vegetotherapy".

Reichian therapy is not fundamentally so very different from psychoanalysis. It is often also verbal, and the verbal approach is much the same in the two therapies: similarly, too, the patient goes through the various psychological stages both energetically and psychologically, from the oral and anal phases to the Oedipal conflicts of the genital phase. Freud's libido theory is confirmed constantly during Reichian therapy. The biggest difference with my approach is that the therapist does not interpret the material that emerges; the patient himself does all the work of discovering and understanding his own inner life. Of course I have my own interpretation, but I keep it to myself. It is always confirmed by the patient, when he grasps the different elements in himself and unites them in his body and his consciousness. My role as a therapist is simply to make it easier for the patient to understand his own depths; the patient's role is to explore and make discoveries.

GROUP TECHNIQUES AND LOWEN'S WORK

After some time in London I began to integrate my own methods with group techniques and Alexander Lowen's system of bioenergetic analysis. In 1970 the Esalen group visited London to give a series of seminars, where I learned many interesting new therapeutic techniques. These did not include bioenergetic work, but not long afterwards John Pierrakos gave a seminar on bioenergetic analysis at Centre 48, where I was living at the time. I was intrigued by these neo-Reichian techniques, and particularly by Lowen's approach.

Above all, I was excited by all the different exercises designed to encourage emotional expression: hitting, kicking, stamping, vibration exercises, shouting, etc. I quickly began trying to integrate these techniques into my work with individual patients. The exercise that interested me the most was one in which the patient lies on his back, hitting and stamping on the mattress with his fists and feet and repeating "Yes" or "No" or "I will" or "I won't", over and over again. This exercise reveals an extraordinary amount about when and how the patient's primary personality was repressed and forced to yield, and also about how the superego came into play. Indeed, a person who is able to take pleasure in saying all four of these short phrases out loud, without the slightest feeling of guilt, will be able to develop his personality to its fullest extent. But if the patient has to be persuaded to do this exercise or demands to know what the point is, this is a clear sign that his primary personality has been undermined; he has lost his spontaneity and has to stop and think before speaking and acting.

I greatly enjoyed working with these exercises, but as I continued to use them I found I was becoming confused about my role as a therapist. I was used to acting as a kind of midwife, encouraging my patients' emotions and abreactions to come of their own accord; but suddenly I felt more like a gym teacher, giving orders and becoming actively involved in the process myself. I found it more and more difficult to integrate this kind of work into my system of biodynamic therapy. Eventually I abandoned these exercises altogether - and it was then that I discovered how to integrate them into my approach. I continued using the gentle method of the "impulse-from-within", telling the patient: "Let your body speak, let it do whatever it wants, let the movement develop", and when a movement had appeared I then used one of Lowen's exercises to help the patient express his emotions. For example, when a "No" or an "I want" formed on the patient's lips, when the emotion was there, I invited him to use the exercise to help him discharge the feeling.

This developed into a new method that was both powerful and at the same time truly biodynamic; that is to say, fully integrated into the patient's own process. When used in this way, there was nothing mechanical about the exercises. For example, if a patient murmured: "I feel lonely" in a small, soft voice, I suggested that he should stretch his arms up over his head and repeat: "I feel lonely!" This would make the feeling of loneliness expand and fill the patient, until it finally discharged of its own accord. I found this technique of repeating a single key phrase - which Lowen also used extensively - an extremely useful way of encouraging the patient to express his emotions and go deeper in his process.

Around this time I met Jay Stattman, a neo-Reichian therapist from the United States who had developed a method that involved using mental imagery in a state he called "creative trance". He simply told the patient to close his eyes and see if an image appeared. This method fitted in extremely well with my biodynamic approach. When an image appeared, when emotional breathing and deep vegetative movements developed, I told my patient: "Describe the image. Talk to the image, express it!" Once the patient was in a state of regression I would ask him questions to evoke more memories: "What room are you in now? In what house? How old are you? Is there anyone else in the room?"

I found these verbal techniques increasingly valuable as a way of helping the patient both to integrate the material that emerged and to explore further. By using the voice as a gentle, reassuring therapeutic tool, I could help the patient to let go of his resistances and lower his defences. Indeed, the effectiveness of the therapy depends largely on how the therapist uses his voice. If he addresses the superego, he simply reinforces the patient's defences; but if he succeeds in speaking to the id, he sets the biodynamic process in motion and supports it. At this point I want to introduce an important distinction between two different levels of being: the tragic and the trivial levels.

THE TRAGIC AND THE TRIVIAL

The tragic and the trivial levels are fundamental concepts in biodynamic psychotherapy. While I was still working in Oslo, I had come to the conclusion that one of the most important causes of neurosis can be a failure to understand or recognise the respective roles of the tragic and the trivial in life. I arrived at this insight after hearing a story that the teller swore was true - although I suspect it is apocryphal.

The story revolves around two psychiatrists who fall into conversation at a party. One of them declares: "I've discovered a new method for treating depression. It works wonderfully!" The other man asks him how the treatment works. "Well", replies the first psychiatrist: "one day a woman in her fifties came to see me suffering from terrible depression. She could see no point in living any more, and could only think of one solution: to jump off the Golden Gate Bridge." "So what did you do then?""I simply said to her cheerfully: ‚Yes, I think that's what you should do!' And she just burst out laughing. I had helped her to change levels, and she was ‚saved'."

The second psychiatrist had quite a different character structure from the first: he was much more rigid and an experimentalist type. He decided to try out this new method for himself at the first opportunity. Not long afterwards he had the chance to treat a similar case: a woman of much the same age presenting much the same symptoms. So when she began to talk about committing suicide, he said to her in his deep, slow voice: ‚Yes, I think that's what you should do' ...and she did just that.

The difference between the effects that these two psychiatrists achieved is difficult to explain in writing, because it hinges on the tone of voice they used. The first man expressed his opinion in a trivial, humorous tone; the second spoke the same words in a serious, existential tone. Arthur Koestler analysed these two levels thoroughly in one of his books, and concluded that it is impossible to live exclusively on either one of them. If someone lives only on the tragic level, he will end up in a psychiatric hospital; if he lives only on the trivial level, his life will become empty and meaningless.

A conversation with my husband's aunt helped me to understand this distinction particularly clearly. She wanted my opinion about a phenomenon that had been puzzling her greatly. "Gerda, it's strange", she began. "Whenever I simply ask someone: ‚How are you?', he starts telling me the story of his life!" I agreed with her that it was certainly strange - and just a few moments later I was startled to notice that I myself was now in the middle of telling her my life story! It was then that I realised that the solution to the mystery was the tone she used when she said: ‚How are you?'.

Unlike most people, she did not simply say the familiar words in an everyday tone, without expecting an answer. She said: ‚How are you?' in such a serious, empathic tone that everyone she spoke to felt that she was genuinely listening to him and encouraging him to tell her exactly how he was!

These observations helped me to make my therapeutic approach more and more subtle. In therapy, as in everyday life, if the therapist asks the patient: "How are you?" in a trivial tone, it is impossible for the patient to reply from the depths of his being. If, on the other hand, the therapist speaks in a tragic, empathic tone, the patient is likely to respond at that level by revealing things that are really important to him. One of my most important therapeutic "tools" is consciously using these two levels to achieve different effects. If I want to plunge a therapy group or an individual patient into the past, into the depths of their emotions, I use a "tragic" tone of voice to help them reach the core of their personality. But if I want them simply to experience bioenergy on the mesodermic, muscular level, rather than on the endodermic, visceral level, I speak in a light, trivial tone.

I was constantly aware how important it was to prepare myself before giving a session, to make sure I was at the right level. After all, if I myself was attuned to a rational, efficient level the patient would also respond at this level, and it would be difficult for me to lead him into the deeper layers of his being. Like a radio, the therapist must modulate his frequency. I am convinced that this concept is crucial, and that far too little attention is paid to it in the therapy world. If only psychoanalysts and therapists would break away from the rational, efficient, functional level, their patients would really be able to enter fully into their own depths.

Once I had fully grasped the importance of these two levels of being, I could also explain various facts about child-rearing and about the origins of neurosis in a completely different way. The case of a small boy sent for psychiatric treatment because of behavioural problems illustrates this viewpoint beautifully. The psychiatrist eventually discovered that everything had begun some time ago, when the child asked his mother: "Mummy, where do I come from?" and she told him: "I bought you." "And how much did you pay for me?" asked the little boy. "Ten pence", was his mother's reply. Some time later his mother presented him with a baby brother, and again the little boy asked: "Where did you get him from?" "I bought him." "And how much did you pay for him?" "Ten pounds", was his mother's reply. So from that moment on, the child became firmly convinced of one thing: "She can't love me as much as she loves my brother; I'm not worth as much as he is!" And his new belief intensified his insecurity and sadness about no longer being the only child even further. His mother had unthinkingly answered his heartfelt question on the trivial level, and undoubtedly no longer even remembered the episode.

When a child comes to his mother and asks her: "Mummy, do you love me?", he expects her to take him in her arms and say sincerely: "Of course I love you!" But if he chooses a moment when his mother is busy and inattentive, he may be bitterly upset to hear her say: "Of course I love you!" in a distracted, trivial tone. A similar misunderstanding can occur if a child breaks a cup - something that is trivial to him - only to find that his mother is annoyed and upset, and snaps at him in a tragic tone: "Oh, you're impossible! You make life so difficult for me!" The child then responds by switching to the tragic level, and can be deeply hurt. So it is important to learn how to use the levels properly when communicating with children. Very similar patterns also occur in adult relationships. For example, if a housewife has spent the whole day alone while her husband has been out at work, and she asks him on his return home: "Do you love me?", serious problems can develop - not only in the couple's communication but also in the marriage itself - if his answer is: "Of course I love you; is dinner ready?"

We therapists can learn to use these two levels effectively and to attune ourselves to the right "frequency" for the people we are with. These subtle techniques, together with a profound, empathic way of being, are the very heart of therapy. It is this way of being itself that is the therapist, that heals the patient. An article I read in a popular science magazine confirmed this view: it reported that Russian researchers had succeeded in measuring the psychic energy that passed from a mother to her child and from the hands of a healer to his patient. This energy, I knew, was bioenergy. And in the same way I knew that a therapy room can be full of this healing psychic energy, or empty and "dry". When I am facing my patient, in contact with the most profound level of my being, psychic energy streams through me and produces a healing effect on the patient.

The experience I had with one of my patients is a very good example of this phenomenon. This man, a television cameraman, came to me one day and asked me to give him "Reichian therapy". He complained about his sex life: he was unable to have satisfying orgasms. In the first session I gave him the kind of treatment he had been expecting: I worked very actively with him, using deep muscular massage, Reichian bodywork and breathing exercises, including Lowen's bioenergetics. This made him very happy during the session, but when he returned the following week he complained that nothing had changed in his sex life. This time he sat on a chair facing me, at a distance of about five metres. He told me he had been rushing around town all morning, and was terribly tired; all he wanted was to sit there and do nothing. His eyes closed, and soon my eyes closed too. I thought to myself: I will look at him through my half-opened eyelids. Then I let myself sink into my own downgoing libidinal streamings, and at once I felt so light, so well. I felt myself bathed in light, with my mind in a state of meditative calm.

Now and again I looked at my patient to see whether he had opened his eyes or wanted to say anything. But there was nothing. He sat there, still and relaxed, with a tiny smile on his lips, his eyes half-closed like mine. After fifty-five minutes I said to him softly: "We must stop now, I'll see you next time." He left without saying a word. When he came back for the next session, he was radiant. He told me that the treatment had achieved extraordinary results and he had enjoyed marvellous orgasms with his wife. He sat down, and exactly the same thing happened as in the previous session. Several more sessions followed the same pattern, and I thought to myself: "This is the new Reichian therapy!" At the beginning of every session he told me how effective the therapy was and how wonderful his sex life was becoming.

In the sixth session, however, I suffered from an attack of conscience. As usual, I began by entering my ecstatic interior world of downgoing currents; but suddenly I began to have doubts about this method of treatment. "Now, Gerda", I lectured myself, "it's not fair that you should just sit there and abandon yourself to your own pleasure when this man has come to you for help and is paying you for it!" So I decided I had better keep my eyes open. "Besides", I thought as I watched him, "if he were to open his eyes he might think I was sleeping!" (I could not help remembering how offended I had been on one occasion during my own therapy with Ola Raknes, when he did in fact fall asleep in the middle of a session.) So this time I did not let myself slip back into my libidinal flow.

The session came to an end, and my patient left. Everything had gone exactly as usual, except that I had not entered into the ‚cosmic ocean'. At the next session, though, my patient grumbled that he did not feel well, and that his orgasms had not been as good as in the previous weeks. I explained to him what I had done differently in the previous session, and at once he insisted that this time he wanted me to give him exactly "the same treatment as usual". So we continued with the sessions as before, sitting facing one another, and each time I re-entered my streaming state. And one day I saw the energy that flowed out of him meet and mingle with the energy that flowed out of me, at a point midway between us. I saw this meeting as an orgasm of energies; or, to put it in Reichian terms, a cosmic superimposition. I did not tell him what I had seen; but when he went back to his home country he declared that he was completely satisfied with his therapy.

I saw this episode as confirmation of the theories I had read in the popular science magazine. I had the "psychic energy" described in the article within me, only I called it "libido". In Reichian terms, the process that went on during my sessions with the cameraman could be described as orgonotic transmission, or the transmission of streamings. This was my first experience of psychic and bioenergetic phenomena of this kind; over the years, however, it became increasingly clear to me that they are an essential part of therapy and healing.

GROUPS

The next thing I did was to start running therapy groups and training courses for therapists. In the therapy training courses I taught massage and a synthesis of vegetotherapy and my own techniques, which I called not "bioenergetic", but "bioenergy". It felt strange to me to be so completely unconventional; in Norway I had worked as a traditional clinical psychologist and physiotherapist, while here in London I had suddenly become a neo-Reichian therapist who "did bioenergy". I set up the Centre for

Bioenergy, which bears my name, in London, and before long large numbers of "people in transition" began gravitating towards the Centre. I was amused to discover that the neo-Reichians apparently believed that it was essential to be nude for therapy. Although I never asked them to do so, the people who came to my groups automatically seemed to assume I would expect them to undress; so often I would arrive for a new group to find myself confronted with twenty naked people. I continued to say nothing about it, and as time went by the group members stopped taking their clothes off. It was simply not necessary.

I myself also learned an enormous amount from my groups. During one of the training groups, which my daughter Ebba had insisted on attending, I was taught a memorable lesson about the importance of the mother's role in the family. At a certain point Ebba found her way to the middle of the room and, as so many had done before her, she lay down on the mattress in a state of regression and began sobbing her heart out. Over and over, through her tears, she repeated: "Mummy has left me, she's gone away to go sailing with Daddy!" And there I was, therapist and mother at the same time, confronted with all her distress. I remembered the weekend she was talking about, and I realised that I had not had the sensitivity at the time to fully understand how much I had upset her. This incident helped me to recognise how tremendously important it is to have an open heart when bringing up children.

I used Alexander Lowen's bioenergetic exercises in my groups. But since I had never worked with Lowen himself, I used his exercises in my own way, and out of them the basic structure of biodynamic group therapy gradually emerged. It consists of a combination of biodynamic exercises and Ola Raknes's "midwife" method: "Let the movement and the feeling come... let it develop...". I used the stress positions developed by Lowen to provoke the stretching reflex, the healing force that can burst the individual out of his neurotic contraction. When this happens the diaphragm is released, and the flood of repressed emotions can be discharged.

It was in this group setting that I really understood how much I had gained from having worked for so long with individual clients. I feel strongly that therapists who lead groups without first building up experience in individual therapy have missed an essential element of their training. I believe they are in danger of making serious mistakes because they do not have a deep relationship with their patients, which is essential in my view. In my biodynamic therapy training programme the student therapists begin by learning massage, and as they do so they begin to develop love and tolerance towards the patient. Later, they give individual massage sessions under supervision, and finally they progress to vegetotherapy and psychotherapy.

As I continued to learn from the groups, I also developed new theories. Over and over again, I discovered that behind all the "horrors" that came flooding out of my group members' bodies and mouths, a marvellous nucleus lay hidden: their true centre, their primary personality, entirely filled with love and goodness. My goal as I worked with these people was to release them from the bad experiences that had held them prisoner; to give them the experience of a "happy ending" so that the ice would melt. Once their barriers of solidified frustration had been breached, these people could begin to open themselves up to good experiences. In this group setting, people are able to clean out the "reservoir" of their unconscious. Then at last the beautiful flower can open: the soul with its qualities of eternity. My work gave me great hope for the future of humanity. Eventually, however, I had to learn to detach myself from my own overwhelming delight, because this in itself became a kind of pressure, a strain on my heart. Yet still, the more I helped to dissolve people's neuroses, the deeper my compassion became.

All human unhappiness is solely and simply the result of what we do to children. All the concepts of education invented by the superego end by destroying the primary personality of the child, and once this has happened spontaneity is no longer possible for the adult. The repression imposed on him by adults forces the little child to deny his innermost self, and he becomes unhappy. When all this suffering comes to the surface again during therapy and is discharged, the child - now an adult - can be happy again, can feel the oceanic wave of his libido circulation and sense the delight of being flesh and blood, incarnated, in touch with his real self.

THE BIODYNAMIC THEORY OF PSYCHOSIS

According to my theory, psychosis is caused by the presence of energetic fluid in the brain. This fluid makes its appearance when the defences fall, when energy rises up into the head and the person is unable to express everything that is happening on the psychological and energetic level. If we bear in mind that energetic fluid not only flows along the muscle membranes but can also follow any membrane of the body, it will be obvious that this fluid can also flow along the nerve membranes. When it does so, it has the ability to create a complete complex of irritant factors together with stasis at the synapses. These conditions in different parts of the brain are the physiological cause of visual and auditory hallucinations. What is more, if we also bear in mind that this fluid is energetically charged - that is, it has the power to create contractions - we can better understand how hallucinations are produced.

In psychotics there exists what we call the "last defence", a strong muscular tension like a ring encircling the nape of the neck, at the level of the atlas bone. It is particularly easy to observe how this avoidance mechanism works in hysterical patients. When energetic fluid begins rising towards the patient's head during the course of therapy, its movement can be followed by watching the colour of the skin change; so when the fluid reaches the tense throat area, it can clearly be seen to change course and surge up into the head, where it causes severe migraines. This avoidance phenomenon not only appears in the skin, but can also occur in any of the various superimposed layers of the body. If the energy does not find an outlet in the form of emotion, or if the provocation has been too strong, or several layers have been reactivated at the same time, the same phenomena that can be observed in any other part of the body also take place in the brain. In psychotics, the pressure of energetic fluid in the brain is the result of unresolved conflicts and repression; so a pathological psychodynamic process arising from the depths of the body takes place in the psychotic's brain. In most cases this process begins with pressure in the stomach; later the energy rises.

It is worth noting that biodynamic theory converges with the pharmacological theory of psychosis at this point, since the two theories agree that psychosis is caused by the presence of energetic fluid in the brain. Pharmacological treatment of psychosis aims to reduce this pressure through the use of drugs. The important difference between the two theories is of course their concepts of therapeutic treatment. According to the biodynamic model of psychosis, massage applied to the excess fluid in the membranes harmonises the energy and helps the body to reabsorb the fluid.

Simply by studying the behaviour of this fluid in the membranes, we can see that the organism has its own safety valve. The antagonistic operation of the sympathetic and parasympathetic nervous systems is a phenomenon well known in medicine: when the sympathetic system becomes hyperactive, the parasympathetic in turn also goes into action. This phenomenon fits in perfectly with my own experience and theories. For example, very often patients suffer from diarrhoea after receiving a massage, and their symptoms are due to the transition from the sympathetic system (building up a charge) to the parasympathetic system (discharging it). This dynamic helps us to understand the aggression/depression polarity better. When someone is unable to express his aggression, he becomes depressed. It is widely recognised in psychology that when someone tries to overcome a block, his energy level rises and manifests itself as aggression. If the expression of this aggression is prevented or held back, the patient may lapse into either depression or inaction and resignation.

It is very helpful to compare the aggression/depression polarity with the antagonistic behaviour of the sympathetic and parasympathetic systems. First the overall level of energy increases: there is hyperfunctioning of the sympathetic system, a rise in the amount of adrenaline in the blood, and the energy begins moving in an upward direction. If these energetic movements become blocked for any reason, they can be transformed into crying; this crying is a parasympathetic phenomenon.

I developed the following theory to explain this pattern: a person can be blocked in the sympathetic expression of his aggression while his parasympathetic expression (crying) keeps functioning. I had noticed that in the majority of cases of manic-depressive psychosis, several layers of aggression and depression were reactivated at the same time. One of the organism's most important safety valves is located in the parasympathetic ganglions of the throat. These nerve clusters halt the upward movement of the emotional energy before it can reach the brain and cause psychotic episodes or even cerebral haemorrhaging. A functional saturation principle is at work here: when the activity of the ganglions becomes excessive, a reversal is triggered; the energetic level of the entire organism is lowered and depression occurs. Through many years of practical experience, I came to realise that the ascending emotional energy not only circulates through the alimentary canal, but also inside the nerve walls, inside the vein and arterial walls, through the lymph circuits and even through all the cells themselves.

When we are giving a particularly urgent case massage treatment, we can place the stethoscope on any part of their body and quickly observe that there is a moment at which the direction of the energy reverses, from an ascending to a descending movement. Similarly, we can explain arteriosclerosis as an energetic disorder resulting from stress. About thirty years ago, an interesting research study was carried out in a rural valley in Norway where the inhabitants consumed a large quantity of cholesterol in their diet, mainly animal fats. However, a biological analysis showed that these people had very little cholesterol in their blood. The main reason for this startling finding was their exceptionally relaxed way of life, indicating good peristalsis. They were known in neighbouring regions as people who generally remained unruffled. Their attitude was: "If I don't come today, I'll come tomorrow."

Exactly why a high level of cholesterol develops in the blood is a question hotly debated in medical circles. I believe that cholesterol plays a similar role to adrenalin. From a purely energetic point of view, cholesterol acts as a negative polarity; that is to say, it promotes resistance in the organism which in turn causes the level of energy to increase. But if the arterial walls are in a state of stasis, exactly the same phenomena occur as when stasis is present in the intestinal walls. In this case all that remains is an empty space with a "transudation pressure" (see page 52), as the energy has been withdrawn. In cases where the energy circulates well, the cholesterol is dissolved in accordance with the plasmo-galvanic principle. However, this process can only take place if the blood circulation is good; if it is not, the cholesterol remains in the arterial walls and the symptoms of arteriosclerosis - infiltrations, calcifications, etc. - eventually develop. To illustrate this concept of stagnant fluid I like to use the image of a sponge completely swollen with water; before new liquid (fresh, purified blood) can enter this sponge, the old, stagnant fluid must first be squeezed out. Normally this squeezing function is performed by the pulsation of energy and the rhythmical movements of the muscles. But if blocks are present, if the energy is withdrawn, this process cannot take place.

One function of psychoperistalsis is to dissolve the excess fluid in the organism and so re-establish a homeostatic fluid balance. As I mentioned earlier, diarrhoea is a strong vegetative discharge that serves the purpose of eliminating excess nervous fluid. In this case, the fluid comes from the intestines; diarrhoea occurs when the intestinal walls become overcharged with energetic fluid and the transudation pressure is at its peak.

These theories also help us to understand a mediaeval custom that seems very strange to us today: the medical practice of bleeding. The only conceivable value of this treatment is as a means of reducing the fluid pressure. By drawing off some of the patient's blood, mediaeval doctors were able to reduce the transudation pressure in the organism.

THE UNCONSCIOUS AND THE ENDODERM

A question to which Freud gave much thought was: whereabouts in the body is the unconscious located? Reich's answer was that it resides in the muscles and bones, especially in the sacrum. Biodynamic theory, on the other hand, says that it resides in the endoderm: that is, in the viscera. But since the circulatory system pervades the whole body, flowing through the arteries, the veins, the capillaries, until it reaches every single cell, it would be more accurate to say that the unconscious is everywhere in the body.

My interest in the neuro-vegetative system was first aroused by Pavlov's theories on experimental neurosis. As I read his work, I was particularly struck by his experiments with dogs. In what is now regarded as a classic experiment, Pavlov gave his dogs a reward - a piece of meat, which caused them to salivate - while simultaneously making a sound. Before long, the dogs would begin to produce saliva as soon as they heard the sound, even if no meat was given. This phenomenon was an experimental neurosis: a state of confusion in the dog's conditioned reflexes, generating a very real conflict within its neuro-vegetative system. According to biodynamic theory, neuro-vegetative conflicts of this kind are at the root of neurosis.

I was also fascinated by a series of experiments carried out with rats. The first stage involved training the rats to jump through a hole cut in a piece of paper; when they jumped, they were rewarded with a piece of cheese. In the second stage of their training, the colour of the paper was varied: when it was white they were still rewarded for jumping, but when it was black they were punished instead. As long as the rats were free to choose whether or not to jump, and so receive a reward or avoid punishment, no experimental neurosis developed. But in the third stage of the experiment the black and white papers were mixed up so thoroughly that the rats became totally confused, and could no longer work out whether or not to jump. At this point they usually stopped jumping altogether. Finally, in the fourth stage, the experimenters forced the rats to jump by frightening them. They found that rats that were forced to jump contracted a severe experimental neurosis; they lay motionless for hours at a time, their eyes rolled upwards. These rats subsequently displayed serious behavioural disturbances towards their fellow rats. However, a second group of rats was allowed to choose whether to jump through the hole or straight down from the platform. Because the rats in this group had a free choice, they did not become neurotic.

From these experiments we can draw an extremely interesting conclusion about the relationship between free will and the vegetative system: when an individual is allowed to follow his own free will, the vegetative system is actually connected to the motor system and works in harmony with it. In the experiment with the rats, the neurosis appeared at the very moment when the conflict between the vegetative and the motor nervous systems became insoluble, producing severe stasis in the internal organs.

In biodynamic therapy our aim is to connect the vegetative system to the motor system and to permit emotional expression and expressive bodily movement, so that stasis can no longer accumulate in the depths of the organism. In order to really cure neurosis, these profound conflicts at the vegetative level must be eliminated. Our biodynamic method unlocks the patient's psychoperistalsis, which in turn dissolves this deep stasis, this conflict at the vegetative level, before it even reaches consciousness. One of the great virtues of this method is that it allows us to dissolve stasis in any part, level or layer of the organism, no matter whether it is in the abdomen, the chest, the head, the circulatory system, the respiratory system or the nerve synapses.

THE MOTOR EGO AND DIAPHRAGMATIC REGULATION

This brings me to an extremely important element of neo-Reichian therapy: the system of bioenergetics developed by Alexander Lowen. Lowen's inspired idea was to devise exercises and positions which, by putting the body under some stress, would help patients to bring their energy down from their heads into their legs and ultimately into their feet: in other words, he set out to "ground" them. This approach seems to be particularly useful in the treatment of neurosis, because the exercises can help to reduce the pressure of energetic fluid in the brain.

Despite the similarity between their names, bioenergetic and biodynamic therapies should not be confused. Because Lowen's method acts mainly on the mesodermic level - the muscular layers - often bioenergetic treatment does not really touch the core of the neurosis. In biodynamic therapy we use Lowen's techniques extensively, but in a biodynamic way. This means that we use his stress exercises to provoke a reaction in the intestines, in the emotional channel; then we allow the cathartic discharge to take place; and finally we also encourage grounding. Grounding gives the patient a feeling of strength and security that comes from using the motor system and the big skeletal muscles. It is a way to create a profound connection between the organism's two main internal forms of energy: the energy of the id and the energy of the locomotor system that is controlled by the voluntary ego. So, in summary, this means: in order to avoid neurosis, there must be no conflict between the organism's libidinal energy and its voluntary movements.

In a non-neurotic organism, the cosmic energy flowing through that organism lends each voluntary movement its own unique force. Neurosis is born when instinctual energy is blocked by the voluntary ego which controls the locomotor system (the motor ego), and this is how muscular armour is created. Eventually all sorts of conflicts between the driving force and its expression spring up at every level of the personality; as a result, the neurotic's power of self- expression is considerably inhibited. I developed the following hypothesis to account for these phenomena: The mesoderm has two sides, one of which is connected to the central nervous system - that is, to the voluntary ego - while the other is connected to the neuro-vegetative system, or the id. Somehow, there must be a mesoderm-ectoderm side and a mesoderm-endoderm side. Paul Boyesen has also given thought to the relationship between the three different levels of embryological development. He expresses it as follows: The endoderm - the embryonic cells that become the digestive tract and the viscera - is the profound organic level. The mesoderm - the cells that form the muscles and bones - is the level of organic contact. Finally, the ectoderm - the cells that develop into the skin, nervous system, sense organs and certain glands - is the conceptual level.[5]

I now want to talk about an extremely important concept: the motor ego. In biodynamic psychology the motor ego is an emotional regulator, which means that muscular armour is also an emotional regulator that has become frozen, solidified in some way. After all, people need to be capable of controlling their emotions rather than being controlled by them. A healthy person is characterised by the fact that, when

5 The ectoderm level predominates in the cerebral type who conceptualises easily but who has difficulty in accessing his emotions.

an emotion rises up within him, he is neither compelled to inhibit it nor to explode. So the motor ego has the extremely important function of regulating the intensity of the emotions. The effectiveness of this function depends on the strength of the ego, acting through the motor system and the skeletal muscles. One muscle in particular is extremely important: the diaphragm.

If we bear in mind that the instinctual emotional energy rises up from the depths of the id canal, from the intestinal walls, we can understand the crucial role of the diaphragm. When this huge muscle contracts and lowers, it prevents energy from rising up into the chest cavity and moving outward into the zones of emotional expression: the throat, the arms, the hands. When, on the other hand, we are willing to express an emotion, the diaphragm pulsates and helps to push energy upwards with a pumping action.

In the event of acute danger, the role of the motor ego must be reduced to the minimum so that the instinctual energy can be given full expression - whether in the form of crying out, fleeing or fighting. In this situation two kinds of energetic interaction occur: the energy coming from the pelvis interacts with the energy emerging from the spongy bones of the cranium, and it also interacts with the energy of the circulatory system. So the role of the motor ego is extremely important. In small children the motor ego is largely undeveloped. We could go a long way towards preventing neurosis altogether if we would only stop educating our children in such a way as to create continual antagonism between the id and the ego, between instinctual energy and voluntary energy. But instead, we impose a "censorship ego" (superego) on them before they become consciously aware of regulating their feelings.

I came across an interesting anecdote that confirms this theory while I was working with a schizophrenic patient. At a certain point in her process, this woman relived an incident that had occurred when she was three years old. Her libidinal energy became totally concentrated in her hands, and she wanted to feel everything, to touch every object in the world with her hands. She experienced an intense feeling of pleasure in her fingers. But her parents interrupted this delicious experience, telling her that she must not touch this or that, and her libido then withdrew completely from her hands and her extremities. Now, the majority of our movements towards the world are produced by libidinal energy; and when physiological energy coincides with voluntary energy, the flow of the libido is complete and the person can experience pleasure in his relationship with the world. When, during the therapy session, this schizophrenic woman re-experienced the sensation of libidinal energy in her hands and could explore the world around her just as she liked, she felt the libido pervading her whole body again, for the first time since childhood. She felt unified and connected; not separated, not fragmented.

LIBIDO CIRCULATION AND INDEPENDENT WELL-BEING

Ever since the appearance of Wilhelm Reich's book "The Function of the Orgasm", a large proportion of its readers have held the firm belief that the only way to rid themselves of their tensions is the orgasm. This misinterpretation of Reich's writings has created a new type of compulsion, a new type of superego that I call the "Reichian therapy superego". During my many years of therapeutic practice, one of the things I have noticed is that the desire for sexual activity becomes an absolute necessity for someone whose ascending energy is blocked and who cannot find a way to transform it and let it melt into a descending, harmonising flow of energy. So I want to introduce the concept of "libido circulation" in the context of this problem.

A person who has his own independent libido circulation is no longer the victim of compulsive sexual urges or of a hyper-symbiotic relationship with another person. But, to achieve this free libido circulation, the person must be able to love himself deeply and to feel love within himself at every moment, not merely love coming from outside.

A baby is born with his own energy circulation, with the feeling of the oceanic wave, which keeps him in a state of deep inner contentment. He is not dependent on other people for his inner peace, only for food and care. It is only when hunger or some other kind of discomfort interrupts his libido circulation that the baby reacts and shows his discomfort, so that his mother will come and give him food or comfort and care for him. Every living being, from the human being to the amoeba, is born with its own autonomous libido circulation.

The most important goal of my system of therapy is to help the patient to re-establish contact with his libido circulation and so rediscover his own inner happiness. There is an extremely close link between this libido circulation and psychoperistalsis. In an emergency, it is entirely normal for the level of adrenalin in the blood to rise and for the organism's energy to become completely focused on action. A principle of "unpleasure", of aversion, then comes into play; its function is to mobilise all the available resources for action and fighting. After this, ideally the energy should disperse and the libido circulation should be re-established. Often, however, this dispersion and harmonisation of the energy fails to occur, and this is the fundamental block, the root cause of neurosis.

In recent years, various branches of therapy have adopted the view that, to be effective, therapy must hurt. This is based on the concept of "breaking down the armour", using painful muscular palpation and stress exercises coupled with heavy emotional provocation. I disagree strongly with this view: indeed, I believe that this concept and the techniques associated with it are often downright anti-therapeutic. When patients treated with this approach enter too strongly into an emotional discharge - an attempt to discharge what these therapies call the "primal pain" - all too often they develop energetic blocks in the throat. And if there is no resolution of the pain, the libido circulation is then actually lost for the second time. In cases of this kind, where patients have developed what I call a "secondary neurosis", the most important thing is to allow this blocked energy to dissolve and circulate, with less pain and more comfort and understanding.

Every session of biodynamic therapy begins with some form of provocation, to set the process in motion; but we always take care to conclude the session with what we call a "happy ending". When psychological comfort is given after an emotional discharge has taken place, the energy released by the discharge is able to flow back into the libido circulation, where pleasure and well-being can finally conquer the pain of the past.

It has often struck me that many people seem to feel deeply suspicious of happy people. This suspicion arises from a phenomenon that I call "the two sides of the looking-glass". Someone on the first side of the looking-glass lives in a reality in which he is overburdened with neurotic defences, he is alone, he is constantly trying to avoid conflicts, and often he is terrified of entering into relationships with other people. When a person is in this state, every smile or cheerful attitude is a palliative, a mask or an idealisation. By displaying superficially happy behaviour, he tries to avoid his profound hatred, his conflicts, his underlying depression and his rage. This is what happens when he is severely blocked. But once the process of unblocking these deep energetic blocks is well advanced, the energy previously "encapsulated" begins to circulate again. Now the patient re-experiences his true libido circulation, his "streamings"; he leaves behind his dependence and enters into a state of independent well-being. He discovers his own inner security and confidence.

The patient is now on the other side of the looking-glass, where the situation is quite different. Here he may very well feel happy, and permanently so. Of course, a person who has discovered his own inner happiness will still react emotionally to the situations and demands of day-to-day life like anyone else; but the difference is that, whenever he likes, he has the ability to re-establish contact with his energy flow, his libido circulation and his vegetative self-regulation, and this gives him a feeling of well-being and security. People who are still living on the first side of the looking-glass often seem to experience negative feelings towards people who have passed through to the other side. They view all this well-being and inner happiness as a sham, a deceptive superficial pose adopted by people trying to escape from their profound inner suffering.

I cannot help remembering a man who came from the United States to consult me. He had heard that I had been doing "primal" therapy long before Janov, and he had come to satisfy himself that there was nothing in this rumour. When I opened the door to him, he looked me up and down from head to toe and finally said: "You look so happy that I feel sure there must be something really painful in you that you're trying to hide." He was on the other side of the looking- glass.

This distinction between the two sides of the looking-glass is particularly important when therapeutic work is done in groups. If one of the participants is on the second side of the looking-glass - that is, in contact with his own independent well-being - the other members of the group may well accuse him of hiding something or of being a fake. For example, when he expresses a desire to be alone for a few moments to have what I call "animal privacy", they may accuse him of trying to run away from his inner conflicts. In this situation the alert therapist must intervene to prevent the person from developing a neurotic conflict as a result of the confusion between the superego that is based on the reality on the first side of the looking-glass, and that things that are really happening on the second side. A person who has passed through to the second side of the looking-glass may sometimes seem to have a cold, detached attitude that others may interpret as an avoidance, a way of escaping from his true feelings. But this interpretation is wrong; in fact his attitude should be seen as a way of protecting his regained libido circulation and so permitting his inner development.

When somebody really makes the transition to the other side of the looking-glass, he becomes both more extroverted and more introverted. As the process of purifying and liberating his energy through psychoperistaltic regulation advances, as his streamings bring increased awareness of the different layers of reality, so his true personality develops, bringing with it higher levels of consciousness. This is what Carl Gustav Jung called "the self"; for the libidinal streamings not only bring a sense of inner well-being, but also an awareness of the energetic circulation through every organ and every cell. This greatly increases the person's energetic potential, especially the vibratory potential of his brain, and so opens him up to different levels of consciousness: the person has access to the level of archetypes and gains a higher awareness of his creative potential.

Difficulties can arise between couples when one of the partners discovers his or her own independent well-being while the other remains stuck in dependency. When this happens, a new compulsion seems to develop in the dependent partner, who feels that the two of them must be together physically all the time. I have introduced the concept of "animal privacy" to describe a new need that develops in people who have fully regained their libido circulation: these people feel a very strong desire for time and space to be alone with themselves. This is because time and physical and spiritual solitude are indeed needed to maintain the libido circulation and enable psychoperistalsis and spiritual development to take place. Often, though, the other partner experiences this desire for solitude as abandonment. The partner who has not rediscovered his libido circulation is permanently dependent on something or someone else.

Total, open libido circulation makes it possible for us to abandon ourselves completely to orgastic melting, to the genital sexual act. In contrast to this, a person who is in a state of dependent well-being must look for love from the outside: he has lost contact with the love inside himself. This creates dependency and the fear that a catastrophe will occur if he does not do everything in his power to hold onto his partner's love. Someone in this situation finds it impossible to remain alone; all his love relationships must be symbiotic and he has no inner freedom.

When, in contrast, a person experiences increasingly intense contact with the love within himself as his libido circulation flows more and more freely, he develops a feeling of self-respect and contentment. He becomes much less dependent on external situations. Someone who has his own full libido circulation, who is in touch with his primary personality, does not need to "suck up" energy from others in a symbiotic relationship; he can give and take as a mature adult. His relationships with other people are greatly improved because they spring from his own centre, from a place where he feels free and independent, and there is no urge to take, to cling, to try to get something from somebody else - urges that destroy so very many love relationships.

We can trace this pattern of dependence back to the child who has lost his independent well-being and feelings of inner contentment - his libido circulation - and instead must rely totally on contact with his mother in order to feel pleasure in his body. Most mothers whose children have lost their libido circulation play games with giving or withholding contact, in order to maintain their power over the child. By using this sort of emotional blackmail, the mother can make the child do whatever she wants. What is more, her own possessive nature and dominant behaviour is undoubtedly one of the main reasons why the child loses his independent well-being in the first place. Once he has lost it, he constantly feels the need to find it again; and he tries desperately to do so by staying close to his mother and pleading for her tenderness and her caresses. Now that the child is in this needy state, his mother is able to influence him in a way that is both subtle and highly effective, by developing in him what I call the "secondary personality" - a condition in which he becomes reliant on others for pleasure and loses contact with the interior of his own body and with his emotions. He becomes very obedient and dependent, but at the same time a feeling of imminent disaster grows within him, because he knows and senses unconsciously that his mother can withdraw her love from him at any moment, whenever she pleas-es and especially when he does something to displease her. A child in this situation responds with telepathic empathy to the slightest signs of approval or disapproval that he can feel emanating from his mother.

In total contrast to this blocked situation, we have the child on the other side of the looking-glass. This child is filled with the energy of love, heart energy, energy in every cell, energy in his genitals, cosmic energy throughout his whole body - all his energy is unified, in harmony, and in it we can see the child's profound oneness with nature. Children on the other side of the looking-glass have very sensitive hearts and a limitless capacity for love. The cosmic energy that surges through all their cells also radiates out to others, and is received from others in turn. But, sadly, it is all too easy for these children to lose their feeling of independent well-being: a loss that occurs when their libido circulation is interrupted or their libidinal impulses are rejected.

THE EFFECT OF INTERRUPTION ON THE LIBIDO CIRCULATION

When a child is at play, he can enter completely into his own world; he is immersed in his libido circulation, in his feeling of independence, in the delight of playing. He becomes deeply absorbed in his game, he forgets the rest of the world altogether and is filled with a feeling of boundless pleasure. So if his mother suddenly appears and asks him: "What are you doing?", her words and most importantly - the tone in which she says them can come as a real shock to the child in its open state. A startle reflex is created, and the child's energy retreats inwards, into the depths of the organism. The incident can leave behind a residual tension, which then inhibits the libido circulation. At the same time, the child also develops a sense of unpleasurable anticipation; now, when he settles down to play, he can no longer fully give himself over to the pleasure of the situation because of his fear that the shock may be repeated. The shock has not only taken place at the physical level, but also - and in fact much more intensively - at the level of the aura. Parents need to be very careful in these situations, because children are so much more open than we adults. In therapy I have discovered that shocks to the aura can be particularly dangerous. To explain this phenomenon with an analogy: if a couple are in the middle of enjoying particularly deep, satisfying sexual intercourse when someone suddenly enters the room and disturbs them, they can suffer a very violent shock.

In therapy groups we often do an orgonomic exercise called "the jelly-fish"; an exercise that generates a libido circulation so intense it can even lead to ecstasy. In this situation, too, if someone is disturbed or verbally attacked by another group member while he is engrossed in the exercise, the effects on his personality and on his whole organism can be disastrous. Such a negative experience disrupts his fundamental organic trust at a core level. It gives him a "psychic shock" in the form of a contraction of the libidinal flow; a shrinking at the level of the cellular pulsations themselves.

I also use the term "auric shock" to describe an interruption of any kind that occurs when we are in a state either of peak excitement, or of extreme sensitivity and vulnerability. Such an interruption will be a psychological shock, and will cause the vital radiance that pulsates outwards from our inner being to "shrink". It also revives unwelcome memories: our "old feelings" of being interrupted, of not being allowed to enjoy our pleasurable feelings and well-being, of coming into conflict with a censorious ego that seeks to repress our spontaneous feelings and sensations. Auric shocks suffered in therapy are just as devastating as those experienced in childhood, because they bring about a "secondary repression" that actually prevents the patient from working out his childhood shocks. When a person regains his libido circulation, he needs to take great care to protect his well-being: the same protection that he so badly needed as a child, long ago.

The theory I have just described is unknown to the majority of psychologists and child specialists. That is why I believe it is immensely important to make it known to parents, so that these severe energetic traumas can be avoided. An adult, watching a baby endlessly engrossed in playing with its own feet and fingers as it lies there in its cradle, may be tempted to wonder whether the child ever gets bored. The answer is simple: when someone's libido circulation is intact, he is never bored because he is truly in eternity. The libido circulation is a sort of nirvana. As far as I am concerned, the main aim of therapy is to help people to return to this level of consciousness. People who are severely blocked and insensitive need intense sexual stimulation, perversions, horror books and films full of blood, sex and violence. A blocked person always needs a great deal of "action"; but once he rediscovers his "tantric", libidinal being, he becomes able to experience the most extraordinary adventures in the simplest things of everyday life. On the other side of the looking-glass, it is impossible ever to feel bored. All our perceptions are altered; we see things from myriad different angles, each more marvellous than the other. This is when the phenomenon that Jung called "synchronicity" occurs: that is to say, life itself comes to meet us.

To an adult, a great many things can seem drab and unexciting; but to a child who has kept his libido circulation or to an adult who has rediscovered his, everything is astonishing and wonderful. This is why the therapist finds his work so enriching, so immensely gratifying, when he succeeds in helping a patient to regain contact with his libido circulation and so reawaken his perception of colours and his awareness of the impact of every single thing on his being. I remember vividly how, when I rediscovered my own libido circulation, it seemed to me that everything - the curtains, the window, the wallpaper, everything - had an extraordinary glow, as if it were a painting, a picture. Yet nothing in the room had changed; it was only my way of seeing that had regained its radiance and wonder.

I must add one more important observation on this subject. Children like it very much when their parents or other adults are close to them, in the same room. Problems arise, however, if those adults believe that they have to communicate constantly with the child, talking to him, playing with him, because often their intrusion in fact interrupts the child's play, the magical world of his libido. If left to his own devices, the child is perfectly well able to keep his magical inner world intact in the presence of adults. Indeed, doing so can strengthen his ability to retain his independent well-being and serenity in social situations; it gives him an inner strength and self-assurance that will benefit him greatly, both as a child and later as an adult.

Life among people who are in touch with their libidinal streamings is easy. I like to use the image of fish in an aquarium; the fish are in a positive relationship with one another all the time, yet each fish also pursues its own journey along its own underwater path. In the same way, people on the other side of the looking-glass are permanently in relationship with others without feeling a constant need to disturb them or to interpret everything they do as evidence that "you don't love me". Wilhelm Reich speaks of the difference between the ‚mechanical' individual and the ‚bioenergetic' individual who is fully alive. He describes the deep envy that the mechanical individual feels towards the bioenergetic individual's radiance, a pattern that he calls "the murder of Christ".

When I arrived in London, I was struck by the fact that mechanical individuals showed two particularly noticeable character traits: they were constantly discontented, or they were envious. These envious people behave like vampires towards bioenergetic people; they literally suck up the energy of those more radiant than themselves, sometimes to the point where their victims become seriously ill. This phenomenon is particularly common among couples; I call it "couple vampirism". Compulsive, mechanical individuals lacking in bioenergetic radiance naturally feel a strong attraction towards people who do possess this radiance. As a result, the following pattern often appears: a spontaneous, bioenergetically vibrant young woman marries a rigid, compulsive man. As time goes by, though, the man feels a growing urge to change his wife, to make her just as rigid as he is and submit her to his compulsive demands. So he interrupts her spontaneity and inner well-being, and as her libido circulation is lost, stasis develops. Then, as the plasmo- faradic principle predicts, the energetic fluid creates a chronic contraction within her; numerous psychosomatic pains accompany these energetic phenomena, and the woman may become obese. She becomes genuinely ill. In the course of my career I have seen many such young women develop serious illnesses and suicidal tendencies. When treating these people, it is tremendously important to give them plenty of support and approval so that they feel they are profoundly in the right.

The following anecdote illustrates this point. A high-powered Norwegian executive took his young wife to a psychiatric hospital, complaining that she was mad. Dr Braatöy, who received the couple, took one look at this rigid, compulsive man and said: "Are you quite sure she is the one who is mad?" His words had a powerful impact; it was at that moment that the executive suddenly realised what he was doing.

A compulsive character makes such unnatural demands both on himself and on those around him that he interrupts the libido circulation of a bioenergetic person, and eventually destroys it.

After this, the bioenergetic person may develop terrible feelings of guilt, because he realises he will never be able to satisfy the demands of the rigid person's superego. Confusion now develops in the bioenergetic person as well; neurotic symptoms grow up all around a core that is still profoundly healthy and alive. The best therapeutic approach for people in this state involves giving them plenty of approval, so that they feel on a profound level that they have a perfect right to be themselves, exactly as they are. Even if they are unable to change their rigid partner, they need to understand quite clearly that he is the one who has created and is feeding the feelings of guilt and confusion from which they are suffering. Once they have succeeded in freeing themselves from this guilt and confusion, the therapist must then encourage them to take enough time for themselves. By doing so, they can rediscover and hold on to their libido circulation and their primary personalities.

At this point I want to re-emphasise an extremely important principle: the dangers of interrupting the libido circulation. This experience, although always unpleasant, is actually much more distressing for someone who is used to having their libido circulation intact than for someone who lost it a long time ago and only occasionally finds it again. The more energy that is present, the more the energetic fluid builds up, creating severe contractions and stasis in the event of such a shock.

This subject brings to mind a case of obsessional neurosis I encountered when I was working in a Norwegian hospital. The patient, a little girl, found it almost impossible to go to the toilet; she felt compelled to wash her hands hundreds of times a day, and it took her two hours to get dressed or undressed. Her mother brought her in to the clinic, and it was immediately obvious that this sick little girl was utterly obedient to her mother. I showed her mother around the clinic, and introduced her to a patient suffering from an even more severe obsessional neurosis than her daughter. On meeting this patient, the mother‘s response was; “What a delightful girl; she‘s so well brought up!“ Her reaction left me in no doubt that her demands had produced her daughter‘s obsessional neurosis. She had imposed her demands on the child so forcefully that she had destroyed her daughter‘s libido circulation. Someone who develops an obsessional neurosis has had his emotional health completely undermined. He has become a compulsive character, and in turn he tries to turn the people around him into compulsive personalities as well, because now he cannot bear the libido circulation.

I must emphasise one thing: when the libido circulation is destroyed, all the wonder and magic disappears from the world. Inner happiness and inner light are destroyed. I once saw an excellent stage production of “Alice Through the Looking-Glass“, which showed so clearly how Alice entered into a magical, marvellous, mysterious world when she stepped through the looking-glass, and how her adventures were constantly being interrupted by a startle reflex as her mother called: “Alice! It‘s tea-time!“. Yet when a mother gradually enters into her child‘s magical world and helps him to return to the level of ordinary consciousness in order to eat or go to bed, no problems arise. Everything depends on how the adult intervenes. If his voice is hard, rigid and mechanical as he calls to the child, he will cause a startle reflex. It is vital to understand that the child‘s magical world is not unreal. When he is in it, he is not outside the real world; he is simply totally absorbed in his activity and becomes one with what he is doing and what he sees around him.

I remember Ola Raknes telling me that while he was writing a book, he felt he was the typewriter. When a person loses this ability to become pleasurably absorbed in what he is doing, all work becomes an obligation, a duty, a painful experience. His efforts to concentrate on what he is doing then generate strong tensions, and his experience is an unpleasant one. To the child, every kind of activity, whether work or play, is fundamentally libidinal. I cannot stress too strongly how deeply we need to rediscover our libido and return to the pleasure principle in relating to other people, making love, speaking, eating, moving - in fact, in everything we do. When our libido circulation is flowing fully and freely, we feel much lighter and stasis cannot develop. When our energy really circulates, we are physiologically and psychologically healthy.

A comparison between this theory and Freud‘s should not lead to the conclusion that we are eager to abandon the principle of reality. Quite the contrary: reality is fundamental to everything, but reality is also marvellous. People whose libido circulation is intact have a much vaster perception of reality and a larger capacity to adapt to it. Both physically and psychologically, they can respond to reality in a more supple, flexible and harmonious way.

"GROUNDING", "UN-GROUNDING" AND HARMONISATION

As I have already mentioned, we use Lowen‘s concept of grounding and his bioenergetic exercises in a biodynamic way: that is to say, we use stress positions to provoke the organism into stretching the startle reflexes that have become embedded into the person‘s structure. It is important to know when to “un-ground“ a patient in order to put his neurotic defence mechanisms out of action. However, it is even more important to know when a patient‘s biggest need is to be grounded and to be brought into closer contact with what I call his motor ego - his strength and his emotional regulator. It is the circumstances and the phase of the therapeutic process that determine whether the therapist‘s goal should be to ground the patient, or to un-ground him.

One thing is certain, though: no therapist should ever “work“ on a patient to such an extent that he regresses outside the therapy session. That is far too much un-grounding. Therapy should be regulated in such a way that the patient can tackle his problems while at the same time also living his daily life better. Sometimes, though, when the therapy is poorly regulated, it comes to dominate the patient‘s life and he lives only for the hours when his sessions are scheduled. This happens when his therapist “pushes“ him to confront conflicts that are still buried too deep within him. The patient responds by becoming compulsive; he wants to “go through“ everything, to “get it all out“.

There is simply no need for a therapist to push his patient in this way; a gentler approach is far more effective. The principle of harmonisation (the “fountain“ of psychoperistalsis) will turn subjective emotional pressure into objectivity and reality. Even if a great deal of deep “material“ needs to be activated and eliminated from the system, when we use psychoperistaltic methods the patient never becomes a victim of the therapeutic process.

As so often, just after I had developed a particular part of my theory I was given information confirming it. In this case, the confirmation came from a completely different realm of knowledge: Indian religious philosophy. This system classifies people into three types:

- Tama, the stone people (with much muscle and tissue armour),
- Raja, the fire people or warriors,
- Satwa, the sunshine people.

This widely-accepted Indian classification illustrates and confirms the methods I use in both individual and group therapy. The Indian system recommends using fire to dissolve stone, and in my therapeutic methods I do use fire - that is to say, very provocative treatment - to break through excessively rigid muscular armour. The Hindus also say that sunshine will soften the warrior. This reminds me of a patient to whom I will come back shortly. For years on end, she screamed: "I hate you!", but in the end she melted in response to the shining of the sun (the melting, descending principle). Lastly, sunshine people need to be given treatment that enables them to enter into the transpersonal dimension of meditation, alpha waves and higher consciousness.

In biodynamic therapy we combine stress exercises with the stimulus-from-within method. This approach is a synthesis of Ola Raknes's techniques, Lowen's exercises, and techniques I have developed myself, so it brings together psychoanalytic practices, vegetotherapy and bioenergetic analysis. Lowen's exercises are mainly used to release the patient's repressions and bring him to a particular level of consciousness. Freud's method of free association is in fact the forerunner of the stimulus-from-within method, but with the focus on the ectodermic, mental level. In biodynamic therapy the stimulus-from-within not only includes mental imagery, but also feelings and bodily sensations, and we encourage expression on the emotional and physical levels as well as in speech.

In biodynamic therapy we are constantly re-discovering the validity of Freud's theories, but we never interpret anything. The patient relives repressed situations with such intensity that it is as if he experiences them at the actual moment they happened. Catharsis is often accompanied by images and exact memories, and it completely involves both body and mind. The cathartic movement emerges from the body depths, the endoderm, then passes through the expressive channels of the mesoderm, and finally connects with thoughts and memories at the ectodermic level.

It is this cathartic movement that distinguishes our method fundamentally from Lowen's. Although abreactions do occur in bioenergetic analysis, the therapeutic goal is different. Lowen's main aim is to bring about bioenergetic trembling movements and fine vibrations throughout the whole muscular system. His work focuses on liberating energy on the mesodermic level. Biodynamic therapy, on the other hand, concentrates on the endodermic level: that is, the id canal and the oldest, deepest repressions. Lowen's work focuses more on the here and now; biodynamic work encourages impulses to emerge even from the patient's most distant past, and helps him to discharge and release them. Our main aim is bring about a profound catharsis to empty the system totally of the anxiety that has become locked into it. Only after this deep cathartic movement has been set in motion do we use Lowen's grounding exercises; at this point they help the energy released from the body depths to enter into the muscular system and the whole mesodermic level, from where it is discharged into the ground. When this happens, the patient recovers his profound vitality.

However, this is not the first thing we set out to achieve. We begin by working towards the abreaction. By using deep regression, we help the patient to bring to light everything that is buried in his body and his unconscious mind. As long as he continues to feel a sense of pressure within him, there is still something more to let out, to abreact. With our method of deep therapy, the patient lies on his back so that his diaphragm relaxes, and this allows the process of purification to continue. Only when most of his fear has been abreacted do we concentrate on helping the patient to discover his vitality. It seems as though a patient becomes a great deal stronger in external situations when he no longer has anything to fear from his own internal world. Once he has rediscovered his independent well-being, his oceanic wave, his inner security, no further danger can threaten him from internal stimuli. Then we can begin to work with him on the vital level.

My own experience bears this out. When I first did the "jellyfish" exercise in the early days of my therapy with Ola Raknes ("Imagine you are a jellyfish, pulsating in the sea..."), I felt nothing at all. The exercise seemed completely pointless to me. My body was "dead" at that time, insensitive to the point where I had no libido circulation, no oceanic wave, no vegetative currents, no independent well-being. Later, however, when I returned to complete my therapy with Raknes after going through the different therapies with Dr Houge and Aadel Bülow-Hansen that I have already described, I did the jellyfish exercise again. This time it was a completely different experience: it brought me to more and more marvellous states of ecstasy and libido circulation. Raknes then said to me: "You don't need any more therapy. Your therapy is complete; you have rediscovered your libido energy." It was only then that I realised how extraordinarily beautiful and powerful this exercise could be, and how dead my body must have been when I found it so pointless.

Nevertheless, although I had now regained my libido circulation, there were still a number of things to eliminate from my organism before I could truly call my therapy complete. This is true for many people. Although their libido circulation may be working well and they may be able to experience independent well-being, often there are still problems to resolve. But at this point, going further in therapy is no longer a necessity for them; it is a luxury. In any case, once somebody has rediscovered his libido circulation, once he is conscious of the oceanic wave, he is so independent, so peaceful in himself, that his own self-regulation can take him further in purifying himself and developing his potential.

At this point I want to explain more precisely how we use Lowen's grounding in biodynamic therapy. The patient lies on his back for most of the time during our therapy. Normally we do not aim to help him find his grounding - or at least, not before the end of the therapy. However, there is one situation in which we do use Lowen's grounding exercises earlier in the course of the therapy: when a patient gets stuck in a primal process so that he finds himself in a state of constant anxiety and dependency. We then ask him to take a standing position, either to give him strength and grounding, or - depending on his individual character structure - to encourage him to abreact.

These grounding exercises can also be very useful where someone has a chronically collapsed chest or habitually lapses into emotional movement patterns. The exercises also help to strengthen the diaphragm in cases where it has lost its ability to function as an emotional regulator as a result of too much primal (pre-verbal and regressive) therapy. With patients such as these we use methods designed to accentuate the in-breath, because when they breathe out, they always get stuck in the same pattern of discharge. We also do a lot of work to strengthen their backs. In fact, grounding exercises are absolutely appropriate where the patient has become permanently stuck in a primal discharge pattern of this kind.

This phenomenon occurs when somebody comes into contact with such deep layers of his being that he is unable to integrate them. The dynamic pressure coming from these deep layers then collides with the barriers of the superficial layers. I do not want to suggest that people undergoing primal therapy inevitably risk running into blocks of this kind in the primary process. I know some primal therapists who have a natural harmonising ability within them and achieve extraordinary results by taking their patients into their arms and encouraging their feelings of love. As long as the primal therapist consciously follows the rule that every provocation must be followed by harmonisation, the therapy goes well and the patient rediscovers his libido circulation. But when the primal therapist provokes deeper and deeper layers, causing too many defences to fall at the same time, the risks are incalculable and there is a serious threat to the patient's health. A number of institutions in the United States have tried using primal therapy to treat drug addicts. In some of these cases, where the therapist has "pushed" the patient too hard, the results have been extraordinarily negative. I have often had participants in my open seminars and training groups who have undergone this kind of intensive primary therapy. They are instantly recognisable: they have a dull expression in their eyes and seem to have aged prematurely, and their auras are damaged.

I had one especially difficult case of this kind: a psychoanalyst who had been through seven years of psychoanalysis and two years of intensive primal therapy. She was in such a state of inner destruction that I had to take a very firm therapeutic attitude to get her out of it. Patients of this kind need a great deal of verbal integration. When I am working with them, I see it as very important to help them to speak about the material that is closest to their ego and so easiest for them to integrate. I absolutely do not push them to levels of deep suffering and screaming.

Primal therapy and Lowen's grounding techniques can be seen as two opposite poles, with our biodynamic therapy hovering somewhere between them. We fully agree with primal therapy's view that activating deep, repressed material is a very important part of the therapeutic work; but we believe it is essential to uncover these repressed layers gradually, step by step, integrating the material as we go along. It is not a matter of trying to provoke a discharge, but of letting whatever is ripe appear and be expressed.

I remember one case where work on grounding was undertaken too soon. The patient, who was suffering from intense anxiety and finding it difficult to cope with her daily life, went to see a therapist in her home country, Brazil. The therapist gave her some grounding exercises, including the classic stress exercise: in this exercise, the patient stands on tiptoe and tries to keep his balance while stretching his arms forward and looking the therapist in the eyes. These exercises proved to be very helpful for her; after she had been doing them regularly for a while, her most distressing symptoms disappeared and she was able to cope perfectly well again in her daily life.

Then she came to London, where she decided to see what biodynamic therapy could do for her. In the very first session she relived an experience from her childhood that was most important for her. Afterwards, though, several of her old symptoms reappeared. She was surprised and disappointed; she had believed that all her problems had disappeared, but now it seemed they had simply been covered over. I explain this phenomenon as follows: grounding exercises strengthen the motor ego, but at the beginning of that first session I had concentrated on lowering her defences again. I used the stimulus-from-within method to do this, asking her to relax and allow her diaphragm to move at its own rhythm, while I encouraged her with little phrases like: "Let the breathing happen by itself, just let it come." At that point, with her defences out of the way, the conflict repressed in the unconscious was able to resurface.

In the second session I gave her a light massage, and she promptly relived a deeply traumatic experience from her infancy in which she nearly suffocated. Her memories of the incident unfolded like a film: she was trapped under a heavy weight, gasping for air as someone jumped up and down on top of her. She then told me the whole story, which she had learned from her mother years later. One evening, when her mother came home from work, she asked: "Where's the baby?" The baby's nine brothers did not answer; they were busy jumping up and down on top of a pile of mattresses. The horrified mother finally discovered their little sister, half-dead beneath the mattresses. Her maternal warmth and tenderness restored the baby to life.

My Brazilian patient relived this incident extremely vividly in the session, and once it was over she was radiant and full of energy. She felt the oceanic wave pulsing within her, and she also discovered an extraordinary capacity for pleasure in her sex life. All the same, she wanted to continue with her therapy. I agreed, on condition that she undertook to come for at least another five sessions.

The next session was equally dramatic. She relived an indescribably horrible experience - this time from before her birth. Her mother had tried to abort her, and she could clearly see an enormous knitting needle coming towards her and trying to destroy her. This memory was particularly difficult to integrate, but I felt reassured by the knowledge that we would have another four sessions in which to work on it. But something went wrong with the arrangements, and she could only come to me for one more session before she went home to Brazil. Right at the beginning she said to me: "Now I regret having wanted to go further with my therapy, because I really wonder how I'm going to cope in my daily life from now on. I feel so unhappy." My only thought was: how could I manage to harmonise her energy in a single session? I gave her a harmonising psychoperistaltic massage, which I call the "emergency massage", and to my relief the treatment was a success. It was when I gently touched her throat by the vocal cords that her psychoperistalsis opened up strongly, bringing about complete harmonisation. Light work in the throat area is often the key to the psychoperistaltic "fountain", because it dissolves unreleased screams.

My patient felt so well after the session that she knew she could go home to Brazil and function normally in her daily life. When I went to Brazil myself the following year, I saw her again. Things were going extremely well for her. She had continued her therapeutic process in Brazil and was no longer troubled by traumatic memories. On the contrary; she had discovered the transcendental levels in herself, and she was living with a fully developed libido circulation and in constant awareness of the oceanic wave. This delightful feeling of independent well-being was also greatly helping her to develop her creativity.

Today a great many therapists from a host of different schools have adopted stress exercises as part of their approach, so I want to emphasise yet again how important it is not to use them in the wrong way. Each exercise should only be used where the therapist clearly understands what point the patient has reached in this phase of his therapy, and what therapeutic principle justifies using that exercise at this point. Under no circumstances should a stress exercise be practised for too long; otherwise, far from helping the patient, it can cause him to regress or develop a secondary block.

Just as medicines should be given in controlled doses, these exercises should only be practised under very specific conditions, and each exercise or series of exercises should be followed by a period of relaxation to allow the "psychoperistaltic fountain" to flow. To sum up, I must make it clear that I regard Lowen's work as extraordinarily valuable. But I also feel that, if the therapist is inadequately trained or insensitive, working on vitalisation at the mesodermic level can simply have the effect of masking the deeper layers of the patient's being. I always seem to encounter the same initial difficulties when I accept former patients of such therapists: as soon as they have come in and taken off their shoes, they stand with their knees slightly bent, in the classic grounding position. When I ask them to lie down and feel what they want to do or say (the stimulus-from-within method), once again they move automatically into a bioenergetic position: lying with their knees bent and the soles of their feet on the mattress, they immediately develop the classic vibrations. They begin to shake all over, and it is impossible to go further. At this point, the only thing I can do is to adopt a very clear, firm therapeutic attitude. I insist that they relax their legs, stretch out their feet, and let their breathing simply happen of its own accord. Basically, my task is to help them to get away from this mesodermic level of energy perception.

A second difficulty that I often encounter with these patients is their tendency to put far too much voluntary energy into the exercises I give them. This is because their level of consciousness is that of the ego, so they want to "push" the process. It takes a great deal of skill to bring them to the point where they can simply feel what is going on in them at that moment. This type of patient is strongly fixated on "doing"; he has great difficulty in simply letting things happen and really abandoning himself to whatever occurs.

An extreme example of this type of patient was a young woman I referred to earlier in this chapter, who came to my centre in London for treatment. She had already been in therapy for some time, but now she was in a particularly difficult phase of her life. She was attending a psychiatric clinic daily as an out-patient, and she was really very distressed indeed. She spent the whole of her first two sessions with me just beating on the mattress with her fists and feet and screaming: "I hate you! I detest you!" over and over again. At the end of the second session I asked her how she felt, and she told me: "Just as bad as ever." So I suggested that we could try something different next time.

At the following session, I asked her to lie down and feel what was happening inside her; she did not need to do anything at all, just lie there and feel. Suddenly, a phenomenon I knew so well occurred: the downgoing energy currents began flowing through her whole body and all her tensions melted away in minutes. She felt better than she had ever felt in her life, and when she came back for the next session she reported that she had felt well throughout the week. She lay down again, as she had the previous time, and once again she began to feel what she called a sweetness, filling her completely. She had rediscovered her libido circulation. But suddenly her face contracted, and she shouted in a voice full of fury: "I came here to work; I didn't come here to feel good!" And in a moment she had gone back to her familiar behaviour pattern, beating on the mattress with her hands and feet and screaming: "I hate you! I detest you!" again. Her case, although extreme, is not unusual. In therapy we often meet people who have been urged to express their aggression, to "get it all out", to the point where they no longer know how to simply let themselves go. They feel compelled to express their anger; a phenomenon I attribute to what I call the "new Reichian superego".

Most of all, it is in groups that I encounter this kind of compulsive behaviour, usually expressed in phrases such as: "You must show your feelings; you must let your feelings out." These people imagine that the more they force their bodies and their whole beings to "let out their aggression", the better they will feel and the healthier they will become. This is a grave mistake. The immediate effect of this compulsive behaviour is a build-up of energy and an even stronger block than before. What is more, because all this discharge activity takes place above the diaphragm, it does not touch the deep layers of repressed material at all. Sadly, the only thing achieved by this kind of "pushing" - that is, exerting pressure solely on the superficial layers - is a phenomenon with which we are all too familiar. It actually creates new layers of armouring.

This problem is beautifully illustrated by the example of a middle-aged man who came to see me at the beginning of one of my groups. He said: "I've been going to groups for years, I've tried every body therapy technique imaginable, and it's all done me a great deal of good. The only problem is, since going to all those groups I've become unable to work. I feel completely incapable of coping with it, and I'm also concerned that my eyesight is getting steadily worse."

Just by looking at him, I could see at once that this man had been over-provoked. He was tired all the time and displayed a complex of symptoms that I always find in cases of hyper- provocation. He was also suffering from energetic stasis in his eyes. I was able to help him to free himself from his compulsive thought patterns. Once again, I want to emphasise this point very strongly: I am fundamentally opposed to all methods that are compulsive in any way whatsoever. Anything that reinforces an individual's compulsive tendencies is intensely harmful. In short, it takes a soft, flexible therapist to produce a soft, flexible, lively patient. Otherwise the patient will very rapidly become even more blocked than he was before - only he will be too blocked to know it.

FROM STASIS TO LIBIDO CIRCULATION

At this point I want to introduce a theory I believe to be exceptionally important. It concerns the transformation of internal energy currents into endodermic energy, and the release of the endodermic stasis that prevents deep energy from moving into the mesoderm. The therapeutic practice that follows from this theory fits in closely with Reich's concept of cosmic superimposition, which I described earlier. The basic idea is to get the patient's instinctual energy and his voluntary energy working together in harmony, so as to end the perpetual conflict between the instincts and the energy of the motor ego. We have developed many different techniques which we use either to provoke or to harmonise the patient's energy, depending on the needs of the moment. By carefully co-ordinating the sequence of these provoking and harmonising techniques, we can make sure the session reaches a "happy ending".

Freud said: "Where the id is, the ego must follow." I prefer to look at things the other way round: "Where the ego is, the id must follow." Freud was a neurologist who worked at the ectodermic level (the central nervous system, the motor ego and the conscious mind). In biodynamic therapy, on the other hand, we work on the endodermic level. "Where the ego is, the id must follow" simply means that the motor ego must be entirely fuelled by the libido. As far as we are concerned, there is no conflict whatsoever between the pleasure principle and the reality principle. In fairness to Freud, though, I must explain that when he spoke of the antagonism between these two principles, he was undoubtedly talking about the id and the superego. In that sense, I agree with him completely; but I also know that reality can be utterly libidinal when somebody is truly able to allow himself to feel the libido circulation in his contact with others and with the universe. The marriage of the id and the ego is a natural one; it can even be called a spiritual marriage.

I must also mention another important therapeutic principle at this point. In biodynamic therapy we prefer the patient to keep his eyes closed when doing exercises to explore his inner state. This is not a rigid rule: the most important thing is for the therapist to be able to work with the patient, whether or not his eyes are closed, and not to become obsessed with one method or the other.

There is however a difference between the two. When the patient closes his eyes, he distances himself from the here and now. He goes back into the past, into repressed memories and images. I call this "the principle of closed eyes". When the patient opens his eyes again, however, he comes back to the reality of the present situation and can integrate the experience he has recalled from the past (the regression) into the here and now. This is "the principle of open eyes". In this respect our approach draws on the Gestalt techniques developed by Fritz Perls; but his method, like many other techniques, needs to be carefully integrated into the biodynamic therapy and only used at the ‚right', ‚ripe' moment.

We need to be very careful not to interrupt the flow of the unconscious in any way once it has begun to express itself of its own accord. In particular, intervening at such a moment by addressing questions to the patient's superego can be disastrous. When the therapist interrupts the patient by talking to the superego, the patient effectively suffers a psychic shock; a shock that abruptly pulls the energy out of the expressive flow of the id, back into the ego. Our therapeutic questions are carefully designed to allow superimposition to occur: that is, to enable the libidinal process to be integrated consciously. The words and the tone of voice we use communicate directly with the deep, essential level; not with the superficial, intellectual level. For example, if a patient starts exploring his hand and you ask him: "What do your hands want to do?", the patient's libidinal flow is interrupted. But if you say: "Try to feel what your hands want to do, let them express whatever they want to, let your hands speak...", the effect is completely different. Yet the difference between these two types of questions is subtle.

There is another important therapeutic principle that I must stress in this context: when the flow of the unconscious has been unlocked and is being expressed, it is the therapist, not the patient, who must bear responsibility for anything that happens. We do not consider that the patient is responsible at this point. In these moments of deep opening, situations that are particularly dangerous for the patient can develop.

One example of this happened during a group in which we used the "seed method"; a technique developed by David Boadella, editor of the Journal of Energy and Character. One person was the ‚seed', in the middle of the group, enclosed by all the other group members; their job was to help the seed to develop and grow. This particular patient went back into an episode from his childhood, when he was about four years old. He remembered how his father was always busy with his work and never showed any signs of affection or interest in his son. "My father was never interested in me! I want so much to have a real father!" he burst out. At that moment he was seeing himself as a child of four, in his parents' living room, as his father came in through the door. I gently suggested to the ‚seed' that he should open his eyes slowly and choose someone from the group who could play the role of his father. He did so. The man he chose as his "father" was himself a therapist. However, this man was a rather insensitive person; he was too heavily involved in the American human potential movement with its principles of scrupulous honesty. So when the patient, who was in a state of regression, asked this man: "Would you like to be my father?", the insensitive therapist replied: "No, I don't want to be your father!" For the patient, this came as a terrible shock.

Dangerous moments of this kind do occur when the liberating impulse makes an abrupt transition from the unconscious to the adult level of the ego. It is essential for the therapist to follow the flow of the process closely. Nowadays we use all sorts of new body therapy methods in our work, but we always use them in a biodynamic way. This means that the therapist must not impose any of his preconceptions or judgements on whatever is going on, and he must have a sense of the right timing.

That is why I make certain in my own biodynamic therapy training programmes that each of the trainee therapists himself goes through a profound and powerful biodynamic process. The biodynamic therapist must reach the point at which he no longer needs to act out of ambition or the desire for power; he must act only out of love. He must be able to recognise the libido flow, and must know how to keep it intact. When a patient who has hidden behind a series of masks throughout his life suddenly opens himself up completely, the therapist must ensure that this vulnerable being is totally protected, never attacked. To help the patient's id flow to truly reach the level of his ego, the therapist must encourage and support every attempt that the patient makes, until he has found his own inner security. Once the patient has reached this level, his id and his ego unite in such a way that he no longer fears anything.

If the therapist is insensitive and fails to recognise that the patient has entered into a libidinal movement, he sets off a new startle reflex and helps to create a new secondary personality in the patient. Secondary neuroses and solidification then begin to develop as well. I truly cannot over-emphasise the importance of this point; I see it as absolutely fundamental to support the re- awakening of the patient's libidinal well-being. Turning now to the use of Lowen's stress exercises in groups, I have often noticed that the more the group members do these exercises, the less they come into contact with themselves. Particularly if the time between the exercises is short, the participants have no opportunity to come into contact with the depths of their organism. Even if the therapist talks about the exercise and explains it, this does not change anything.

The biodynamic approach enables us to avoid the pitfalls that can be caused by using Lowen's stress exercises inappropriately. Our method involves adapting these exercises according to what we want to achieve with the group or patient. In other words, the therapist continually modulates the movement of energy. For example, when I lead a group of people who have never had therapy or who are too used to being "pushed", I talk to them and get them to do a series of exercises in rapid succession, to keep them on a vital level. If, on the other hand, my intention is to bring the group members into contact with profound realities, both Freudian and Jungian, then I act accordingly. During the course of therapy, extraordinary things can happen at the consciousness level of the self. To help my patients reach this level, I speak in a tone of voice that I call "essential". For example, I may begin by getting the patient to do a stress exercise with his eyes closed, and I then speak directly to the id, to the unconscious. I speak with a light but sincere tone, in a slow rhythm, and the inner stimulus surges up of its own accord in response. This stimulus, which emerges from the body, moves slowly. It takes a long time to rise into consciousness, to reach the motor ego and the level of expression. The stimulus starts within the endoderm; it then passes through the mesoderm and finally reaches the ectoderm. For this process to follow its natural course, the patient must feel that there is no danger of being interrupted, no need to guard himself against the risk of suffering a startle reflex. In moments such as these, security is fundamental. The therapist's job is to protect the patient from all unpleasant outside influences: whether from the external world, or from other group members.

I recall using this method on one occasion to get into contact with deep, spiritual levels in a group that was more accustomed to stress exercises and violent abreactions. The scene was a peaceful one: the group members were simply sitting or lying there with their eyes shut, and apparently nothing at all was happening. If a therapist of the active, impatient type had come in at that moment, he might have imagined that the whole group must be bored. But in the feedback that followed, all the participants told me how, for the first time in their lives, they had experienced simply being there in the moment, expecting nothing of themselves or of others, and how they felt they had come into contact with something truly essential in themselves. Several of them said they had felt freed from their inner compulsions: freed from the urge to be constantly doing something, or constantly demanding that other people push them into action or abreaction. It is at moments like this that we experience the truly "magical" side of this work. These group members rediscovered within themselves the miraculous world they had inhabited long ago, before grown-ups had snatched them out of it. At such moments, a person rediscovers his own centre, which he experiences as a moment in eternity.

Of course, the likelihood that these phenomena will occur depends on how heavily armoured the organism is. But as therapists, we must always be aware that if we have too many expectations, if we want to make too many things happen or to push the patient in a particular direction, instead of dissolving his armouring our efforts will actually reinforce it, or even create secondary armouring. Unfortunately, far too many therapists still continue to push for a discharge, as I have observed in numerous groups. In conclusion, I would like to say that any technique that allows the unconscious to express itself and makes room for the profound biodynamic process to unfold will produce positive results. If the unconscious is in a static state, "encapsulated" in the body, the majority of the psychotherapeutic work can only take place on the surface, above this layer of stasis, where the only thing it can reach is the patient's defences.

Often, as a result, the therapy simply creates new defence mechanisms or increases the conflicts between the existing defences, without the unconscious ever manifesting itself. The libido is unable to re-emerge, and any apparent changes cannot last; no purification occurs. Although any number of noisy abreactions may take place, they are all superficial: everything happens above the diaphragm.

PAIN

I must now speak about pain, because I am fundamentally opposed to any kind of pain ideology in psychotherapy and bioenergetics. Wilhelm Reich's daughter, Dr Eva Reich, is scornful of any form of neo-Reichian work that claims pain and suffering have a therapeutic value. She often says: "My father would never have wanted anyone to suffer in order to get well." In particular, Eva Reich uses a technique in her work that she calls the "butterfly touch": an extremely soft bioenergetic method. For my part, I believe that no matter how heavily armoured an organism may be, the way in which we touch it must never cause any kind of suffering.

So I must make it clear that I am against the use of some of Lowen's techniques - or certainly against the ways in which I have seen them used in groups. One such technique involves exerting extremely strong manual pressure on the patient's jaws and tense facial muscles as he stands in a stress position. The patient "attacked" in this way reacts with bloodcurdling shrieks. It seems to me that methods of this kind will only succeed in strengthening the patient's defences, and I find them deeply masochistic - especially if the patient must not only remain standing throughout this violent procedure, but also thank his therapist afterwards. No matter how I try, I am unable to see the therapeutic value of any technique that involves using violence. As far as I can judge, the effects of such techniques are limited to a momentary abreaction that has no real connection with the buried events of childhood.

Certainly, it seems to me the most natural thing in the world to yell out if somebody hurts me. At the same time, it seems equally self-evident to me that a yell that does not really come from somebody's depths - that is, a yell that comes from above the diaphragm - will be no more effective than singing. Letting out a hearty yell from the lungs can have a certain value as an affirmation of the self in the here and now; but it is important to distinguish between something that reaches the depths of the person's unconscious, and something that does not. If self- affirmation in the here and now is what the therapist wants to achieve, these techniques can be very useful; but

I do not agree that they have great therapeutic value.

I am strongly opposed to all physical therapy techniques that cause pain. I vastly prefer acupressure, a method that involves applying simple finger pressure to a painful part of the patient's body and releasing the pressure when he reports that the pain has diminished. I use this technique methodically, in a biodynamic way, and particularly in conjunction with the stethoscope in a specific type of massage. Working in this way, I have often managed to make pains caused by lumbago or blockages in the spinal column disappear completely. All the same, as biodynamic therapists we never allo the level of pain to increase in these treatments, which we give regularly. I am convinced that this whole pain ideology arises from nothing more than the insensitivity of the therapists who argue in its favour; therapists who adopt powerful techniques and use them in a violent way. It would be good if every patient were aware of this. The era of redemption through suffering has had its day; it is time for it to end.

Moving on to another aspect of group work, it is immensely interesting to observe the phenomena that occur when the participants are not used to coming into contact with their own dynamic process. Often these people do not have the slightest idea what we mean by an inner stimulus; they have only worked in groups where the leader is constantly telling them what to do next. So when they find themselves confronted with a biodynamic therapist who gently suggests to them: "Try to feel what you want to do...", they are completely nonplussed! They want to follow instructions, they want somebody to tell them what they have to do. They have no awareness of what is happening in the depths of their being, and when they are unable to understand the group leader's instructions, such as: "Try to feel...", they simply wait for the next order.

Here we have a classic confrontation between the authoritarian and the obedient character types. But in biodynamic therapy the last thing we want is to repeat familiar role patterns of this kind. We want the patient to discover his own identity and spontaneity. We use all the therapeutic tools at our disposal to help him to come into contact with his own uniqueness, his originality. That is why we begin our groups with exercises designed to bring deep impulses into consciousness. Once this has begun to happen, of course, we must give the patient whatever space and support he needs to follow these inner impulses; otherwise the work simply ends up by reinforcing the superego. In my view the group leader's level of awareness is crucially important; he must not be driven by his own irrationality, must not work in a way that expresses primarily his own ambitions, his desire for power or his aggression.

Yet another danger can arise in poorly led groups. For example, let us consider the situation where a group member asks the group leader and the other group members to surround him and provide resistance so that he can feel and show his own strength.

This can go badly wrong if the therapist does not keep a careful eye on what is happening; instead of merely offering passive resistance, many of the group members may use the opportunity to express their own needs, their aggression, their hatred, their desire for revenge. They pit all these urges against the strength of the person in the middle of the group, and they quickly overcome him. Under no circumstances must this be allowed to happen. In this specific situation, both the therapist and the group members must be detached from their own reactions; they must give their unconditional support to the person who is descending into the depths of himself. The whole group's task is to support that particular individual's therapeutic process, not to further their own processes. If the therapeutic objective is not clear, exercises of this kind can degenerate into pure expressions of violence.

It seems to me that all of this is also an ethical problem. If the group leader and the group members truly have the goal of helping somebody to free himself from his defences, they must recognise that in consequence, that person will become intensely vulnerable. Once in this defenceless state, he will need to receive their unconditional support; under no conditions must he be subjected to further aggression, which will only plunge him into deep confusion. I myself, and the therapy training school that I direct, believe in the fundamental principle that every therapist who works with the mind and the body must himself be "pure". By this I mean that he must be totally there for his patients and must keep his own needs and conflicts to himself, or work on them in his own therapy. He must also protect his patient from attack.

I disagree absolutely with the theory, which has become so popular in recent years, that the patient is responsible for his own therapeutic process. From the moment that the patient enters deeply into himself, the therapist must accept responsibility for him; otherwise a deplorable confusion develops between the principles of Gestalt therapy and those of biodynamic psychology. It would be totally untrue and unfair to say to a patient in whom, with the help of his therapist, a powerful biodynamic phenomenon has just appeared: "You are responsible for what is happening!"

I believe that the therapist has a duty to be at his patient's side, to give support to his unconscious and to his primary personality which has been buried for so long. It would be completely immoral and unethical to help somebody's unconscious material to emerge and then, immediately afterwards, to turn that material against him. A therapist who blames his patients for their unconscious desires is not worthy of the name. It is tremendously important to draw a clear distinction between the "encounter" level of therapeutic work, and the profound biodynamic level. Certainly, the "encounter" level can be used to help the patient enter into contact with his unconscious; but after this, the therapist must give his unconditional support to the unconscious and the impulses that arise from it.

THE OPEN AND CLOSED PRINCIPLES

It is impossible to avoid all tension during the course of the day. However, it is best when periods of tension alternate with periods of relaxation, like the natural alternation between night and day. Our lives would be unreal if we lived them in a permanent state of relaxation; and besides, excitement is a positive, pleasurable sensation. Psychoperistalsis only goes into action to dissolve residual tensions and prevent energy from accumulating and stasis from building up - conditions which encourage neuroses to develop. All sorts of different residues are dissolved by psychoperistalsis: residual tensions in the muscles, metabolic residues from the emotional circulatory system, and residues between the membranes and residual tensions in the membranes themselves.

When I look at photographs taken of Wilhelm Reich towards the end of his life, I am struck by a very noticeable accumulation of energetic stasis in his face. If only Reich had known about psychoperistaltic self-regulation, he would have been able to transform the upward movement of his energy into a downward, harmonising flow. This feeling of harmony in his body would have made it much easier for him to cope with the chronically hopeless situations in which he found himself throughout his life, and particularly towards its end. But we must never forget that Reich was not only a pioneer of the concept of cosmic energy in the West, but also a martyr to it. Even his earliest writings clearly show that he was searching for the principle of self-regulation. He knew that the key lay hidden somewhere in the abdomen, but he was unable to discover the ‚fountain' of harmonisation, nor did he recognise intestinal peristalsis as the regulatory mechanism he was looking for. I am certain that if he had known about the function of psychoperistalsis, he would have been able to dissolve the stasis in his face and so avoid the excessive energetic provocation that had such a disastrous effect on his heart.

At this point I want to explain in more detail exactly what I mean by the open and closed principles of peristalsis. When the psychoperistaltic system is closed, energy accumulates in the whole organism and disturbs its self-regulation. At certain times the system should naturally open and start working. This should happen at night, during sleep, but also during moments of relaxation in the daytime: drinking a cup of tea, reading a newspaper, or simply sitting and relaxing in a comfortable chair. But if someone goes straight from one stressful situation to another without pausing in between to relax, the psychoperistalsis does not have time to function, and it stops. This is what happens when a person is under non-stop pressure, both at work and at home. The build-up of energy and stasis predisposes him to develop neurotic symptoms.

I experienced this phenomenon myself many times during the period just after my arrival in London. This phase of my life was both highly significant and highly stressful. My workload was huge, and at the same time I also had to pay extra attention to my children, who found themselves transplanted into an environment very different from their former home in Norway. I discovered that I was able to cope well with all of this as long as I could dedicate a little time on Saturdays and Sundays to my own psychoperistaltic self-regulation and spiritual development. But whenever I was unable to spend this time on my own, I could feel the energetic pressure within me starting to build up. As my busy weekend wore on, the pressure just carried on growing. By the time Monday arrived, far from feeling refreshed, I often felt worse than I had at the end of the previous week.

I also discovered that it took me much longer to recover if I had been through a long period of stress and pressure. After a full week of activity and tension I needed to have at least an entire morning to myself. After three or four weeks of constant stress it took me at least one full day - and sometimes several days - to harmonise my energy. That is why I insist that a natural alternation between times of relaxation and times of tension is so important; without it, a person's energetic balance can be irreparably ruined, or at least damaged so severely that it takes a very long time to re- establish itself. Yet so little is needed to keep the system in balance: simply taking a bath is enough, or even washing your face or spending a few moments with somebody you love.

These regular pauses for self-regulation are even more vital for people who are involved in a therapeutic process, since they are particularly vulnerable to the danger of developing new neuroses if their energetic balance is disturbed. For example, I had a patient who had experimented with a variety of Reichian and neo-Reichian therapies before coming to me. During the course of these therapies her body had swollen up progressively, till by the time I saw her she looked like a balloon. An intensely powerful biodynamic process had been set in motion in the depths of her organism, but because her tissue and her superficial membranes were still armoured, her system could not open to allow harmonisation to take place. Instead, the energetic fluid had stagnated, causing the swelling that was distressing her.

In the first session with this woman I began to look for the ‚keys' to open her psychoperistalsis: in other words, I touched her lightly in different places to identify the spots that would respond with peristaltic sounds. For some time I could find no sounds at all, but finally I heard a faint response as I gently massaged her behind her right ear. Gradually these faint peristaltic sounds grew louder, and suddenly she started screaming, clutching her hands tightly over her ears. She relived a horrible experience from her childhood: she was seven years old, and there in front of her eyes her father was strangling her mother. Her ears were filled with the dreadful sounds of her mother's screams, and she was shaken with an intense feeling of fear and horror. This event had traumatised her very deeply, and she had blocked and repressed an enormous amount of terror. The tension had become concentrated in her ears, because she had been unable to bear the intensity of her mother's screaming.

Finding the keys to the psychoperistaltic process is a fundamental part of our therapeutic practice. To apply this method, it is helpful to keep in mind the image of an over-inflated balloon and Reich's theory of the organism's urge to explode and so release the accumulated tension. This explosive pressure can build up at various points in the body, such as the throat, where the energy is blocked and unable to find an outlet. With our psychoperistaltic method we can discover the keys to unlock the patient's discharge processes on both the vegetative and emotional levels, as in the case I have just mentioned: peristalsis acts as a guide that shows us the way to go. In my patient's case, it was not surprising that there was no psychoperistalsis, because the emotional pressure was extremely strong. This was an example of the closed principle of psychoperistalsis: a principle that we always keep in mind in our work.

This same principle can also be seen at work in the case of Wilhelm Reich himself. Reich's own energetic flow was exceptionally powerful, but the hostility that he encountered in the outside world created a strong pressure in his membranes and residual tensions in his muscles. Naturally enough, a conflict soon developed and became anchored into place in the form of stasis.

I want to mention one more example of the closed principle at work; a situation that arose in 1968, just before I left Norway. At that time public opinion in Norway had been stirred up over the issue of pensions for victims of the Second World War. A law granting pensions to war victims was passed in 1945, at the end of the war, but only a small number of people applied for the money at that time. Suddenly, though, a flood of claims for disablement pensions on the grounds of psychosomatic or neurological disorders came pouring in to the Ministry of Health in 1968. Although the ministry at first refused to accept these claims, the pressure of public opinion soon forced it to reverse its decision. The claims were paid, but the Norwegian authorities remained mystified as to why these symptoms had suddenly made their appearance more than two decades after the war.

Biodynamic theory and the closed principle of peristalsis can offer a solution to the mystery. When people are subjected to the pressures of war for weeks, months or even years, in a permanent state of stress and a perpetual startle reflex situation, their psychoperistalsis stops working altogether. There is no downward movement of energy, no harmonisation; instead, nervous energy continually accumulates within the organism. This situation is like trying to pour more and more liquid into a glass that is already full to the brim: the body is unable to hold all the accumulated energy. The body's response is to lapse into a state of nervous depression, and the dynamic pressure then stops. This is easy to understand. I have worked with many people who have taken part in encounter groups in the past, and I have noticed that it takes at least two months for their psychoperistalsis to open. That is not surprising, if we bear in mind that encounter groups can create multiple startle reflexes in their participants, as well as new armouring and secondary neuroses.

A good example of the effects of permanent stress is the case of a New York hospital manager. This woman and I had known each other for some time as professional colleagues, and when she visited London for a few days' holiday she took the opportunity to look me up. She was suffering from a severe pain in her back, and asked me if I could relieve it. Normally I do not give treatment to people whom I know well, but on that particular afternoon one of my sessions had been cancelled and I had some free time. So I gave her a treatment. At the start of the session she was so tense that she made no peristaltic sounds whatsoever. As I went on massaging her I hunted for the ‚keys' to open her peristalsis, and eventually I found three: the area around her eyes, on her nose, and between the thumb and index finger of her right hand. From that point onwards her psychoperistalsis grew steadily louder and more vigorous.

At the end of the session she said to me: "I had a wonderful sensation of floating in a warm, pleasant stream, and I heard noises coming from my belly that I've never heard before in my whole life." She looked fifteen years younger, her hair tumbling loosely around her face, and her eyes were shining as she said to me gratefully: "This has been a real holiday!" Yet all I had given her was a single treatment. But its dramatic effect can easily be explained by the three keys that unlocked her peristalsis. The first key was the area around her eyes, which had to do with concentration: I could picture her sitting at her desk, her eyes fixed on a pile of papers. The second key was her nose, an area associated with will-power and the direction she gave to her work. Finally, the third key was the place where she held her pen in her right hand.

Most people have difficulty in really resting and enjoying themselves during their holidays. Their systems have been closed and blocked for such a long time that they no longer know how to find a way of being in which their ascending energy can be transformed into descending, harmonising energy. As a result, neither the residual tension in their muscles nor the tension in their membranes is able to dissolve.

THE DIFFERENT SOUNDS OF PSYCHOPERISTALSIS

Now I want to describe the different peristaltic sounds that we encounter when working with the stethoscope. When I first started experimenting with this method of massage, I was constantly astonished by the variety of sounds I heard. In those days I was working with extremely highly charged people, and in particular with psychotics such as Oscar, whose case I will describe later in this book. The sounds I heard from these patients were like claps of thunder; their intensity helped me to recognise that I was dealing with a phenomenon of cosmic energy in the interior of the human organism. Exceptionally highly charged and blocked people with a huge backlog of repressed aggression tend to produce these thunderous sounds. Sometimes they also make sounds like the roaring of a lion. I am particularly fond of these sounds; they often occur when I am using a biodynamic massage method I call ‚psychoperistaltic osteopathy', especially when I am working on the vertebral alveoli. They can also be found on the surface of the skull and in other parts of the body. These sounds are of course associated with deposits of energetic fluid, which the massage gradually releases to be dissolved in peristalsis.

Quite different sounds are produced when we work with ‚energy distribution', another of our biodynamic massage methods. These sounds are usually much more harmonious and a pleasure to listen to; I call them ‚the sounds of the enchanted river'. Very often we also hear watery sounds during a massage. We try not to interrupt or influence these sounds because they tell us that a powerful flow of energy is circulating; if we interfere with this flow we risk stopping it.

Another sound resembles a gust of wind. I prefer not to come across this sound, because it seems to be the sign of a flow of energy that is circulating without real psychoperistalsis. This sound is often found in hysterics and in cases where excessively deep layers have been touched. Mechanical sounds like the ‚tac-tac- tac' of a machine-gun also fall into this category; they are associated with layers of aggressive impulses that are not really ripe. These layers are still too alien to the consciousness and to the ego.

Another very distinctive sound that I sometimes encounter is one that I call the creaking door. The first time I heard this sound was while working with my manic-depressive patient Oscar. Each time I passed to a layer of older, deeper material I heard this characteristic creaking sound, which made me think of a rusty door opening to reveal hidden rooms full of long-repressed conflicts. The image that came to my mind was the ancient houses on the west coast of Norway, which date back to the age of the Vikings. Massive and studded with rusty iron, their doors emit the most horrible sounds.

An inhabitant of one of these houses once told me of an incident during the war; when the invading Germans came and opened the door, the hideous sounds it produced made them flee in terror. When massage opens these ancient doors, a flood of unconscious, repressed material is suddenly liberated and returns to consciousness in the form of images and memories. Often the doors do not open fully at the first attempt: they seem to be opening, opening... only to close again abruptly. In the end, though, they will open.

A classic example of this process is a South American psychiatrist who came to consult me. He told me: "Everything in my life is going splendidly. I have plenty of patients, my professional life is flourishing, I have a good relationship with my wife and with my whole family, and I am perfectly happy. All the same, I have a sense of something inside me that I am unable to contact. Can you help me?" I thought to myself: "Right, I think I must find this man's rusty doors and open them." I started the massage session, and before long I began hearing the creaking sounds I was looking for; but the ‚doors' kept slamming shut again. I simply carried on massaging, until suddenly my patient's peristalsis opened up completely and he recalled an event that had frightened him severely when he was three years old. He shuddered with fear as he relived the experience: he was living in the jungle with his parents, it was night time, and he was terrified. He wanted to run to his father for comfort, but he knew that his father never had a moment to spare for him. So my patient relived the intense conflict between his fear and the resentment he felt towards his father for neglecting him. As the session continued, he began murmuring softly in a child's voice, repeating the same words over and over like a litany: "Papa prefers reading books, Papa prefers reading books..."

During the following session, this man had a strong emotional discharge in which he relived an indescribable horror that completely paralysed him with fright. In yet another session he was again overwhelmed by feelings of fear as he recalled a bitter quarrel between his parents. He remembered his mother hurling reproaches at her husband, accusing him of being useless and an inadequate father. His repressed feelings of love for his father then surged to the surface, and it was tremendously poignant to hear him slowly and deliberately declare: "Papa, you are a very good father. It's Mama who is not a good wife to you; why don't you leave her?" He had kept all of this repressed; he feared that saying these words could be fatal for him. A moment later he was filled with joy; it was all over, and he said: "Oh, I couldn't care less about my father, my mother and all those old stories. I have my wife now, and in a few days' time I am going to have another child. I feel fine!" This is the kind of thing that can happen when we open those creaking doors.

IV THE FIELD OF BIODYNAMIC THERAPY

PUBLISHING MY THEORIES

One of the things that frustrated me most when I came to England was the lack of time to write. At first I threw myself into studying English, as I eventually hoped to be able to write about my work in that language. Before long, though, I found I had so many psychotherapy clients that I was working nearly every day of the year. I hardly managed to sit down and write for so much as a moment: something that I regretted, because I very much wanted to keep a full record of my experiences and theories, not just a set of hurried case notes. I only managed to produce three articles, on the subject of "The dynamic relationship", "The primary personality and the vegetative streamings", and "Oscar: a case study of manic- depressive psychosis" (reproduced at the end of this book).

So I was delighted and relieved when my daughter Mona Lisa offered to help me set down my theories on paper. Her offer came after a London newspaper published an article which was supposed to be about biodynamic work. Mona Lisa was so shocked by the inaccuracies in the article that she vowed: "If other people are going to distort the theory like that, we are just going to have to write down the fundamentals of biodynamic psychology ourselves." I was equally grateful to David Boadella, who so warmly agreed to publish Mona Lisa's articles in his ‚Journal of Energy and Character'. Their publication was a great help in making the theories and methods of biodynamic psychology more widely known.

Another problem strengthened my daughter's resolve to write. In my training seminars I used to talk about different theoretical aspects of biodynamic psychology. But my theories were quickly taken up by some of the participants, who wrote them up in reports and, of course, presented them as their own discoveries. This meant that, much to my annoyance, on several occasions I came across my own theories masquerading under someone else's name. Mona Lisa's biggest fear was that someone would also appropriate and distort the theory of psychoperistalsis in this way. So she set herself the goal of studying the physiology of what she called "neurological digestion" in depth, and eventually she managed to formulate a precise explanation of many aspects of bio- dynamic theory and put it down on paper. By this time, the need for an organisation to provide training in biodynamic psychology was becoming increasingly clear. As a result, the Institute of Unitive Psychology was founded in the Netherlands, followed in 1973 by the International Foundation of Biodynamic Psychology.

PERISTALTIC MASSAGE IN CARDIOLOGY

At this point I want to describe how the work of one of my trained therapists, Peg Nunneley, resulted in a truly spectacular demonstration of the use of peristaltic massage in cardiology. Ms Nunneley is a trained nurse and psychologist who also spent many years as the director of a children's home. After training in the psychoperistaltic method, she developed a particularly gentle and light form of this massage which she used in her own practice. One day a journalist came to her for treatment, and was so favourably impressed that she wrote an article for an English newspaper with a very large circulation. The response to the article was so huge that Ms Nunneley found herself answering literally hundreds of letters. One of these letters came from the manager of a leading London hospital, inviting her to come and give a demonstration in the cardiology unit. When she arrived, Ms Nunneley was ushered into a demonstration room equipped with an impressive array of instruments to measure any physiological changes that might take place during the massage. The doctors asked her to work on a patient suffering from extremely high blood pressure which no drugs had succeeded in lowering. So she began giving this patient a gentle peristaltic massage, and before long the instruments did indeed record a clear drop in the patient's blood pressure. The head cardiologist was so impressed that he left the room with a cry of astonishment. Two weeks later Ms Nunneley received another invitation to the cardiology unit, where she succeeded in considerably reducing the effects of a heart attack within a few hours. Another highly effective method of energy harmonisation that I want to mention here is a technique I call "mirror breathing" or "esoteric breathing". It involves breathing out as slowly and gently as possible, as if trying to create a delicate film of steam on a mirror. I often use this simple breathing technique in groups. I usually begin by getting the group to do one of Lowen's bioenergetic stress exercises in a biodynamic way, after which I ask them to try the mirror breathing. In this way the participants can experience the transition from a state of stress to a state of harmonisation.

THE PREVENTION OF NEUROSIS

How can neurosis be prevented? When a psychotherapist spends many years working to free people from their neurotic patterns, this is a question which haunts him continually. In my view we ought to spend far more time than we now do educating parents about ways to prevent their children from developing neuroses or even psychoses. So when I met Eva Reich, Wilhelm Reich's daughter, my delight knew no bounds when I learned that she shared my view. Eva Reich is a doctor specialising in paediatric and obstetric medicine. She has worked with Frédéric Leboyer to develop non-violent birthing techniques, and for many years she has championed the principle of natural birth in numerous clinics. In this way she has been pursuing the goal defined by her father shortly before his death: to protect children from neurotic environments and to give them the ability to preserve their primary personality.

Without any exaggeration, conventional childbirth can be described as the "cradle of neurosis". During depth therapy we often find that patients relive birth experiences, and I have even had patients who regress so far back that they can recall being their father's sperm as it entered their mother's vagina and uterus. Everything that I have observed has also made me more and more convinced that when souls incarnate, they are drawn towards a mother whose level of spiritual development matches their own. As a general rule, the higher the mother's spiritual level, the more spiritually advanced her child is likely to be. But this statement does need qualifying, and this brings us to the topic of "Karma".

I can think of several examples of people who came to me to train as therapists, and went through an intensive process of professional and spiritual development during their training. These people became excellent therapists, yet they came from particularly difficult family backgrounds. It is my belief that, leaving aside the thorny question of "karmic debt", direct personal experience of neurosis is essential in order to become a really good therapist. This may explain why many people who have extraordinary qualities, but who have not passed through this process, are not interested in therapy in the slightest. I must make it clear, though, that all these explanations, questions and answers are purely speculative. All that I can say for certain is that I have been present during many, many therapeutic processes in which patients have recalled the experience of their birth, their pre-natal time in the womb, and sometimes even the moment of their conception. Since I now believe in the existence of the soul and reincarnation, I do not find it difficult to understand that the soul waits for the right moment to incarnate.

A number of my patients have described phenomena that closely resemble the phenomenon known in esoteric literature as "astral projection". Most particularly, I remember a man who relived certain moments in his childhood when his father was so cruel to him that he went out of his body to escape the pain and distress. I am deeply convinced of the reality of these phenomena, because many of my patients, after they have "opened up" through therapy, have found that they can easily leave and re-enter their bodies while in a state of meditation. I have also experienced this myself many times.

All of these are phenomena about which we can only speculate. One thing is certain, though: we adults simply must understand that children are open to an extent that we cannot even imagine. Once we understand that the soul is pure consciousness, we can also understand that children are conscious on a higher level. They experience all the events of their birth consciously, and so, inevitably, when they arrive in a sterile, cold environment they feel a tremendous longing to return to the womb. Whatever we may think about these phenomena, the number of patients who say they experience them in therapy seems to me to argue in favour of their reality.

All the phenomena I have described here play their part in biodynamic psychology. The psychoperistaltic process, for example, is closely bound up with the birth process. This is because birth is a more or less severely traumatic experience for every child, so a residual tension remains in the child's body after birth. It was while I was treating my manic-depressive patient Oscar that I first realised how important it is for the psychoperistalsis to open immediately after birth. Once the child has emerged from the birth canal, someone must intervene if the peristalsis does not begin of its own accord. If the birth is a normal, natural one, the mother of course does this simply by taking the baby in her arms. At the moment, though, most deliveries are carried out far too mechanically, and the child is taken away from its mother at once.

Happily, things are now starting to change as the work of Frédéric Leboyer becomes more widely accepted. His "birth without violence" approach is an essential step towards the prevention of neurosis. But the mother's psychoperistalsis during pregnancy is also an important factor. If she is happy during this time and in contact with her own libido circulation, her baby will also be nourished with good energy. During therapy many patients enter into regressive states in which they remember hearing the sounds of their mother's psychoperistalsis while in the womb. They describe these memories as intensely pleasurable and reassuring.

One of the most important things to be aware of, both during the birth process and afterwards, is not whether or not to touch the child, but how to do so. Babies are so sensitive, and adults so insensitive, that there is a risk that the adult's touch may become too mechanical, too "efficient". This mechanical touch quickly causes energetic fluid to accumulate within the child, laying the foundation for neurosis even at this early stage. The way in which the mother holds her baby is also crucial. He can only let go and relax when she too is relaxed; otherwise he senses her inner tension, feels insecure, and contracts and fidgets. He cannot then enter fully into his libidinal flow, and rapidly loses contact with it. Only when his mother feels well and happy can the child experience independent well-being.

There is a special kind of libidinal circulation that unites a mother with her child. Often, after the delivery, the mother is overwhelmed by an extraordinary feeling of sweetness and tenderness which I call "the mother's libidinal feeling". She should not confuse this pleasurable sensation with feelings of sexuality or incest, nor allow these or any other anxieties to prevent her from abandoning herself to the flow of sweetness. If she blocks it off, she also blocks the flow of psychic energy towards her child and severely disturbs his aura.

I am particularly unhappy with the kind of advice that many paediatric nurses give to young mothers. Their emphasis on sterilising equipment and materials and using the right medications is all very well in its place, and I certainly do not want to deny the importance of hygiene; but I must say that this "efficient", hygienic way of looking after children is totally lacking in libido. This can severely disturb the child's libido circulation, or even destroy it. The child needs to remain in profound contact with his inner impulses, and his mother's demands must not interfere with his libido circulation in a rough or mechanical way. Rather, it is up to her to adjust to the child's rhythm, because he is still in direct, natural contact with the ocean of cosmic energy, connected to the rhythmical pulsations of the universe. His mother, his father and anyone closely involved with the child can benefit enormously from this. Through him, they are able to rediscover their own connection with cosmic energy that may have been suppressed by their upbringing. Adults often feel puzzled and helpless when they take a crying baby in their arms to comfort him, only to find that he does not calm down. The baby carries on crying because he cannot find what he is seeking if the person holding him is not sensitive enough to understand his needs, and merely holds and moves him in a mechanical way.

Facial expression plays an equally important role in contact with children: even very young ones indeed. A mother with an anxious, fearful or angry expression on her face will induce a startle reflex in her child; as a result, his muscles contract and the first symptoms of tissue and visceral armouring begin to develop. The child's aura also contracts, and its rate of vibration diminishes.

Often, it is not the major traumas in a person's life that cause neurosis, but rather the small, frequently repeated everyday events. If a child grows up in an atmosphere of rigidity in which feelings of guilt or his parents' demands, expectations and ambitions push him to become something that he is not, he is exposed to a constant series of shocks. Although to us these shocks may seem tiny, in reality they can have extremely serious consequences. The child suffers from the same kind of confusion as that between the tragic and the trivial levels, which I described earlier.

This confusion is also related to the two hemispheres of the brain. Each hemisphere is connected to the opposite side of the body: in other words, the right hemisphere is connected to the left side of the body, and vice versa. In our Western culture people tend to make much greater use of their left hemisphere, which is associated with rational, mechanical, intolerant, efficient behaviour. They tend to suppress the functions of the right hemisphere, which is associated with the left side of the body, the side of the heart, the side that is in direct contact with cosmic energy. But this bias towards the left hemisphere eventually destroys other levels of consciousness in the child.

Of course I do not deny that major traumatic events have a powerful effect on personality development; but I am always profoundly astonished by the ability of "little things" to produce neuroses as well. It is these "little things" that create resignation in the personality and cause the libido to retreat into the deepest layers of the body. This can happen on countless occasions in a child's life. It is particularly likely to happen during the developmental stage in which the child wants to touch and grasp everything he comes across. If his parents are constantly telling him not to touch this or that, perhaps accompanied by a slap on the fingers, the child's libido will eventually withdraw and he will begin functioning in a way that is much more strictly controlled by his central nervous system. The withdrawal of the libido can have serious consequences. It can retreat from the hands, but also from the heart: when the world around him is too hostile, the child will close his heart. Similarly, if his parents bring him up in an atmosphere of sexual taboos, the child will withdraw his libido from his sexual organs.

It is often difficult for us to grasp the full extent of the damage done by this withdrawal of the libido. The child abandons his primary personality - the purest essence of who he is - in favour of a mechanical secondary personality. Because he has lost his libido circulation, he becomes dependent on others, and is completely at the mercy of their approval or disapproval. This creates a feeling of imminent catastrophe in the child. He becomes convinced that if he fails to do what his parents demand of him, then "that will be the end of everything". This fear can become so strong that it eventually comes to rule his whole life.

Parents do need to understand that their child does not "belong" to them. Rather, he is a gift of nature to whom it is their role to give support, help, and the very best of themselves. The belief that children are possessions or objects gives parents so much power over their child that he has no choice but to become a victim. The most appropriate attitude we adults can take towards a child is to look at him and listen to him as if we had something to learn from him. And we do have something to learn from him! The child is still in contact with the ocean of cosmic energy. He knows its essence - not intellectually, of course, but his whole organism "knows" it. When an adult follows a child's inner stimulus without worrying that doing so will harm his social development, the child is able to develop harmoniously, because he naturally wants to learn and imitate.

I want to emphasise the particular importance of two aspects of education: integrity and identity. In early childhood, no matter what his parents want to make of him, the child fights to protect his integrity and his identity: and this is where things often begin to go wrong. He tries to show something to his parents, but they are busy and have no time to take an interest in it. Or he starts to cry, and his parents tell him to be quiet. Through many small dramas such as these they destroy his inner joy.

Repressing joy, laughter and creative play in this way can cause many illnesses to develop. This may seem strange or hard to understand, but it is easy to make sense of it when we look at it in terms of energy. The same energy flows through the cells, the muscles and the brain, and neurosis is simply the effect of an interruption to the flow of energy. The child gives up the fight for his integrity and identity; he becomes resigned, encapsulates his energy and becomes established in his secondary personality. If his parents can only realise that their child is profoundly good just as he is, that he comes into the world full of cosmic energy, with the purest qualities of soul and the highest vibrations, they will understand that their task as parents is to protect and assist their child in his development. Instead of this, most parents believe that their child is full of faults; they are convinced that they must pay close attention to these faults to prevent them from getting even worse.

All of this raises a question in my mind: what are we to think of an approach that aims to stop the child from becoming what he is presumed to be by nature (that is, bad), and force him to become what he is presumed not to be (that is, good)? Can we really call this education? Looking at a photograph of a foetus, we might imagine that we are seeing some kind of deformed monster: and yet this "monster" will grow into a marvellous little child. With this example I want to make it clear that many of the things we regard as abnormal are, in fact, completely normal for a particular age and stage of development. Most parents are so frightened by their child's vitality and expressiveness that they rush to suppress it with a mass of rules and educational principles. The list of rules seems almost unending: feed the child at fixed times, forbid him to touch his genitals, leave him to cry so that he will develop "good lungs", toilet train him as early as possible... All these practices, and many more besides, have only one effect: to make the child neurotic.

Of course, like anyone else, parents cannot be "perfect". But if they surround their child with an atmosphere of love and do their best not to implant feelings of guilt in him, his psychoperistalsis will continue to protect him with natural self-regulation. It will eliminate all these small sources of conflict and stress from his organism before they can cause the contractions that eventually lead to neurosis. The deepest-rooted neurosis springs from a permanent feeling of guilt, of insecurity, of not being loved. If emotional expression is not usual in the family setting, or is even banned altogether, and the child is not given the time and space to himself that he needs for his libido circulation, he becomes neurotic. He gets into the habit of repressing all the traumatic experiences, conflicts and obstacles he encounters.

If, on the other hand, the child's environment is rich in love and security, his psychoperistalsis can open and become established. Bearing in mind the special function of psychoperistalsis, which is to digest the residues of neurovegetative activity, it is easy to understand that children in a secure, loving environment will not accumulate energetic fluid and layers of repression. In many cases, when children suffer from "inexplicable" pains in the stomach or other parts of the body, these pains are actually their reaction to a conflict which they have just repressed. This is why old pains such as these often reappear during therapy, when the original conflict situations are re-experienced, and can finally be eliminated from the system.

This brings to mind an anecdote about a little boy of four-and-a- half, whose parents were in the process of getting a divorce. When his mother told him that she was going to go away and leave him to live with his father, he began suffering from severe attacks of colic. Now the child's grandmother was familiar with the theory and practice of psychoperistalsis, and she asked him if he would be willing to let her listen to his stomach with a stethoscope. She found that there was no sound at all; the little boy's peristalsis was completely blocked. She then gave him a very light massage, which re-opened the peristalsis. After this, each time that the child suffered from stomach pains during this difficult time of his parents' divorce, he asked his grandmother to "telephone his tummy to tell it to stop hurting him". This approach worked so well that there was no need to call the doctor in again. Eventually the little boy got into the habit of fetching the stethoscope himself, lying down and "telephoning his tummy". By relaxing and listening he allowed the peristalsis to open, and the pains disappeared.

I also remember an anecdote that Ola Raknes told me. A family asked him to come and treat a child who simply would not stop crying. The little girl was in bed, and Raknes noticed that she had her hands between her thighs. He looked at her and gave her a little sign of approval with his head. She then put one hand in her mouth and moved the other hand closer to her genitals. She calmed down at once and fell asleep. What she was doing was not exactly masturbation, but rather a polarisation of energy.

By using her hands to connect the oral and genital poles of the libido in this way, she was causing soothing downgoing currents to flow. She was caressed by sweet waves of libidinous pleasure coming from her mouth and from her genitals. But whenever she approached her mother for a cuddle, her mother continued her frantic daily hyperactivity and reminded her of all the chores she had to do.

This kind of hyperactivity in the people around the child has an extremely destructive effect on his libido circulation. It is often accompanied by a torrent of words and phrases addressed solely to the rational part of the self. Anyone who has daily contact with a child should be aware that this can cause repression if the child responds by blocking his in-breath. But if the child is able to let a good out-breath follow, he will discharge his tension and relax. The most important thing is never to interrupt the child's libidinal movement abruptly, no matter what form it takes: play, verbal expressions or gestures. The child should also be allowed to follow his own rhythm. If his parents respect this rhythm, they can easily persuade the child to do what they want without imposing their will by brute force.

These principles are illustrated very clearly in Margaret Mead's study on the Trobriand Islanders, which I mentioned earlier.

Whenever a Trobriand mother wants to introduce a new idea to her child, she does so in a playful, enjoyable way. For example, when she wants to wean the child she repeats to him in a soft, melodious tone of voice: "This is orange juice, this is good for you, this is good, this is juice...". Or to accustom him to a new adult, she sings to him gently: "This is your auntie, she is very nice, this is your nice auntie...". The Trobriand mothers' custom of devoting extra attention to their children after they have spent some time away from them also seems particularly relevant. Although the mothers cannot replace the quantity of time that has been lost, they can compensate their children fully by giving them good quality time instead.

All these small points are so simple, and yet they play such an important role in preventing neurosis, just as the fundamental principles of psychoperistalsis do. If only parents and everyone involved in looking after children were aware of these principles, far fewer neuroses would develop. I believe strongly that all mothers should learn some of the simpler psychoperistaltic treatment techniques, such as polarisation, light head and face massage, the right way to hold their child in order to open his psychoperistalsis, and so on. Two more treatment techniques, the "energy distribution massage" and the "self-help method", are also particularly helpful as a means of preventing neurosis.

Many of my students and therapists whom I have trained use these massages on their children. They tell me that their children adore the treatment, and are always clamouring for more. When asked what she wanted for her birthday, one little girl of six unhesitatingly replied: "I want a massage!" Massage is a way of restoring the contact that children are constantly seeking. Many parents express their affection in words, but that is not what their children need. Above all else, children need physical contact; contact that is provided in a very careful, sensitive way. Massage is an ideal medium for this kind of contact, because it is impossible to massage somebody without coming very close to them, and it is this closeness that encourages love to blossom. What is more, as I have stressed throughout this book, massage is the best therapy there is - both for the person giving it, and for the one receiving it. It enables parents and children to "find" one another when they are unable to do so in any other way.

THE EMERGENCY TREATMENT

Now I want to describe a method of treatment that is used to help patients in crisis: people whose psychological and physical defences have suddenly collapsed, allowing a powerful flood of anxieties and unconscious material to rise to the surface. At moments such as these, the pressure of the energetic fluid emerging from the body depths is so great that the ego and the organism as a whole are unable to regulate it. There are two possible causes for this state: either the person has been provoked too strongly, or the defences have simply "given way" spontaneously.

The situation of these patients is very different from that of obsessional neurotics. In obsessional neurosis the energy is encapsulated, and the best way to treat it is to create an imbalance in the vegetative system in order to dissolve the defences and "de- encapsulate" the blocked energy. This sets in motion a biodynamic process with which it is possible to work. It can be compared with an abscess, which has to be "opened" before treatment can proceed. With patients in crisis, however, the abscess is already open. The therapist's job is to remove the "pus"; but it is extremely important to do so without ripping the wound even further open.

I developed my "emergency treatment" one summer when several patients in crisis came to consult me in my clinic in London. These people were feeling suicidal and desperate for help. During my sessions with them, the method gradually evolved. The first rule of treatment is that the therapist's manner must be calm, professional and reassuring to the patient. I do not let these patients talk about their situation for too long, because doing so could provoke them even more. Instead, I listen to them for a few minutes and then ask them to lie down: not on their back, but on their left side.

This position helps the psychoperistalsis to open. I support and intensify the process by "polarising" their energy: this means that I stand behind the patient with my left hand resting on the nape of his neck and my right hand on his abdomen, as I listen with the stethoscope to the peristaltic sounds. In every case, the psychoperistalsis is closed at the start; I hear no sounds at all. Gradually, as I make slow, gentle massaging movements on the patient's belly, I begin to hear sounds as the peristalsis opens. I use my hands very lightly, with almost no pressure at all; I simply follow the movements of the patient's breathing as his abdomen rises and falls. Often I remain in this position for half an hour or even longer, according to the patient's needs. The patients experience a melting sensation and say that they feel better and better as the session progresses. If the peristalsis is reluctant to open, I apply very light pressure to the membranes of the nape of the neck, head and shoulders. Sometimes I also gently tug and press on the membranes of the forehead to encourage the energetic fluid to circulate more freely.

In the second session I give the patient's hands and fingertips a very light massage. During this massage the patient can slowly begin to talk while I listen to him, or sometimes I may talk while he listens. The verbal expression helps to reduce the pressure within the patient's chest, while the fingertip massage works on the acupuncture meridians to regulate the mass of accumulated energy in the chest cavity; it is this accumulated energy that causes the emotional overload.

As a general rule, by the time the patient comes for his third session he is ready to lie down on his back and receive a light massage. In most cases, it is at this point that he is able to feel the pleasurable sensation of the downgoing, harmonising vegetative currents.

My understanding of the crisis situation is as follows: once the defences collapse, the pressure of the energetic fluid in the chest increases sharply and throws the whole vegetative nervous system out of balance. The sympathetic system becomes hyperactive, and the parasympathetic system becomes hypoactive. This deeply uncomfortable sensation arouses feelings of desperation in the patients: Wilhelm Reich talks of the urge to explode.

In these crisis situations, it is useless to invite the patient to speak at length about his problems, because he is unable to make contact with the deeper levels of his being and cannot be objective. Nor does it help to use vegetotherapy techniques or to try to provoke a discharge; in fact these tactics are downright anti- therapeutic, because it is important to avoid any further provocation while the patient is in this state. But the moment that the patient emerges from his desperation and re-establishes contact with the harmonising, calming sensation of his descending vegetative currents, he rediscovers the value of life and the pleasure of existence, and the crisis is over. Once this has happened, the therapist can begin working with vegetotherapy techniques without causing any problems.

"SELF-HELP" AND THE BIOFIELD METHOD

The International Foundation of Biodynamic Psychology organises "self-help" groups, where people are taught techniques that they can use to regulate their own energy. Not everyone in need of help can find a therapist, and in any case psychotherapy is relatively expensive. So I hit upon the idea of developing prophylactic techniques that can be used by anyone, and that are also useful for people in hospital and for medical and psychiatric out-patients. These techniques can be practised alone or with a partner. The training groups consist of about thirty people who meet once a week. At these meetings the trainer teaches the participants various techniques that they can practise each day at home, and each participant also has a chance to tell the group about his experiences and anything he has learned about himself in the preceding week. This is a therapeutic approach that uses absolutely no provocation, yet it gradually and gently brings about fundamental psychological transformations. We do not touch the muscular defences at all; instead we act solely on what we call the "biofield", also known as the aura. The discovery of Kirlian photography has made it possible to speak openly about the energetic field that surrounds the body. Our special massage technique only touches this biofield in order to re- establish its harmony. According to biodynamic theory, if the energy in the biofield (which Russian scientists call bioplasma energy) is blocked, the density of the field around the organism interferes with the libido circulation. In particular, this energetic charge in the biofield suppresses the downgoing vegetative currents that have such a healing, harmonising effect. The psychosomatic effects of this imbalance are distressing, much like those of the excess of upgoing emotional currents that we find in patients in crisis.

I talked earlier about the constant sensation of pressure that people feel when their upgoing flow of emotional energy is blocked. Our treatment method in such cases aims to re-establish the libido circulation by restoring the harmonising descending currents. With the self-help method we can achieve similar therapeutic results by working purely and simply on the biofield around the organism. I have tried out this method in all sorts of different groups in different countries, and the feedback from the participants has always been excellent. They report that it makes them feel lighter, in better physical condition, and, above all, happier. Their bodies respond with extremely pleasant sensations and gentle discharges such as belching (a very light form of emotional discharge) and yawning (our natural relaxation reflex).

Various methods of biofield treatment have emerged from the original self-help techniques. I used one of these methods for the first time in a group that I led in Brazil. It happened on a day when I had spent hours working with all sorts of different techniques. Suddenly I was overwhelmed by the feeling that absolutely nothing was happening, that none of my techniques was having any effect. I know this feeling of uselessness and helplessness very well; in fact I welcome it, because for me it always signals the birth of a new discovery. So on this occasion I got the group to practise the self-help technique not on the trivial level, but on the deep, essential, "oceanic" level: that is, not in a rigid, mechanical, rational way, but in a slow, essential, fundamental way.

The six therapists who made up this group had just finished doing one of Lowen's bioenergetic exercises. This involved lying on the back with the legs raised, the heels pointing up towards the ceiling and the toes pointing down towards the face. One of the participants now showed all the signs of a strong upward flow of emotional energy in the id canal: she was about to have a powerful emotional discharge. I asked her to lie down and simply relax: at this point her breathing had become particularly rapid and spontaneous. Then I explained to the other members of the group that I wanted to demonstrate a process of provocation followed by harmonisation without the need for an emotional discharge. Instead of encouraging an emotional abreaction, as we normally do in vegetotherapy, I showed the group how it was possible to remove the charge from the solar plexus and so completely harmonise the movement of the energy and re-establish the libido circulation.

After a while, I asked my patient how she was feeling. She replied: "I feel terribly sad. I want to cry." I then began working within her biofield with a particular hand movement as she lay in front of me. Suddenly she began to speak: "I feel that I am truly meeting myself for the first time. It's as though my heart and my sexuality are melting together, and I finally feel unified with myself. Gerda, you have taken an octopus off my solar plexus! Now I feel pure and truly happy, strong and gentle at the same time."

That was how my biofield method came into existence. From then onwards, I used it in numerous sessions, and I always got the same kind of feedback: "You have taken away the worst part of me... you have freed my heart from the bad mother... you have removed my monster father..." All I was removing from these people's biofields was energy, but it seemed as if I was taking away something on the psychological level as well. Other patients said: "You have taken away my paranoia... you have relieved me of my false sense of responsibility..." All of them reported that they felt purified and freed.

As I continued to work with this method, I discovered that it acts on the energy centres of the body. The "bad mother" or "monster father" is "internalised"[6] in these energy centres. When a child, or even an adult, has a bad relationship with his parents, he not only suffers from conflicts on the psychological level, but he also internalises certain energies that have a negative effect on his organism.

I had long suspected that this psychological phenomenon of energy internalisation must exist. It seemed to me that its existence was confirmed when I heard about the results of a series of experiments in Russia. There, a group of parapsychologists and scientists managed not only to photograph the flow of energy passing from the hand of a healer to his patient or from a mother to her child, but also to measure it. But, just as the organism can absorb this "good energy", it can also internalise negative, "bad" energy. Negative energy can accumulate at several different places in the body at the same time; however, it can be eliminated from the whole body by withdrawing it from just one of the centres. For example, when I "pull out" this negative energy from the "third eye", in the middle of the forehead, the patient may also find that negative energy anchored at the throat, the heart, the solar plexus or the genitals is released at the same time. The internalised negative energy creates a split within the personality; when this energy is removed, the split starts to heal and unification occurs. One of my patients described this experience: "Now I feel I have become myself again".

This biofield method calls for a very different way of giving treatment. The theory on which this technique is based runs as follows: when the negative energy in the biofield is removed, the energetic charge of the fluid in the organism is neutralised and the fluid can be "emptied out". It is much more effective in certain cases than our more conventional massage methods, because when we work on the muscles the energetic fluid may simply move around and reappear in another part of the organism, where new symptoms then emerge. Consequently I want to stress that the biofield method enables us to avoid the undesirable side-effects of deep vegetotherapy treatment. It is also a highly effective way of treating psychotic patients.

Each time I discover a new method, destiny seems to send me particularly difficult patients on whom to test its effectiveness. One such patient was Oscar the manic-depressive, whose case study you will find in the appendix of this book. Another was a member of a group that I led in Germany. I had not intended to work with the biofield method on that day in Munich, but at a certain point this group member entered into an extremely deep and intense emotional abreaction. His jaws were so tightly locked

6 The psychoanalytical concept of „introjection" only partially covers the biodynamic concept of „internalisation", which emphasises the energetic aspect of introjection.

that the energetic impulse boiling up within him could not pass through them to be expressed in crying and shouting. The strong masseter muscles held back the energy. I massaged his jaws and neck vigorously in the classic Reichian way, but the emotional abreaction stayed trapped in his throat. At that point, one of the group members - a young Chinese girl - intervened to help. With a circular movement of her hand just above the patient's forehead, she "pulled" the energy out of the area between his eyebrows. The results were wonderful to see; the patient relaxed and smiled, and told us that he felt very well indeed. He could feel the flow of downgoing, harmonising energy throughout his being. I asked the girl whether she had learned this technique in China. Her reply came as a great surprise to me. She said: "But I learnt it from you, Gerda! Yesterday, when you showed us the "self-help" technique!"

The next day I travelled on to Vienna to lead another training group. There, too, I had a chance to try out the biofield method. A young girl, who I later discovered had already been severely over- provoked before she came to my group, went into a psychotic state while doing an extremely light, gentle exercise. She panicked and started to hallucinate: she thought she was being pursued by gorillas, gigantic apes. She would not let anyone go near her. All the group members looked like monsters to her. She pressed her hands against the wall and tried desperately to escape. I approached her and tried to touch her very gently, hoping that she would allow me to give her an energy polarisation, but she reacted with even greater panic. My efforts only served to give her a new startle reflex. In approaching her, I was following my own human urge to help; but if I had paid attention to my intuition and my knowledge, I would not have made the attempt. Her boyfriend, who was also in the group, then tried to make contact with her by touching the tips of her fingers; but even this terrified her. Then she tilted her head forward, and at last I saw an opportunity to intervene by working with the biofield method on the area around her head. I began drawing the excess energy out of her biofield, and after a few minutes - without having seen what I was doing - she returned to full awareness of reality. She hurled herself into her boyfriend's arms and began to sob, quite overwhelmed with gratitude and relief.

I was astonished by all of this, until I remembered my theory that psychosis results from an excess of energetic fluid in the head. What I had done was to remove some of the energy from the biofield around this girl's head, which neutralised the energetic fluid inside her brain. By doing so, I had "removed" the psychosis! Once the fluid inside the brain had lost its excessive energetic charge, it no longer had the power to irritate and create hallucinations.

The next day the girl felt much better, although she still had difficulty in expressing herself. She murmured: "I feel much clearer and cleaner inside myself." But she was almost in a catatonic state, had trouble in moving her hands and forearms, and walked in a stiff, rigid way. With her permission, I gave her another light biofield treatment, and suddenly she burst out laughing. She laughed and laughed; all the remaining excess energetic charge melted away, and she reverted to a completely normal state. A few minutes later she ran outside to pick some apples for the friends who had taken care of her that morning.

The biofield method is so well-suited for treating people in a state of psychosis because it is both gentle and powerful. The classic methods of vegetotherapy or bioenergetics cannot be used to treat psychosis: treatment that is excellent for "normal" or "neurotic" people is too strong for psychotics. Lighter, more subtle techniques are also needed for people who have reached an advanced stage in therapy and personal development. When somebody has reached the point where he has truly given up his defences and rediscovered his libido circulation, great care is needed when touching his body, his mind and his aura. Only a therapist who is himself very advanced can assist these patients on their inner journey, by working with methods that are in fact an extension of his own sensitivity.

THE METHODS OF BIODYNAMIC PSYCHOLOGY IN PSYCHIATRY

For many years it has been one of my most cherished dreams to change the way in which psychiatric patients are treated. The first time that I fully recognised the potential offered by the methods of biodynamic psychology was while treating my manic-depressive patient Oscar. With an adequate understanding of the theory of psychoperistalsis, it is simple to predict what will happen when someone's peristalsis is closed: the dynamic pressure within him will build up continually, and he will feel a growing sense of desperation and an urge to explode. As a result, he will also develop psychosomatic pains of ever-increasing intensity. In this situation, the goal of psychotherapeutic work is to open the patient's "shell": that is, to relieve the tension in the membranes around the muscles (not in the muscles themselves) so that the trapped energy can flow through them and melt away in a process of harmonisation. So it is very important to find what we call the "keys" - which are unique to each individual - to enable us to open his shell.

During the time when I was working in psychiatric hospitals in Norway, I often used to listen to the patients' abdomens with my stethoscope. Most of the time there was no sound at all. I am convinced that the time that psychiatric patients spend in hospital could be used a great deal more fruitfully if the nurses, and in fact all the psychiatric staff, were trained in the techniques and methods needed to open the patients' psychoperistalsis - and in the method I call the "emergency treatment" in particular. Patients in psychiatric hospitals spend so much time lying in bed that the nursing staff should have no difficulty in giving twenty minutes or so of psychoperistaltic massage to those who need it - especially those who are completely blocked. This would also make the staff's job more enriching and satisfying, and above all, more effective. In some cases a full massage would not be needed; a check to see that the peristalsis was open, perhaps followed by a short energy polarisation or a few massage strokes, would be sufficient. The biofield method would also be immensely useful in this setting. Once a psychotic patient's psychoperistalsis starts functioning and remains open, this marks a considerable advance in his healing process. His conflicts then begin dissolving one after the other. Hypnosis could also be used much more effectively in the treatment of neurosis if the patient's psychoperistalsis were to be checked regularly and opened if necessary: because unless a vegetative discharge takes place, the neuroses do not disappear.

All these techniques help to achieve the same objective: that is, harmonisation of the patient's energy. Returning to my theory of psychosis: in psychotic patients the defences have fallen, the muscular tensions have slackened, and many layers of repressed conflicts have begun pushing their way simultaneously towards the surface, into consciousness, so that they can be abreacted. A pathological biodynamic process has been set in motion to eliminate all this repressed material from the energetic system and the organism. Because these layers are very numerous and also very old, the energy emerging from them collides with the barriers of the superego on its way towards consciousness, and becomes blocked there. Energy and fluids then accumulate at these new blockage points, in keeping with Wilhelm Reich's fundamental law: energy attracts fluid.

At this point in the process the build-up of energetic fluid creates considerable pressure within the organism, which tips the neurovegetative system even further out of balance. The fluid attracts still more energy and this increases the pressure within the membranes from the inside towards the outside; however, the contractive effect produced by this accumulation of energy also increases the pressure from the outside towards the inside. This sets off a pathological process in the tissue that causes pain. At the same time, the energetic fluid continues to cross all three layers (endoderm, mesoderm and ectoderm), and finally reaches the brain. There, because of the fluid's irritant properties, it awakens layers of repressed memories. As the brain and sensory and motor nerves become irritated, the different symptoms of psychosis then appear.

According to our biodynamic theory of the emotional circulatory system, which I described on page 41, the flood of metabolic residues and repressed emotions that has been unleashed disturbs the circulation of the blood; old emotional cycles are reactivated and an intense fluid pressure develops throughout the whole body, which the patients experience as their feeling of "nervousness".

If we consider how the organism reacts when it suffers an injury by flooding the wounded tissues with fluid - we can see that this confirms the biodynamic theory of nervousness as the result of excessive fluid pressure. We can also observe how, by simply working to reduce this fluid pressure, we can reduce the patient's nervousness considerably. His anxiety, excitability and depression eventually disappear altogether as we continue to work in this way, together with his psychosomatic pains. By using the appropriate massage techniques to control the process of psychoperistalsis, which we monitor with the stethoscope, we can encourage the organism to complete the old, repressed emotional cycles so that their irritant effects finally disappear.

We reduce the fluid pressure within the organism, and so help it to digest and eliminate the emotions that have remained blocked. I see mental illness as a phenomenon that develops when the organism becomes "overloaded" with repressed material and tries to eliminate everything at once. However, this is almost impossible to achieve unaided. with suitable therapeutic help, however, the patient can avoid the danger of repressing everything for a second time and confining himself within his secondary personality again. Instead, he can be what he truly is. He can rediscover his primary personality, his creativity and his independent well-being. In biodynamic psychotherapy, we do not see the libido as a force against which we must constantly battle: we believe that it can and should become harmoniously integrated into the ego. I myself consider that there is only one fundamental, authentic impulse: the one that impels the individual towards self-realisation and self-expression. The psychotic's problem is that his organism's desperate efforts to break free from conflicts and repressions are blocked.

Our job as therapists is to bring an end to this tragedy by helping each of the repressed layers to move from a state of provocation to one of harmonisation and integration. It is therefore important not to think in terms of muscular tensions, but in terms of fluid pressure within the organism. With this approach we can create a link between psychoanalysis, biochemistry and physiological changes within the organism.

PEOPLE IN TRANSITION

I have been enormously fortunate in recent years to be able to work in London and elsewhere in Europe with what I call "people in transition". My day-to-day experience has given me total confidence that it is possible to change our world. Seeing all these people rediscovering their primary personality has left me with an almost religious belief in the existence of a core of goodness and love within every individual. In young people, in particular, I see a profound need and a determined will to make this world a better place. All their inner impulses spring from this urge. Their desire for honesty is so strong that they are unwilling to accept the compromises of the mechanical world any longer. I meet a great many students - particularly in the fields of medicine and psychology - who tell me that they are thinking about dropping out of conventional society for this reason. Each time, it makes me very happy to be able to tell them that there is no need to drop out; that they can continue their studies while still remaining open to the new age that is dawning. Often they discover in therapy groups that they can do something in their professional capacity to help this new world emerge.

Many of the young people whom I meet pursue their principles to the point where they refuse to register with their country's social security system because they do not want to become trapped by society. Yet they are bursting with energy which is only waiting to be harnessed for some meaningful activity. Behind all the revolutionary fervour of youth and behind the distress that leads many youngsters to take drugs, I see the same deep desire to believe in the power of goodness. The problem is that most of them do not know how to go about realising this desire. Often they become ill when they start to open up, because they have no idea what direction they should give to their lives.

I have seen this pattern in many of my patients as well: when their energy begins to circulate, they can find no meaning or direction in life and they fall ill. I use the concept of "creative stagnation" to account for this phenomenon. Jung himself suffered from psychosomatic illness during a phase in which he could not write. Life energy, the flow of cosmic energy within man, needs to be expressed; it needs to be transformed into action, to offer something to the world. A process of exchange is needed: give and take is one of the fundamental cosmic laws. The stream of libido energy must flow in harmony with the energy of the cosmos and give something out to the universe; otherwise stagnation sets in.

In our mechanical, neurotic world we are cut off and divided, so that all we can do is to fight against each other. We are locked into our upgoing, instinctive energies, which inspire us to subjective, irrational and egotistical behaviour. Not until we come into contact with our downgoing vegetative currents and the harmonising movement of cosmic energy do we experience independent well-being and what I like to call the "qualities of eternity": that is, patience, universal love and compassion. People who have rediscovered their libido circulation are capable of collaborating closely and harmoniously. However, people who are restricted to their upgoing emotional currents can only experience envy and suspicion. Their aggression is so strong that it makes them quite incapable of co-operating with each other. I see this over and over again in my training groups. By harmonising people's inner energies we create peace between human beings, and this profound harmony comes to us when we are in touch with our vegetative energy flows.

In Reich's earliest works he talks about patients who became able to feel pleasurable vegetative currents when their muscular tension was dissolved. These vegetative currents occur underneath the muscle armour, and their appearance heralds a process of purification characteristic of the organism. According to the plasmo-galvanic principle (see page 79), this process works by eliminating metabolic residues. If the vegetative currents are very strong, they inundate the emotional channel and are abreacted in a catharsis of everything that has been repressed. Psychopathological symptoms only develop when this cathartic movement is blocked. When the vegetative currents are able to flow freely, they push a person who has reached the other side of the looking-glass to seek self-realisation. All the energy in the person's being then follows an intense urge to express his intrinsic talents for singing, dancing, writing, composing, or any other form of creative activity, whether artistic or not. So I use the term "creative stagnation" to describe a blockage of these energetic currents.

Creative stagnation develops when a person fails to follow his stimulus from within, and two forms of depression can then occur: either classic depression, or a second type which I call "spiritual depression". Spiritual depression is produced when a person's spiritual development comes into conflict with either an excessively rational superego, or a therapist whose approach is too mechanical. At this point in the therapy it is essential to give the fullest possible support to the patient's efforts to become the person he truly is. When a neurotic person undergoes this kind of transformation, it is often a difficult time in which many ambiguous situations may arise. For example, if his friends and family have got used to coping with his neurotic but at least predictable behaviour, it is often hard for them to adapt to the spontaneous, libidinous new person who is now emerging.

All of this can be summed up in one statement: "The vegetative currents always speak the truth". And this leads to the astonishing conclusion that a human being's fundamental truth springs from the depths of his body, from his "soma". When the deepest impulses within a person rise to the surface, become integrated and begin to flow harmoniously, his spiritual development is also greatly assisted. And psychoperistalsis is Ariadne's golden thread that guides us in our spiritual development. If a person develops his higher consciousness and follows the movement of his psychoperistalsis, a permanent process of deep purification will aid his spiritual development, even after his therapy has come to an end. With an "open" body and sensitive tissues, it is easy to tell the difference between things that are good for us and things that are not: if the psychoperistalsis opens, the activity we are contemplating is good for us, while if it remains closed, that activity is one that we should avoid.

Luckily this cannot develop into a new superego, because the peristalsis closes as soon as the superego is activated. The "rules of conduct" that a self-regulated person follows bear no relationship to the iron-clad rules that constrict an individual who is still governed by his superego. Like an animal or a child, a self-regulated person is guided by the mixture of feelings and sensations that Jung called "intuition". He is completely at one with himself, and all of his organic perceptions help to shape his actions. Since spontaneity governs his actions, he is prompted to behave in a way which he cannot always explain logically, but which guides him in a sure fashion. And this intuition carries him into the world of "synchronicity", the realm of meaningful coincidences of which Jung spoke.

Before this stage can be reached, though, there may be further obstacles to overcome. The following example sums up a problem that we often encounter in therapy. One day a patient said to me, looking me straight in the eyes: "If you take away my hate, I won't have anything left at all." That patient's feeling is shared by many others at a certain stage in their therapy: when their hatred disappears, they feel only emptiness. This is an awkward phase: although the patient recognises that he is now free of the countless compulsions that his superego used to impose on him, he does not yet know what he really wants in this life. Over the years I have met a great many rebellious young people - drug users, drop-outs, hippies in the days of the "flower power" movement - who have also faced this dilemma. All of them said much the same thing to me: "We know what we don't want, but we don't know what we do want..."

Therapy, and most of all psychoperistaltic self-regulation, can be a tremendous help to people who have reached this stage of self- discovery. This is because psychoperistalsis follows the pleasure principle. When someone rediscovers his flow of vegetative energies, he enters into the marvellous world of "synchronicity"; his being is in harmony with all that is, and his life becomes truly full. Self- regulated people encounter the people and situations that are exactly right for them, and this enables them to develop their creativity without any hindrances. They are in contact with their true, authentic selves, not with their neurotic secondary personalities.

I myself entered into therapy and went on to train as a therapist because I wanted to develop myself and rid myself of my neurotic patterns; but in those days I could never have imagined that my life would be as rich, fulfilled and full of surprises as it is now. And it becomes richer every day. The person who entrusts himself to the guidance of his psychoperistalsis and his libido circulation makes new discoveries all the time that help him to come into harmony with himself. When someone is truly open, life unveils itself before his eyes in all its richness and reveals its mysteries to him.

Then a subtle balance develops between creativity and action, between the left and right hand sides of the body, between the pleasure of being in harmony with oneself and the pleasure of being in interaction with the world.

EPILOGUE: THE THERAPY OF THE GIRAFFE

To conclude, I want to dip into my treasure-chest of therapeutic anecdotes for one last story: something that happened recently, just before I sent my manuscript off for editing. One of my students in London had always been renowned for his terrible posture; but when I saw him that day, I could scarcely believe my eyes. He looked totally transformed. He held his head beautifully free and erect, and his neck and shoulders fell harmoniously into place. I asked him what had happened to bring about this change, and he told me the following story.

He had been treated for several months with one of our special massage methods called "deep draining". Shortly after stopping this treatment, he had a dream: he was in Africa with his girlfriend, and they were admiring a herd of magnificent giraffes. "Just look how harmoniously they hold their heads and how gracefully they move", he said to his girlfriend. "How about you?" she replied. "You could do the same. Just try!"

So he started to move his head as the giraffes were doing, trying to find the right position. Suddenly he discovered exactly the right posture. Everything fell into place on its own. "Tell me what I'm doing right now!" he exclaimed excitedly. "Oh, that's easy to answer", said his girlfriend. "You're doing the therapy of the giraffe!"

I wanted to tell this story because it seems to me to demonstrate beautifully the variety of benefits that biodynamic treatment brings: in this case in the form of a postural change. After a large number of sessions - both massage and psychotherapy - this young man had reached the point at which he was "mature" enough to discover his free, graceful posture for himself.

The story also illustrates how biodynamic treatment continues to operate in dreams, even some time after the therapy has ended.

Thanks to the principle of psychoperistalsis, the organism's natural self-healing process, all the therapy takes place in a gentle, gradual way; the body slowly learns self-awareness, and the therapist constantly supports and encourages it in its own self- regulation.

Therapy is simply a way of helping the organism to help itself.

APPENDIX I

SPONTANEOUS RHYTHMIC ACTIVITY IN THE SMOOTH MUSCULATURE

There are two ways of looking at intestinal peristalsis. The first, and most obvious way is in relation to the digestive process: peristalsis encourages food to pass through the alimentary canal. But the second way is in relation to a separate phenomenon that deserves further study in its own right: the more or less spontaneous rhythmical contractions that also occur in the intestines. Researchers have long puzzled over the significance of these apparently unprompted contractions; their studies have mainly concentrated on the electrical activity of the cells during the contractions. Professor Johannes Setekliev reported the following findings in a Norwegian journal (Tidskrift Norske Laegeforen, 1964):

"Numerous factors can influence rhythmic contractions during experiments, such as variations in the temperature and location of the cells... changes in blood pressure and nervous influences... In particular, its reaction to passive stretching is a remarkable property of the visceral musculature. It responds to a sudden elongation with a contraction, an anti-elongation; at the same time, its rhythmical activity also changes... Elongation and dilation are factors that play an important role in the activity of the autonomous hollow organs... The dilation of a hollow organ up to a certain point acts as a natural stimulus for the smooth musculature... The frequency of spontaneous rhythmical contractions seems to depend on the degree of tension, while their amplitude depends more on the length of the musculature. However, these observations mask a great deal of ignorance about this subject, which becomes apparent upon taking a closer and more detailed interest in the mechanisms underlying the reaction to the elongation... Electrical phenomena are difficult to observe, due to the fact that the cells are small and continually moving in rhythmical contractions..."

"Different research studies have shown that the potential of the membrane in the smooth musculature varies according to the organ, the species of animal, the hormonal balance, and various external influences such as temperature; but also, equally significantly, according to the degree of stretching. It differs from the membrane potential of the skeletal muscles in two respects: it is weaker, and it is unstable. However, it is very similar to the potential of other tissues that display spontaneous activity, such as the sinus venosus and the cardiac musculature of the foetus... The action potentials display different patterns: depolarisation may take place rapidly (‚point type'), or more slowly (‚plateau type'); or a protracted depolarisation may be followed by a positive charge (‚undershoot'). Besides these three main types, another pattern that sometimes occurs is slow oscillations in the membrane potential (slow waves), either in a regular rhythm or interspersed with periods during which the potential remains stable. One or more action potentials can form at the peak of a slow wave of this kind. Moreover, potentials similar to those found in the cardiac sinus can be detected: these are known as the ‚pacemaker potentials'. They consist of a gradual depolarisation (pre-potential) which releases an action potential when a certain limit (the threshold potential) is reached. This threshold potential is also known as the ‚level of ignition' or ‚zone of firing'."

"Variations appear to occur in the potential of the membrane that cells of the visceral type use to regulate spontaneous rhythmic activity. Each of these smooth muscle cells has its own individual zone of firing and is activated as soon as the membrane potential falls within that zone. Consequently, the smooth muscle cells are activated according to the alternating fluctuations in the membrane potential, depending on whether the potential falls within the cell's zone of firing or outside it..."

"The action potentials give rise to contractions in the smooth musculature... Cold, acetylcholine, parasympathetic nervous impulses and elongation depolarise the intestinal musculature, so that the cells reach the release threshold. Once this has occurred, adrenaline and sympathetic nervous impulses raise the membrane potential, hyperpolarise the cell and make it less excitable..."

"We are only just embarking on the enormous amount of work that will be needed to cast light on the phenomena that occur in this heterogeneous group of muscles."

Professor Setekliev makes all these observations from a strictly neurological viewpoint, and does not take psychological factors into consideration. His findings leave the question of the origin and function of spontaneous rhythmical activity in the smooth musculature unanswered. For me, the answer lies in the psychoperistaltic process of stress "digestion", breaking down the residues of nervous tension. To explain my view, I draw on the concepts developed by Reich: energetic fluid, bioenergetic circulation, and the principle of tension - charge - discharge - relaxation.

As I see it, the process involves three separate zones within the intestinal walls: the id channel, through which ascending energy moves (energy mobilisation); a second channel through which descending energy moves (harmonisation); and finally a zone where the energetic currents reverse direction. The pressure within the intestinal walls is the factor that triggers psychoperistalsis. The bioelectric moment of transition from an ascending to a descending flow, from "flood" to "ebb", corresponds with the zone of firing[7] and the production of the peristaltic sound. This moment produces a bioelectric effect on the whole organism; it gives a sensation of pleasure and contentment.

7 Cf. David BOADELLA, „Firing Zones", in: Journal of Biodynamic Psychology, no. 2.

In fact the bioelectric discharge takes place in all the cells of the body, but the intestines are a particularly privileged region: they represent the most primitive system for energy conduction, and they also provide the most feedback. But the phenomenon of discharge - relaxation involves the brain, the muscles, the respiratory system and the internal organs just as much: in other words, the ectoderm, the mesoderm and the endoderm.

APPENDIX II

TREATMENT OF NEUROSIS WITH THE PSYCHOPERISTALTIC METHOD: A CASE HISTORY

A young girl was sent to me for treatment after being discovered by the police unconscious in the road. She had taken an overdose of barbiturates in a suicide attempt. She told me that when she came round in hospital, she was attended by two psychiatrists. They gave her my name and telephone number, and advised her to come to me for psycho-peristaltic massage treatment.

The girl was twenty years old. She told me that, for the last three years, she had suffered from migraine headaches so severe that they kept her from sleeping. At most, she was able to sleep for just two or three hours a night, and she explained that she had taken the barbiturates because she could no longer stand the pain. Her migraines and insomnia had started when she left boarding school and went back to live with her family. A few months later, she took a job as an "au pair" in another town, hoping that the symptoms would disappear once she had put some distance between herself and her family: although in fact she voiced no complaints about her home. She insisted that her parents were very kind people who loved her with all their hearts. However, the painful headaches persisted even after the move.

As I talked to this patient, I realised that I would not be able to take a psychotherapeutic approach with her. Her psychological defences and her idealisation of her family were so strong that she would be quite incapable of "working" on her conflicts in a psychological way. What was more, she was firmly convinced that the two psychiatrists had referred her to me strictly for massage; she thought I would massage her head to relieve the headaches and help her to relax and sleep. My opinion was that various conflicts relating to her sexuality must be giving rise to her physical symptoms, and that these conflicts probably began in puberty. She was a "nice" Catholic girl, and I could easily imagine that her conflicts had been aggravated when she left boarding school to return to her family. As I continued talking to her, I also discovered that she had no interests at all: she did nothing all day long, and fundamentally, she had no desire to live.

I began treating this patient by massaging her head very gently, particularly on the right side where the symptoms were the most severe. There were no psychoperistaltic sounds at all, which indicated to me that she had an extremely powerful fear contraction in her alimentary canal (the id canal) and that, as a result, the energy in her head was blocked. I spent some time simply supporting the nape of her neck and stroking her skull very lightly and carefully with my fingertips, at the points where the energy was blocked.

Suddenly the psychoperistalsis opened, and at the same time she began to speak. She talked freely about herself, and told me how much she was enjoying the massage. All of a sudden, she announced that she wanted to learn to play tennis; that she had always wanted to do so. She glowed with enthusiasm as she carried on talking about this idea, and I could scarcely believe that this was the same girl who, half an hour earlier, had seemed so depressed and defeated.

When this patient came back a week later, she told me that she had enjoyed eight hours of sleep every night. She reported that the pain had completely disappeared from the right side of her head (where I had mainly worked), but she was still experiencing a little painful pressure on the left side. I remembered that during the previous week's session she had described how her pain was steadily decreasing as I continued to massage. This was because when the psychoperistalsis opens, it reduces the pressure of the energetic fluid. As the pressure gets less, so does the pain. During this second session, although I continued to work very gently on the girl, I used slightly more pressure on the parts of her head that were the most highly charged. Since the treatment was somewhat deeper I expected her to experience some kind of reaction to it; but since I had still been fairly gentle, I hoped her reaction would not be too strong. For safety's sake, though, I took the precaution of asking her to ring me or come to see me if anything seemed too hard to bear.

In the third session it became clear that she had indeed had a reaction. She complained that it had been a terrible week: not only had she "not had a wink of sleep", but she had also been greatly upset by two horrible nightmares. In the first dream she was pursued up endless flights of stairs by a gigantic serpent, as big as the Loch Ness monster. Finally she reached the refuge of her bedroom, but although she struggled desperately to keep the door shut, the creature succeeded in forcing its way in. At that point she woke up with a start.

I saw this dream as confirmation of my hypothesis about this patient's sexual conflict. The serpent was a menacing phallic symbol, and it illustrated the conflict that I felt was raging between her superego and her id: a conflict whose symptoms often include feelings of horror and a sensation of pressure at the top of the head. The sexual energy and the combination of pleasure and terror that this young woman felt towards the monstrous serpent (a phenomenon that I call the "gorilla syndrome") rose up her back and lodged at the base of her skull. People's hair is often said to stand on end when they are confronted with something terrifying; I can confirm that this is not just a saying, but a real phenomenon that I have frequently observed. The second nightmare was also highly expressive: in it she had given birth, but the baby was spastic, symbolising her fear of "falling" pregnant.

After experiencing these two memorable nightmares, my patient began to show rapid improvement. Her insomnia disappeared altogether, as did her migraines. She felt herself becoming a normal, happy young woman, and she discovered new interests in life: her ambition now was to become an actress or a dancer. She and her parents were very grateful to me for this transformation. At that point I had to end the therapy, as I had to go away for some time. However, I felt that this was a good moment at which to stop, since she was not yet ready to go further.

I feel that this patient's case demonstrates particularly well how effective psychoperistaltic methods can be on a psychological level. But I must emphasise that the therapist using these methods also needs to be a psychologist or a psychotherapist; he must be capable of guiding and controlling everything that arises, both during the massage and afterwards.

APPENDIX III

MANIC-DEPRESSIVE PSYCHOSIS : THE CASE OF OSCAR

Introduction

While I was working at the Dikemark psychiatric hospital I saw many fascinating phenomena. One of the most intriguing was the sudden and spontaneous changes that occurred in manic-depressive patients. Not only did their personality and their symptoms change, but their whole physical appearance also changed dramatically between the manic and the depressive phases of the cycle. During the manic phase the surface membranes became greatly distorted, causing the skin to puff up. Then, with the onset of the depressive phase, the skin suddenly became wrinkled, as if no more fluid remained in the tissues.

To help me to understand what was going on, I studied the phenomenological reports on the patients' sensations. They described feelings of movement inside the head that began without warning and disappeared equally abruptly. These sensations seemed to me to illustrate the concept of a flow of energy that is continually alternating in direction: first inwards, then outwards, then inwards again... from the depths of the body to the surface, and back into the depths. This flux occurs in every cell of the body. I realised then that Reich's principles of bioenergy could be applied to manic-depressive psychosis: orgone energy moves towards larger concentrations of energy, then, when it reaches a peak, it changes direction.

This corresponds with the clinical symptoms of the manic phase: hyperactivity, frenzied optimism, euphoria, diminished critical faculties, and indefatigability. The manic patient seems to have all the energy in the universe at his disposal. In a certain sense this is true, since all the chemostatic layers that have been created by repressing energy are suddenly activated and thrust their way towards the outside in search of release. As a result, the membranes of the intestines and other internal organs become flooded with pathological fluid.

This theory of pathological fluid can also be applied to the membranes of the nerve cells. The excessive build-up of nervous tension makes the patient virtually ready to explode, and this is why he bursts into bouts of psychomotoric hyperactivity. During the manic phase of the cycle, the chemostasis moves in a centrifugal direction. The energy presses outwards, seeking release, until it reaches a point of saturation in the peripheral region; then, once the tissues are full, it returns towards the interior in a centripetal direction. This leads to depression, with its characteristic contraction of the peripheral membranes.

Looked at in this way, the cycle of manic and depressive phases symptomatic of this illness is due to the alternating centrifugal and centripetal flows of energy, which follow a rhythmical pattern influenced by the production of chemostasis. This concept can be pursued even further, by relating it to the pulsating rhythms present in all living cells. So, when treating a manic-depressive patient with psychoperistaltic massage, the treatment must be given during the manic period: that is, when the surface membranes are full of chemostasis. This promotes an abdominal discharge which eliminates the accumulated toxins, before saturation point is reached and the chemostasis becomes inaccessible. The membranes of the interior organs cannot, of course, be massaged directly.

Case study of Oscar

Oscar had been diagnosed as intellectually retarded. His mother said that she had been severely depressed during her pregnancy because bitter conflicts blew up at that time between her husband and his father, who was also his boss. Eventually the couple were forced to move to another town, where they had to set up home again from scratch. The whole experience had been so fraught that Oscar's mother had not had time to enjoy her pregnancy or the birth.

Oscar did not have an easy start in life. He was a blue baby at birth, and it was not until he was five years old that he began to talk. He managed to complete primary school without problems, but once he had reached secondary school age his parents had to hire a tutor for him. He had always been very close to his mother, who both dominated and protected him, whereas there had always been a great deal of tension between him and his father. Because of this, he had not lived with his father since the age of eighteen. But shortly after his thirty-sixth birthday, circumstances forced Oscar to live with his father again. Under these stressful conditions, Oscar developed strong, conscious feelings of aggression which subsequently escalated into a manic-depressive psychosis. He was given drug treatment for this, but to little effect.

Eventually we decided to try massage therapy, on condition that the treatment was private and that Oscar was not admitted to psychiatric hospital, where the staff had said that nothing more could be done for him. The first time I saw Oscar, he scarcely seemed human; he was a totally unresponsive vegetable. We resolved to keep him out of hospital no matter what happened, and to treat him at home. I had never thought of treating a case such as this, but I reassured Oscar's mother that I believed I would be able to help him and perhaps even cure him. I had complete confidence in my theories about manic-depressive psychosis.

One night, after Oscar had received two treatments, we were shocked to hear a strangled, agonised groaning sound, as if someone was dying. When I reached Oscar's room, he was sitting bolt upright on his bed. My first thought was that we must rush him to hospital and that he was not a suitable subject for this type of treatment. In my anxiety, I did not notice at first that the painful sounds rattling their way out of Oscar's throat were actually words. Eventually, though, I was able to make out what he was trying to say, over and over: "I hate him! I hate him!"

I realised then that the emotional energy of hatred had been activated by the treatment, but was now stuck in his throat as chemostasis, causing an oedema to form. Oscar was in danger of suffocating. I quickly got him to lie down, and began massaging the membranes of his neck with stroking movements. His stomach responded with loud, explosive sounds, like thunderclaps, indicating an intense psychovegetative charge. At the end of two long hours of treatment, I was heartily relieved to see the last traces of stasis and oedema disappear; Oscar could breathe normally again, and he fell asleep at once. The Oscar who greeted us the next morning was a completely different person. Instead of a lethargic, absent "vegetable", we saw a lively, happy, active, normal individual, interested in everything around him and taking part in the conversation. I realised that he had been forced to repress his feelings of rage, because otherwise he would have been in real physical danger of suffocating. He really, literally had his father wedged in his throat. Oscar received no treatment for several weeks after this episode, because I had to go away. During this period he developed very marked manic symptoms, with increasing irritability and hyperactivity: he had never gone through such a strong manic phase before. But when I treated him on my return, and during subsequent sessions, the massage completely relieved his symptoms and he became normal again.

One day I gave Oscar his treatment when I was feeling particularly tired and stressed. I was irritable and impatient as I worked. Evidently I must have set emotional material from the depths of his body in motion without first eliminating the layer on top. This time the treatment did not help him in the usual way. Within two weeks he had entered into a full-blown phase of mania, during which he made arrangements to hire the concert halls in the nearest town for a series of piano recitals, as well as ordering a monumental quantity of children's books. He took to waking up at four in the morning and racing around the house, knocking on all the doors.

As I lived in another town, Oscar came to see me by train, accompanied by his mother. During the journey his body began swelling visibly, like a loaf of bread rising. He was scarcely recognisable by the time he arrived, and I started the treatment without delay. I felt that I needed to empty the chemostasis from the outer layers before the process reached saturation point and reversed direction; otherwise the energetic fluid would return into the depths of the body and would then be unavailable until the next manic phase.

By this time I had started using the stethoscope in my work, and since I had two of them, Oscar's mother was able to listen as I worked on her son. It was the first time she had been present during a treatment. I listened to Oscar's intestines with the stethoscope before beginning the treatment, and found that there was no peristalsis at that point. A few moments later, though, his stomach began responding with extremely loud sounds like thunderclaps and explosions, which were almost more than our ears could bear.

Typically, Oscar's skin was so charged with chemostasis that I did not even need to work at a deeper level, on his muscles. Such a potent peristaltic discharge of nervous energy was taking place that it helped me to understand why people become hyperactive during phases of mania. When energy is being released outwards on such a scale, the person has no choice but to behave in a hyper-energetic way.

After two hours of uninterrupted abdominal discharge - although I only treated Oscar's back and legs - he calmed down to such an extent that he gave me a smile of gratitude and fell into a serene sleep. I felt that we had just achieved a scientific miracle, and I was delighted that Oscar had given me an opportunity to confirm my theory. The next morning I was even more delighted when I went to the hotel where he and his mother were staying, to ask how he was getting along. His mother told me that Oscar had woken early and was calm, normal and happy. Later he had entered into a polite conversation with some English guests in the hotel, speaking their language fluently; it was clear that his knowledge of English, which he had learned years ago from his tutor, was now coming back to him. It seemed to me that Oscar had entered into a state of well-being that so-called "normal" people seldom experience. Observing his experiences helped me to understand more clearly the process that transforms a healthy individual into a manic personality, escalating through a series of states of pre-manic euphoria. This process is triggered when energetic fluid released from layers of repressed emotional material is activated, but remains trapped by the outermost layer which acts as a sort of shell, preventing an abdominal discharge.

Since that time, I have taken to using the concepts of "open" and "closed" to describe the state of the outermost layer. In Oscar's case, it seemed as though all the layers of chemostasis repressed since his birth were activated in a frantic quest for satisfaction and release. So the peak of intensity in the manic phase could be likened to a kettle under such high pressure that it was on the point of exploding. At the time, though, I took a purely theoretical approach, since I could not begin to guess what the emotional content of the different layers might be. I could only wait for it to be revealed during the course of the treatment.

At the end of five months of treatment, it seemed clear that Oscar was finally free of his excessive manic energy. He was in such a healthy, balanced state that I felt that it would be safe to take a bolder approach in the therapy. So I now began using a deeper form of massage designed to loosen his muscular armour, dissolve his inhibitions and free his breathing. The effects were quickly visible: one day, after the session, his mother gasped: "One of his shoulders has dropped!" I explained to her that this phenomenon often occurs in dynamic physiotherapy when the therapist is working directly on chronic muscular tensions, and that the other shoulder would also drop eventually.

During this period Oscar was living with his mother and a domestic help in a summer home near Oslo, so that he could come to me for treatment more often. After one of these treatments he fell asleep, but he quickly woke up again in floods of tears, sobbing that he wanted to go back and be with God. He lamented: "Why was I born if I can't do what I was destined to do?" He would not stop crying. When his mother and the domestic help came into his room, they found him urinating on the floor. They thought he was doing so because there was no chamber pot, so they rushed to fetch one. But Oscar went on urinating on the floor, saying that he liked doing it because it was such fun. That night he began crying again, and by the next morning he had regressed so much that he was like a three- month-old baby. He could not even hold up his head; he just lay there, staring at his fingers and making baby noises.

I was called at once, and when I saw Oscar I was shocked by his sudden regression. I put the stethoscope on his abdomen, but there were no sounds at all and he was feverish. At that point he recovered the ability to speak, but the outermost layer of his organism remained completely closed. Although I massaged him for hours, nothing happened, and it became clear that Oscar was now resisting the treatment strongly.

At around one o'clock in the morning my patience was finally rewarded. The first intestinal sounds came as I was working on the membranes of the left sternocleidomastoid muscle. This part of Oscar's neck seemed to be the key; if I could only manage to open this "door", the whole organism would then be able to eliminate its excess energy. But Oscar was so uncooperative that each time I came close to succeeding, he would escape again. In the end we found that, by doing exactly what he wanted - that is, feeding him with an unending supply of bananas - we could calm and quieten him enough to enable me to treat him. He kept calling out "Mummy, banana!" in a childish voice, over and over again. The heart-rending sight of such a big man lying there like a baby, consumed with such an immense oral craving, really brought home to me the characteristics of the oral phase: omnipotence and megalomania. "I can get whatever

I want if I yell loudly enough!"

As I mentioned earlier, my hypothesis was that all the layers were activated simultaneously; so far, though, we had only encountered the oral layer. The anal phase made its appearance the next day. I found it very difficult to treat Oscar during this phase because it was so disgusting, and I could not deny my negative feelings towards him. He had tremendous resistance to the treatment and fought so hard that the only way to carry on working was, once again, to pacify him with vast quantities of cakes and sweets. Even so, he kept poking his fingers into his anus during the massage and trying to smear his faeces on my face. His eyes lit up with malicious glee each time he succeeded. I could feel all my most irrational emotions surging up inside me. It was only thanks to his mother's help that I was able to continue; she was so tender and patient with Oscar that I felt huge admiration for her as she calmly let him wipe his hands on her face. I, on the other hand, wore myself out trying to treat him with the gentle movements of the massage, when I would really have liked to hit him!

After I had succeeded in eliminating much of the visceral pressure, Oscar was able to sleep peacefully. By the next morning he had almost become a normal adult again, and seemed calm and contented. But since his normal adult personality did not want to receive treatment and we were reluctant to force it on him, his energy level soon rose again and he reverted to a manic phase, running around the house, hammering on the walls and generally making as much noise as he possibly could. He kept pulling aggressive faces at us and shouting that he wanted to kill us. Things continued like this for some time, and it became more and more difficult to keep him at home. It took all his mother's patience, as well as a large supply of sweets and threats to withdraw the sweets, to get Oscar to co-operate with the treatment. But he went on teasing me, trying to push me to explosion point. For example, he quickly discovered that by scraping his fingernails along the rubber tube of the stethoscope, he could produce sounds that hurt my ears.

One day, after I had been massaging Oscar under these trying conditions for a good five hours without producing a single peristaltic sound, I felt that the situation was hopeless. Suddenly I lost my temper and I hit him. At once I felt terrible about having hit a defenceless "baby". Through my tears I tried to explain to Oscar: "I hit you because you don't want to get well!" To my great surprise, he answered in a normal, sincere tone of voice: "You're right. I don't want you to give me this treatment because you can reduce me to nothing." That incident proved to be a turning point in Oscar's treatment. From then on he allowed me to massage him without resisting, and the events of his life unfolded during the therapy like a film being projected in reverse. This "film" presented a fascinating picture of the conflicts underlying the manic-depressive syndrome. We were able to trace specific patterns of behaviour back to the reactions that caused them, and in turn we could see the relationship between these reactions and the accumulations of chemostatic toxins that preceded them.

For example, Oscar would often wake early in the morning with the symptoms of abdominal closure and in a state of full mania. But as soon as the peristaltic sounds began and his system opened, he would fall back into a peaceful sleep. When he reawakened after this, he would be like a child; a child who might be happy (if enough of the chemostatic build-up had been eliminated by the peristalsis), or unhappy and restless, or in a manic state again. If the pressure within his organism became even more intense, the transformation would go a stage further; he would then become a manic adult. His aggression became very visible; he would defecate on the floor saying: "I'm doing this because you don't love me, Mother!" We could now clearly see his ambivalence towards his mother. Sometimes he wanted to do everything for her; he would run around like a three- year-old child, picking up anything that caught his eye and announcing: "This is for Mummy!" He would repeat manically: "Mummy, take this! Mummy, take this!" During this phase his faeces were a gift. On one occasion, when his mother scolded him, Oscar reproached her: "Don't you understand that this is a present for you?" But when the treatment had "emptied" the excess pressure from his system again, he reverted to a normal three-year-old child with all of a young child's concerns and fantasies. One day he was given a glass of milk. Instead of drinking it, he poured it over some flowers, saying: "The flowers must have their milk too!" And he marched around, sprinkling milk on all kinds of things that he thought needed it.

Apart from his height, Oscar's appearance corresponded surprisingly well with his "age". His mother and grandmother were able to recognise each phase of his development, and soon learned to predict what would come next. Throughout the process, his behaviour showed such continuity that neither of them was at all worried. In fact, we had Oscar's development almost completely under control. Both his mother and his grandmother began talking in terms of energy: "Have you "emptied" him today?" "Is he "closed"?"

Another curious phenomenon that we noticed during the treatment helped me to understand the relationship between stasis and fluid: if I was only able to treat (or "empty") one leg, Oscar felt so light on that leg that he lifted it higher than the other when he walked. If both legs had been treated, he felt so light that he pirouetted around like a ballet dancer, singing: "Aren't I marvellous?"

Based on the course that the treatment had taken up to that point, Oscar's mother predicted that the next stage would be crying, since her son had not cried when he was born. I expected the missing birth cry to come bursting out in a massive abreaction of the trauma, but instead it developed very gradually, beginning as an almost inaudible, hesitant sound in his throat. Oscar was almost unconscious when this happened, his eyes sunk deeply into their sockets. Each time the birth cry emerged, his body automatically adopted the characteristic position of a new-born baby. If he had been sitting on a chair, he would suddenly find himself on the floor with no recollection of what had happened. This continued for several days until, one morning, a really loud cry came, accompanied by all the sounds and bodily reflexes of birth. Then Oscar started wondering: "Am I alive? I'm not alive!" And if one considers his life up to that point, it is true that Oscar had never really been alive until that day. Then, as he gradually began to realise that he really was alive, he became overwhelmed with a terrible sadness. He declared that he wanted to go back to God, and said he could hear voices in his head telling him to kill himself, to go to the sea and drown himself. He became preoccupied with questions of life and death, expressed in terms of a child's philosophy: "Are flies aware that they are alive? Does Spot (his dog) know he is alive? Should we feel pity for dead things?"

After this phase, Oscar regressed into the womb. He protested: "I don't like water, I don't want to be inside Mummy." And each time he did so, he lost consciousness and his eyes retracted within their sockets. At the same time, he emitted strange sounds whose meaning we could not understand. Then, suddenly, a new personality emerged from the midst of these sounds; the voice of a child could clearly be heard, announcing that his name was Little Oscar. He repeated constantly to his mother that he did not want to live because she had never loved him. The only thing he wanted was to go back to God, who loved him. In the evenings Oscar's mother and the newcomer, Little Oscar, curled up together on the bed and talked together for hours. During these conversations Little Oscar told his mother, over and over again, that he regretted having been born. She in turn told him that she had always worried terribly about him because he had been so ill, but that she had always loved him very much indeed. Finally, after many days of this, she succeeded in convincing her son that her love for him was real. Gradually he began to trust her, and he declared that, in spite of everything, he would try to live.

While all of this was going on, the adult Oscar was also present; but he was unaware of what was happening and wanted nothing more than to lie passively in bed. Little Oscar, on the other hand, was full of vitality; now that he had decided to live he developed a wide range of interests, and before long he had grown into a completely normal little boy. Watching him blossom in this way was very moving; at last we were able to see what Oscar would have been like as a child if only the circumstances had been different. He was enthusiastic and affectionate; in the evenings he would sing: "I love you all so much!" and "We are a little family!"

One evening, when, as usual, Oscar and his mother were curled up together for a conversation, another voice emerged: the deep voice of an adult, who spoke in a highly intelligent, philosophical way. This personality introduced himself as Oscar the Intelligent Unconscious, and said that he was a part of Oscar that had been repressed. All he wanted to do was to meditate and ponder on the mystery of the stars, to develop his wisdom and express it. He explained that he had never been able to influence Oscar because Oscar had been too badly damaged during his childhood. He had lost contact altogether, and that was why Oscar had always been so obtuse. But now he had succeeded in re-emerging into consciousness because he saw that there was hope, since Little Oscar, for the first time in his life, wanted to live. He had also come to offer his support to Oscar's mother and Little Oscar; he would help the child to grow up and develop his talents as a composer. This situation demanded careful handling. We were now faced with three personalities: the adult Oscar, Little Oscar, and the Intelligent Unconscious - or Mr Hansen, as he asked us to call him. Mr Hansen began appearing more and more frequently; his personality became more substantial, and he was delightful company. He was charming, sociable, polite and warm; when he dined in company his table manners were excellent, and he could tell stories that made everyone rock with laughter. From time to time, though, the original Oscar with his blank gaze would suddenly reappear and ask bluntly: "Why are you laughing?" Then he would start eating with his old, atrocious table manners, licking the plate and stuffing five potatoes into his mouth at once.

When I visited Oscar one morning, I was worried by what I saw. The original Oscar had not appeared for several days, and the Intelligent Unconscious, Mr Hansen, seemed exhausted. The next day Oscar's mother told me that she had had a long conversation with Mr Hansen. He had said to her: "I am extremely concerned about Oscar, because there is no sign of life in him and he is gradually disappearing. None of you help me to make him get out of bed and become active. He needs to have a daily routine and some kind of occupation. He needs to work. As things stand now, I have to bear the whole burden, and I was not made for this kind of work. My task is to meditate and to guide the inner self. I am so tired that I cannot go on any longer. And if Oscar dies I will die too, because I depend on his body." Mr Hansen was so distressed that he burst into tears, and implored Oscar's mother to help. Finally he told her that he was going to sleep, and that he would try to find a solution to the problem as he slept. Sure enough, at four o'clock in the morning Oscar's mother was aroused from sleep by a deafening shout which heralded the birth of a new personality: Oscar the Giant by name. A little later Mr Hansen reappeared, and confirmed that this new being was the solution he had found as he slept. Oscar the Giant was neither intelligent nor cultured, and had no interest in the stars, but he was ideally suited to his task, which was to help Little Oscar to grow up and protect him from harm - both from others and from himself. Oscar the Giant was the kind of person in whom one could have complete confidence.

The Intelligent Unconscious told us that it was now very important for the adult Oscar to start taking part in social life. We should take him to parties, he explained, and see to it that he got plenty of stimulation. At first we were really worried by this prospect: what if Little Oscar were to appear suddenly? But at home, each time Little Oscar was about to defecate on the floor, Oscar the Giant now appeared and took him to the toilet instead. And now, whenever Little Oscar seized objects and was on the point of throwing them, Oscar the Giant would intervene and stay his hand. Then Mr Hansen would also appear, and ask us proudly whether this solution suited us.

It did suit us; after a few weeks Oscar's mother was able to take him with her to social gatherings, where he behaved very well. But each time, an hour before setting off, Oscar the Giant would sit down deep in thought, and gather all his strength so that he could make sure that Little Oscar did not emerge for a single moment. And the moment they got back home, he would tell his mother that he was so tired, he needed to sleep for several days. At that point Little Oscar would be given free rein again. Around this time, the different personalities began to merge into one another. For example, when the adult Oscar was running errands, he would ask for fresh lemonade for Little Oscar, massive portions of beef for Oscar the Giant - and only the Intelligent Unconscious wanted nothing at all.

One day, while I was treating Oscar, I got a strong impression that a deep trauma he had suffered at around the age of four lay at the root of all his problems. During the following night his mother rang me up to tell me that her son had been vomiting violently, and was now experiencing such severe stomach pains that she suspected he might have appendicitis. But I was sure that his symptoms were simply a reaction to the treatment, because I had used stronger techniques than usual. I hurried round to see for myself what was happening. When I arrived, Oscar's face was distorted by the pressure of vomiting, and the room was filled with the smell of ether. Oscar gasped that he was afraid of the knife. At last we had the explanation of a symptom that had been puzzling me greatly. In recent weeks, Oscar had developed an intense preoccupation with his nose. He would say: "When I can see my nose, I know I'm alive". He declared that he envied the sheepdog, because it had such a long nose that it could see it all the time.

Finally the story behind this strange preoccupation emerged. When Oscar was four years old, he underwent a tonsillectomy operation. His mother was not allowed to accompany him into the operating theatre, but had to stay in the waiting room. Only his father witnessed the operation. Oscar's mother heard her son screaming, but she consoled herself with the thought that he was anaesthetised. But now, as Oscar relived the trauma, his mother told me: "I've had a dreadful shock today. The domestic help came to me and said she had a confession to make. She told me that on the evening after the operation, Oscar's father came to her, terribly depressed, and confided in her that the surgery had been carried out without an anaesthetic. It had taken four nurses to hold down the child's arms and legs and a fifth to keep his head still; even so, he fought so desperately that his father had also had to use all his strength to help them. Oscar shrieked like an animal in the slaughterhouse."

At last we were able to understand Oscar's obsession with his nose. The child must have been convinced that he was going to be killed, and it was only by looking at his nose that he knew he was still alive.

This final revelation seemed to represent a crucial point in Oscar's therapy. From that day onwards, he became an integrated person and began to grow up. We were able to follow the different stages of his development from eight or nine years old to around sixteen. But it was clear that he would still need to remain in treatment for some time to come, and since he and his mother lived some distance away, I taught her the method so that she could continue treating Oscar herself.

By this time, Oscar's behavioural patterns had become neurotic rather than psychotic. He displayed marked aggression towards his mother, but each time she massaged him the aggression would disappear and instead his sense of humour would come to the fore. During this phase he called himself Happy Mr Hansen, and before long this cheerful disposition became an integrated part of his personality. More and more, he now refused all medication, because it made him ill.

This, in broad outline, is the story of Oscar. I would simply like to add that his creativity continued to blossom. The last time I heard from him was when he got his mother to ask me whether what he was experiencing was normal. He said that, as in the past, he could "hear" the music that he composed in his head; but now he had also begun to "see" musical notes in the air. And when he wrote these notes down and played them on the piano, he found that it was the same music.

Conclusion

We associate Little Oscar with the id, so we can describe him as the id-personality - that is, the primary, inner being that possesses tremendous creative talent. This is the raw libidinal force which all too often becomes frustrated and encapsulated. In Oscar's case, due to the difficult conditions during his mother's pregnancy and the trauma that he suffered at birth, his life got off to a bad start. The anxiety prompted by the birth trauma and the chemostasis that this produced paralysed his throat to such an extent that he was unable to feed properly from his mother's breast; the milk ran out of his nose instead. His speech organs were weakened by the oedema in his throat so that he could not speak, and he also developed a thyroid problem that halted his growth at the age of three. He would have become a dwarf if he had not been given growth hormones, enabling him to develop to a normal height.

Oscar's entire libido circulation had come to a standstill at birth. As a result, the personality of Little Oscar had to be repressed: that is, the libido became encapsulated. The true, vital Oscar became imprisoned in his body and his unconscious, and the ego-personality then took over.

The ego-personality - Oscar as he was before he developed his psychosis - was resigned and apathetic, mentally retarded, and always bad-tempered. He had such difficulty in adapting to his environment that he grew up without any interest in anything. Pre-psychotic Oscar developed a pseudo-neurosis and a defence system based on amiability and compliance; he never complained. This system of defences enabled Oscar to survive into adulthood, but it collapsed abruptly when he was forced to confront the conflict with his father again. When the manic phase of his illness occurred, his aggressive feelings towards his father surged up violently. Stripped of his defences, the Oscar who now became visible was mentally ill, a pitiful manic-depressive patient who was numbed and tranquillised by drug treatment.

At this point I became involved in Oscar's treatment, and began applying the principles of psychoperistalsis. My aim in doing so was to suppress and remove the excessive levels of chemostasis that Oscar's organism was constantly generating. As we cleansed his system of stress products, we were eventually able to discover that Little Oscar was the driving force of the psychosis. Little Oscar, who carried within him all of Oscar's native creative potential - his musical talent - was the libido-personality. He longed to emerge so that he could achieve self-fulfilment and express his creativity; he did his utmost to reject and overcome the accumulated frustration and aggression that he had suffered.

Eventually, as we saw, the libidinal part of Oscar succeeded in shaking off the repression that was crushing him, and Little Oscar emerged. But it was clear that this id-personality was scarcely integrated at all with the rest of Oscar; as the emotional vasomotoric cycle was completed, Little Oscar invaded the ego and assumed control of the psychomotor system.

Mr Hansen, the Intelligent Unconscious, represents the latent potential for integration that developed within Oscar; integration of the mind, body and personality. Mr Hansen also emerged from the depths of Oscar's being, took command of the ego and of the psychomotor system, and functioned as an autonomous personality.

To explain these striking changes in the ego consciousness, we must turn to the theory of energetic regulation of the Self. The Self is the superconscious and the guardian of the whole person, in contrast to the unconscious id. The Self - that is, Mr Hansen in Oscar's case - witnessed everything that happened, knew each of the different personalities, and was rich in wisdom, grace, charm and humour. But the Self was unable to influence Oscar's personality while so much of Oscar was lost to himself under multiple layers of neurosis and chemostasis. However, when the retrogressive blood distribution system was mobilised, reactivating these layers, the new circulatory system brought the whole organism back under control and the repressed material was finally able to penetrate the consciousness of the ego.

The mechanism by which the different personalities "took over" the ego in Oscar's case is a fascinating one. First the ego was overwhelmed by a pathological condition; later, though, we witnessed the emergence of healthy, constructive elements that produced lasting behavioural changes. In a certain sense the encapsulated id- personality, Little Oscar, had always been present within the pre- psychotic ego; but he became more and more frustrated, and consequently less and less able to influence Oscar at all.

When Oscar succumbed to manic-depressive psychosis, the stifled id-personality burst out in its full fury. This was actually a desperate attempt by the primary personality to break free from the yoke of the secondary personality. The Intelligent Unconscious, Mr Hansen, was encapsulated too, but in some way he was continually aware of everything that happened. As soon as he was able to emerge, he helped to co-ordinate and activate the therapeutic process. He became the main driving force behind Oscar's recovery.

When Mr Hansen created Oscar the Giant, he did so to solve the stream of new problems that had become too exhausting for him to handle on his own. He found his role as co-ordinator of the personalities too demanding and unnatural for him, since his natural mode of being was in contemplation and meditation (the function of the Self, the superconscious). So, instead, he delegated control over the co-ordination process to the rock-solid, dependable Oscar the Giant. This control is closely linked to the will and the psychomotor system; parts of the total being that are less spiritual and more material, making them more suitable for the job.

Only by understanding the activity of the circulatory system is it possible to explain how the physiological dynamic affects and transforms the ego. The key to this understanding lies in the physiology of the retrogressive blood distribution system; in its cycles and rhythms, and in the need to complete old cycles once they have been reactivated. So the blood circulatory system can be viewed as the connecting link between the conscious and the unconscious, between the id and the ego.

Oscar remained in treatment for three years, and when he returned to the psychiatric hospital for a subsequent check-up, the doctors could find no trace of manic-depressive tendencies. They concluded from this that their original diagnosis must have been wrong.

NOTE: PERISTALSIS CONTROLLED BY THE STETHOSCOPE

This therapeutic technique involves stimulating the intestinal peristaltic response in such a way as to facilitate the elimination of stress products. To achieve this, a stethoscope is applied in various ways to appropriate points in the region of the navel. In this way even the smallest intestinal movements can be detected, amplified and followed with precision. This enables the therapist to maintain close contact with the patient's visceral tension and to monitor his reaction to the treatment continually. The treatment may take the form of massage, or of other somatic techniques. The series of treatments brings about a gradual relaxation of muscular contraction and an increase in tonus. It also restores the patient's capacity for spontaneous functioning and vegetative self-regulation. Self-regulation depends on the state of all the visceral organs.

BIBLIOGRAPHY

BOYESEN, Gerda:	Collected Papers of Biodynamic Psychology, Vols. I & II, Biodynamic Psychology Publications, 1980. Journal of Biodynamic Psychology, 1980-1981.
FREUD, Sigmund:	Three Essays on the Theory of Sexuality, Metapsychology,
GÉRÔME, Paul:	Les Anatomies Fantastiques, D 3, Collection Vibrations, Geneva, 1983.
JUNG, Carl Gustav:	The Roots of Consciousness,
RAKNES, Ola:	Wilhelm Reich and Orgonomy,
REICH, Wilhelm:	Character Analysis, The Function of the Orgasm, Cosmic Superimposition,

Dorian Bøyesen - Publisher's Note

The meaning that this book will have in future, and has had, I still cannot comprehend. Doubtless it belongs on the book market, and I am glad to finally make it available, so that it can serve as a reading and have its well-deserved place within the history of idea, philosophy and psychology. Here are insights and theories that were, and still are, groundbreaking research, enlightening and their time far ahead, envisioning with splendour the presence, past and future of psychotherapy.

She was provident of her time in that she also had philosophical thoughts about her time; the individual in society, yet always with solutions.

As an example, I can refer to these passages:

On blockades:

> "When someone is unable to express his aggression, he becomes depressed. It is widely recognised in psychology that when someone tries to overcome a block, his energy level rises and manifests itself as aggression. If the expression of this aggression is prevented or held back, the patient may lapse into either depression or inaction and resignation." (Gerda Boyesen - The Biodynamic Theory of Psychosis).

These and many other passages form for me the quintessence of the work of my grandmother Gerda Bøyesen. These are observations that have written and will write history.
One thing I have discovered amongst many via publishing the work of biodynamic psychotherapy: Expression is important and part of the healing process, and in addition, the expression in art also plays a significant role. Expression and impression are two important factors that characterize us as human beings, who have a psychology, whether we are aware of it or not.

Some people, e.g. as a manager, may have a lot of stress in their everyday lives, seek a balance, find a place, where they can be themselves, maybe during squash, or like my grandmother Gerda Bøyesen during tennis, before discovering massage and her methodology. In times of resilience research and self-regulation, this book constitutes an important time-travel to the beginnings of body psychotherapy.

This book is one of the standard works of body therapy and it is an honor to republish it. The passage quoted above, for example, reminded me of a song by the British music group Oasis:

Go Let It Out - Oasis

For me, this song text describes this expression, expressing it, not letting one's emotion stay inside and fester, but letting the expression get out, through whatever valve, and also accepting feelings; to become conscious of what is seething in oneself and not to suppress it; searching for awareness, of what also maybe was or has been, in oneself. As we have learned from the work of Gerda Bøyesen, muscle armor, blockades, stress. Many of these phenomena have their cause in reprisals that we experienced in childhood, adolescence, and adult life, and if not processed, perhaps re-experience, until this structure becomes aware, resolved, and cured.

There are many anecdotes in the book that have contemporary historic value, so it reads like a piece of contemporary history: i.e. the Emancipation of the Woman, the Civil World/Society in Norway, her Journey to London, from Reich, Jung ... in short - it is a book that is publicly heard and should stand/be in any book shelf. As the song by Oasis is referring to former music culture, to The Beatles, and again to the Blues, Biodynamic Psychology, from the Beatles era, also influences new currents today in the form of holistic body psychotherapy, mindfulness, attentiveness, permaculture.

Also today the title of "Spiegel" Edition 27/2019 "Gesundheit: Helfer im Bauch – Wissenschaftler erforschen die enorme Bedeutung des Darms (und seiner Bewohner) fürs Leibeswohl" (EN: "Health: Helpers in the Stomach - Scientists Research the Great Meaning of the Intestine (and its Inhabitants) for Body Health", the Film by Cécile Denjean "Der kluge Bauch – Unser zweites Gehirn" (EN: "The Smart Stomach - Our Second Brain") or the book "Das zweite Gehirn: Wie der Darm unsere Stimmung, unsere Entscheidungen und unser Wohlbefinden beeinflusst" (EN:"The Second Brain: How the Intestine Affects Our Mood, Our Decisions and Our Well-Being") by Emeran Mayer.

Gerda Bøyesen had already in 1985, published via Payot Publishing, Paris, "Entre Psyche et Soma", and 1987 at Kösel Verlag, "Über den Körper die Seele heilen" (EN: "Healing the Soul through the Body, Between Psyche and Soma"), developed and envisioned theories that were foreseeing and provident.

The research has long recognized that biology, psychology, massage, physiotherapy, yoga, sports in general, nutritional science (ecotrophology) and meditation can all contribute to health, and holistic healing processes can be achieved by applying different treatment methods.

Here we dive into the world of body psychotherapy and its emergence, the discovery of the significance of psychoperistaltics for psychology, the stethoscope application, the discovery of the Gerda Bøyesen method, and how much of this is related to the vegetative nervous system; the sympathetic-parasympathetic (SNS and PSNS) and enteric nervous system (ENS = intestinal or autonomic nervous system).

It (psychoperistaltics) also, in my opinion, has an affinity to and provides additional insights when (re)-studying Japanese/Oriental medicine: the knowledge of Tsubos, of pressure nodes/points that could be utilized by massage along the meridians, to relieve stress and muscle tension, to release the Chi or Ki, respectively, the flow of life energy, and through a methodology, such as Shiatsu, Qigong Taiji, acupressure, acupuncture and the 5 elements and 5 seasons show very old traditions echo or resonate in some of the theories, especially of biodynamic massage.

With Gerda Bøyesens's analysis and the use of the stethoscope, this Chi suddenly becomes audible. In addition, Gerda Bøyesen was the first body psychotherapist, a psychologist & physiotherapist, who established a bridge between physiotherapy and psychology.
That the meaning of the intestinal noise/psychoperistaltics is scientifically verifiable during the massage stands for me outside of question, since I have experienced and listened to it (psychoperistalsis) myself. Stress reduction/relief and relaxation as well as emotions associated with the noises of peristalsis are fields that require much patience, but I am convinced that it is measurable, empirical and scientific.

Even the Stoics, who cultivated absolute control of the affects/feelings, knew that they must first understand the affects in order to master them. So if we want to understand biodynamic psychology better, more insights and articles, as well as established researchers, are needed concerning its field of study.

From certain evidence-based medicine's viewpoint, Biodynamic [Psychology & Psychotherapy] is not always recognized as a scientific method (e.g. https://en.wikipedia.org/wiki/Gerda_Boyesen, chapter "criticism", 19.10.2021), although combining Psychotherapy & Massage, 2nd Brain-Theory, Neurosciences, Psychoperistalsis and Mindfulness exercises are increasingly being recognized as therapeutic methods. [Source: https://neuroscience.ubc.ca/our-second-brain-more-than-a-gut-feeling/, 25.01.2022]

I'd like to respond to this criticism with a simple answer:
The non-recognition of Biodynamic [Psychology & Psychotherapy] as a scientific method [by e.g. AOK - one of the German Health Insurances] is for me symptomatic of much of the current situation in the health sector, although progressive changes are appearing gradually, this also concerns the pharmaceutical industry, which clearly has an economic interest in "keeping the symptoms" instead of curing the cause of some illness. I am not saying that this applies to all medicine, I am just questioning, from a philosophical viewpoint, the method of treating one illness by prescribing drugs that again have maybe an addictive character, maybe side effects. Here (body-psychotherapeutic) insights can help get to the core of problems.

It is easier prescribing psychiatric/psychotropic medication, a psychoactive drug, where the symptoms are alleviated or aggravated, as this used to be standard treatment for men in clinics, whereas women were treated with psychotherapy in the 60s, [Source: https://www.gbpev.de/gerda-boyesen-eine-kurzbiografie/, 25.01.2022] instead of working on the cause, thinking about it, breaking up patterns, or even acknowledging that the system in which we live in, might be in dischord [faulty]; that piecework, the ongoing pursuit of money and recognition, neoliberalism, capitalism, Darwin's theory of evolution, all this competition, speed, time pressure, exorbitant rents and elbow society [dog eat dog competition]; yes, all this may also cause stress – bringing togetherness and social order to topple over.

So what is the solution: Cooperatives or Cyber-(Post)socialism as an answer to Hypercapitalism? [More on this topic: http://www.imaginaryfutures.net/2007/04/17/cyber-communism-how-the-americans-are-superseding-capitalism-in-cyberspace/] Of course these words have connotations, and I do not want to drift away from the topic. Of course stating such radical criticism on society and the medical system might not always apply, and medication and psychotherapy combined, be needed in individual cases. I am not a doctor and generalizations might seem inconvenient here, and do not reflect my more moderate opinion, as a critique, I find it important to discuss these sociocultural aspects; the individual, relations and society are reciprocal.

The effect of Modern Society on the individual's health is also something Gerda Bøyesen described.

Criticism of Modern Society & Sociocultural Thoughts & Solutions:

> "In our mechanical, neurotic world we are cut off and divided, so that all we can do is to fight against each other. We are locked into our upgoing, instinctive energies, which inspire us to subjective, irrational and egotistical behaviour. Not until we come into contact with our downgoing vegetative currents and the harmonising movement of cosmic energy do we experience independent well-being and what I like to call the "qualities of eternity": that is, patience, universal love and compassion." (Gerda Boyesen - People in Transition)

Fortunately, we have 365 days a year to change this, and to change for ourselves and the society in which we live in. For some, this book may help as well. Just as the body has around 365 Tsubos, and Shiatsu in Asia is a recognized method, Biodynamic [BPP] here in the West should receive more recognition. It is scientifically quite easy to prove that the body in the state of relaxation causes digestive noise from itself, during the massage you hear the peristalsis and these noises are distinguishable, e.g. when tensions have been resolved/the moment of resolving tension.

I hope very soon that new scientifically proven studies, if not already available, will support my grandmother's work. As mentioned before, she was provident of her time in that she practiced social criticism, yet always with solutions:

> "Over the years I have met a great many rebellious young people - drug users, drop-outs, hippies in the days of the "flower power" movement - who have also faced this dilemma. All of them said much the same thing to me: "We know what we don't want, but we don't know what we do want..." Therapy, and most of all psychoperistaltic self-regulation, can be a tremendous help to people who have reached this stage of self- discovery. This is because psychoperistalsis follows the pleasure principle. When someone rediscovers his flow of vegetative energies, he enters into the marvellous world of "synchronicity"; his being is in harmony with all that is, and his life becomes truly full. Self- regulated people encounter the people and situations that are exactly right for them, and this enables them to develop their creativity without any hindrances. They are in contact with their true, authentic selves, not with their neurotic secondary personalities."
> (Gerda Boyesen - People in Transition)

There is no doubt that some theories were very avant-garde and still are, thus, as a thinker, as a therapist, Gerda Bøyesen shaped (and had impact on) her time, has written emancipation history (for man and woman, namely for humans!) and laid a foundation for exciting work.

The fluidity of existence and the principle of freedom, embedded in the writings of Jean-Paul Sartre and Simone de Beauvoir, are also reflected in her work, which has truly gone new groundbreaking ways. What the Libido flow exactly means, cosmic energy, life energy, Chi or Ki, may not be exactly measurable, but happiness and health can be felt, and finding a balance, where our Chi flows, and we are in synch with what is good for us, can only be said to be worthwhile to be achieved.

To explain this with the psychology by/of Gerda Bøyesen, it is also about finding a harmonious connection here, to solve polarities and bring in concord/compliance/concordance:

> "The basic idea is to get the patient's instinctual energy and his voluntary energy working together in harmony, so as to end the perpetual conflict between the instincts and the energy of the motor ego. We have developed many different techniques which we use either to provoke or to harmonise the patient's energy, depending on the needs of the moment. By carefully co-ordinating the sequence of these provoking and harmonising techniques, we can make sure the session reaches a "happy ending"."
> (Gerda Boyesen - From Stasis to Libido Circulation)

> "Freud said: "Where the id is, the ego must follow." I prefer to look at things the other way round: "Where the ego is, the id must follow." Freud was a neurologist who worked at the ectodermic level (the central nervous system, the motor ego and the conscious mind). In biodynamic therapy, on the other hand, we work on the endodermic level. "Where the ego is, the id must follow" simply means that the motor ego must be entirely fuelled by the libido.
> As far as we are concerned, there is no conflict whatsoever between the pleasure principle and the reality principle. In fairness to Freud, though, I must explain that when he spoke of the antagonism between these two principles, he was undoubtedly talking about the id and the superego. In that sense, I agree with him completely; but I also know that reality can be utterly libidinal when somebody is truly able to allow himself to feel the libido circulation in his contact with others and with the universe. The marriage of the id and the ego is a natural one; it can even be called a spiritual marriage."
> (Gerda Boyesen - From Stasis to Libido Circulation)

How much the unconscious is connected with the audio reception of peristalsis is explained in the chapter `The Different Sounds of Psychoperistaltics`, to which I am also referring, because I can only repeatedly emphasize the significance of this science, especially this discovery. Here, in particular, I refer to "Chapter 4. THE FIELD OF BIODYNAMIC THERAPY, 1) Publishing my Theories." of this book. The chronological order of who published what is part of this publication, as some credit to Mona Lisa Boyesen as part of founding and coining the concepts of/with Gerda Boyesen, and based on Gerda Boyesens theories and findings, is not being mentioned sufficiently in public. Also anecdotes from Ebba like the presentation at Sorbonne with professors explaining the "Bio-dure - Lowen", "Bio-douce - Gerda" differentiation are interesting. The concept "Biodynamic Psychology" was finally conceptionalized and founded by Mona Lisa in spring 1973, together with and based on Gerda Boyesen's theories, later presented by Mona Lisa with Jay Stattmann at The Institute Of Unitive Psychology in Utrecht (The Netherlands), in 1974 Gerda Boyesen founded the "Center for Bioenergy" in London. My research shows that she (Gerda) pioneered in Scandinavia, combining psychology, psychotherapy and massage/physiotherapy, and as early as 1947, Gerda Boyesen encountered analytical Vegetotherapy, and from about 1956 she used the stethoscope as a "Biofeedback-instrument" to accompany massage techniques with psychotherapy. [Source: https://www.gbpev.de/gerda-boyesen-eine-kurzbiografie/, 25.01.2022]. An accurate historical chronology of Biodynamic Psychology would be a vast undertaking in itself, so maybe this can be a beginning, and hopefully inspire the digitization of much work in the field of Body-oriented/ Biodynamic Psychology & Psychotherapy.

These are just some of a variety of passages, I found especially important, that can be highlighted. After having been available in other languages for decades, now finally, the original version in English can be read and studied.

In my opinion, and I am sure many share this: Gerda Boyesen was ahead of her time, and science will gradually understand what she already understood as a pioneer.

"On the Enjoyment of Healing" An Obituary of Gerda Boyesen

Dipl. Psych. Peter Freudl

After a long and fruitful life, Gerda Boyesen, the Norwegian clinical psychologist and body psychotherapist, died in her London home in December 2005. Gerda Boyesen was probably the most famous female Reichian body psychotherapist. In the second half of the past century she founded a body psychotherapeutic school, which became well-known under the name "Biodynamic Psychology." Gerda Boyesen was a big star in the therapy scene outside of the established therapy associations. At the height of her professional career in the 1970s and 80s, she enjoyed an absolute cult status. In 1986, a much trumpeted article of the German weekly paper "DIE ZEIT", vaunted her as a leading figure of the then contemporary psychotherapy.

How did she establish her fame? Gerda Boyesen was not only a mistress of her thera-peutic craft; she enjoyed an icon status even during her lifetime. In short, she embodied the archetypal female. She represented a non-feminist and yet self-conscious femininity and motherliness and had thus a great attraction for both women and men alike. She stood for the archetype of the great mother, who gave her blessing to the daring and vocal revolt against the all-too-narrow bodily confines and societal conventions so typical for the therapy experiments of the 1960s and 1970s.

Gerda Boyesen was no untouchable goddess. She was open, tactile and blessed with a warm and affectionate vibrancy. She let herself be touched and replied in turn. She was on first name terms with all. A previously unknown gentle anarchy reigned in her therapy room free from any fearful or moral misgiving and without any trace of societal code of behaviour. Everything was possible, everything permitted and through everything hovered Gerda's deeply embodied trust, that it is good to allow the free, autonomous organically anchored living process just to happen, because this path would find its good and healing way as though automatically, as long as it was given scope.

She stood for the great Yes to animal wildness and the power of the creature in man, freed from all repression and tyranny. She stood for the quest for vitality and happiness and did not contradict when a patient assured her that with her technique, she had found the "key to happiness." She stood for the beauty and the healing power of the free and authentic life movement. She stood for unconditional love to her patient, for placidity and tolerance, for acceptance and respect for the uniqueness of the fate of the individual soul. She was a fearless pioneer of a holistic body and soul medicine, who knew how to hold its ground against resistance.

This is an amazing upshot for a women whose future was intended to be similar to that of Nora in Ibsen's dolls house; the virtuous and decent lady in the fine circles of Oslo high society.

Gerda Boyesen was born as Gerd Monsen in the Norwegian Seaport town of Bergen on 18th May 1922. Her maternal family could trace its ancestry back to Vikings, something of which her mother was very proud. Her father was the son of a wealthy businessman from the Norwegian upper class, who had come to considerable prosperity through the sale of school materials. As a result, Gerda enjoyed a childhood free from material worries. The housework was performed by staff; the children were looked after by a nanny.

The paternal ancestry included a much-travelled Dutch captain, who counted Polynesia amongst his many destinations where he fathered a child, who he brought with him to Europe so that a measure of Polynesian blood was in Gerda's veins. It could also be possible that aspects of the Polynesian earthly nature, their hearty and innocent gaiety and light-heartedness left traces in Gerda's nature. Many who knew her would be ready to affirm it.

Gerda Boyesen's recollections of her own childhood were however less cheerful. From her own autobiographical descriptions, we know that she was devoted to her natural and warm hearted mother, and was conscious of her close nature. She once described her mother as "an instinctive pedagogue." Yet as so many other leading representatives of the therapeutic guild, she also quickly learnt the shadowy side of life. Above all, she suffered under the austere upbringing of her - never satisfied - father, a firm follower of the then influential German doctor D. Schreber. The class conceit and the high standards of the man whom she herself described as "vain" belonged equally to the structuring of her childhood educative routine, such as the Schreberian sanctions including rigid table rituals and blows.

Gerda Boyesen was the eldest of four siblings. After her came two brothers and a sister. This role of the eldest of four shaped her: care for others and a great feeling of responsibility for her loved ones counted amongst her most prominent characteristics. Her family background foresaw the role of the women as that of caring for the children, and laid little value on female intellectual development. Gerda's intellectual gifts were however recognized early. She was an exceptional pupil and read both avidly and widely. A well meaning doctor, who once examined her as a child recommended much sport and movement outside the house as a remedy to the studiousness of the young girl. Gerda solved the dilemma presented by the ban on reading in the house in that she climbed a tree in the garden to read in secret.

Altogether, the sons and heirs seem to have received a great deal more attention, encouragement and attention than Gerda.

Aged seven, Gerda contracted colitis, an inflammation of the intestinal tract. In the same year, her youngest sister was born, for whom the father had a particular affection. He regarded her as the "prettier" and "attractiver" of the two sisters, whilst the young Gerda possessed the role of the "intellectual." As Gerda said herself, the fatherly austerity and narcissistic slights arising from of the favouring of the sons and her sister was for Gerda a great source of sadness for many years. As a teenager and young woman she was shy, virtuous and insecure.

Aged nine, the family moved to Oslo. Financially things became a little tighter, as the father proved himself to be less enterprising as previously. Aged 19, Gerda married the five year older Carl Boyesen, the son of one of the richest men in Oslo. Carl Boyesen earned his living as an extremely successful composer of Norwegian hit music. Three years later, in 1944, Gerda's first daughter, Ebba was born, and shortly afterwards, in 1945, the second daughter Mona Lisa. The girls were followed in 1948 by her son Paul.

Gerda was not suited to being a housewife. Aged 25, she made a self-diagnosis of a obsessive compulsive disorder and after short consideration, began to study psychology. She visited the theologian and psychoanalyst Ola Raknes (who had studied further under Wilhelm Reich during his Oslo period, 1934-39, in order to become a vegetotherapist) for therapy. Further therapies followed. However, the meeting with Raknes and his analytically influenced and body-oriented therapy style was to influence Gerda's life decisively. She took her diploma as clinical psychologist and completed her training as a physiotherapist. Additionally, she received instruction in massage techniques from Aadel Bülow-Hansen, who at that time co-operated closely with the renowned psychoanalyst T. Braatoy. From Bülow-Hansen she learnt that it was possible to break up the vegetative basis of the neurosis through treating the body directly with massage. After initial experience in diverse clinics, she opened her own practice in Oslo, which went very well. Her exceptional professional competence proved itself in that she held for a while the position of the chief psychologists at Oslo's university clinic.

Gerda Boyesen saw herself as a scientist, and her entire professional and therapeutic career was indeed accompanied by sizeable scientific interests. Against the backdrop of strong resistance from her family and the established professional psychologists and doctors, she devoted herself to her subject, posed questions and wanted to get to the bottom of matters. She was especially fascinated by the connections between the body and soul, which seemed obvious to her in her own work and her own therapeutic experience. The previously little-researched field of the constitutional relationship between the physiology and the state of the soul became her central topic of research.

Although her insights often fell on deaf ears or were met with mocking or pitying laughter, she continued to be highly creative, original and fruitful in her chosen field. Independently and autonomously from Reich, she re-discovered much of what he had already described.

Moreover, we owe to her many techniques and terms which have helped us to understand how to heal the soul via the body. The discovery of a mellow, corporeal, self-regulating mechanism located in the bowel which she named psychoperistalsis is surely just one of her exceptional contributions to the doctrine of psychosomatics. I am sure that these related insights and techniques will take their deserving place within any medical science worthy of this name.

This path was not made easy for Gerda. The chasm between the demands of her husband and family for a representative and adapted female, and Gerda's independent spirit, her urge to research and her enjoyment of her therapeutic work became ever greater, and in the end was not to be bridged. It culminated in a divorce from Carl and in 1968/69 a move to London, where Raknes had offered her the opportunity to take over his practice. London was to become her residence and new home for the rest of her life.

Gerda's daringness and trust showed itself most clearly at this decisive point in her life. With very little money, she took on a completely new start in a country, the language of which she had little command. But she was at the right place at the right time. It seemed as if though London had just been waiting for her. As the only Reichian therapist, she quickly had overwhelming success. She exercised great influence on the neo-Reichian founder generation such as Pierrakos, Boadella, Brown, Stattmann, Liss and others and in turn received impulses from them. Her bio-dynamic psychology developed explosively. She also trained her children in the discipline, who soon became colleagues and collaborators who began to formulate their own creative points of view. Supported by her children, in a creative field of reciprocal inspiration, in the early 1970s, Gerda began to impart her own experiences, insights and techniques in instruction groups. Already at the beginning of the 1980s, under Gerda's leadership, the family Boyesen supervised about 30 instruction groups with often more than 20 participants in not only Europe, but the whole world.

How was this possible ? What was so special about Gerda Boyesen ? I mean that she was unique because she was granted the ability to make the uniformity of the living process with its energetic, corporeal, emotional, intellectual and spiritual aspects, immediately experiencable for everyone who came into contact with her. One could feel that one was complete, and that life pulsed autonomously in a way that the intellect could not grasp. Under her hands, or lead from a friendly "let it come" the unconscious was no longer an interesting phantasm of Freud: it was directly perceptible in one's own body, it became alive and moved independently, without that the conscious understanding had either planned or deliberately evoked it.

As her patient, one knew that one was liked and could marvel at the development of the spontaneous body-soul process, in which one was gripped and moved in one's personhood. Her presence, her charisma, her touch, her economical and precisely employed voice did one good. She was a mistress in creating an atmosphere of trust in which one could be unconditionally who one is. Courageous and un-shocked, she allowed her patients his or her experience in their inner chaos, and accompanied people, without judgement, in their Dionysian self, their body tremors approaching madness, animalist aspirations and abysses of the soul. She was able to do this, I think, because her strong faith and knowledge, that the beautiful, healthy, and salutary aspects of man would assert themselves and that everything would turn out for the best. Thus she was able to accompany people in their most august apollonian moments, leading to their inner bliss and ecstasy and share the experience of the wonderful with them. Nietzsche would have liked Gerda very much.

Gerda Boyesen loved her work, and one could feel it. She worked a lot and avidly, sometimes 14 hours a day. She understood how to combine human warmth and sincerity with professional abstinence and neutrality. The basic principles of her work were humanity, love, tolerance, no judgement, no criticism. Gerda practiced this attitude long before the calls for a "user friendly" therapy of esteem, as is practiced in contemporary psychoanalytical self-psychology. She did this long before Grawe's neuro-psychotherapeutic insights, which encourage psychotherapists to an open and explicitly warm hearted friendly and optimistic bearing, and much longer before ever-louder calls for a stronger resource orientation in therapy. She worked towards healing the body and soul of her patients, not just alleviation of the symptoms. She hated therapists who made the patient responsible for breakdown or failure of the treatment, who arrogantly placed themselves above their patients and who thought themselves to be better informed as to where they had to go. She never tired of attacking pseudo-therapeutic pushing and the practice of pressure and compulsion in therapy, as being harmful instruments for the establishment of a secondary casing in the formation of neuroses in the patient. She regarded it as a great privilege, to be able to help others and exhorted her pupils and colleagues to humility and gratitude.

Gerda's life was dedicated entirely to her bio-dynamic. She left us 25 essays and lectures and 4 books, in which she described the development of her thought in close connection with her biography. She sought little communication with representatives of other therapy directions outside body psychotherapy. Never-the-less, she regarded herself as standing in the tradition of Freud, Jung and Reich. She once said, "we are standing on the shoulders of giants."

Of the three, she probably stood closest to her great predecessor Wilhelm Reich. Like Reich, she placed unconditional trust in the healing and constructive power of body-soul self-regulation. Like Reich, she believed in the operation in humans of a life energy, and dedicated her life to the study of this energy. Like Reich, she believed in freedom, healing and happiness as attainable goals of human endeavour. She shared Reich's optimistic conception of man and believed in the basic fairness and goodness in the essence of man. Like Reich, she believed in the spiritual meaningfulness of organic, bio-energetic life movements. And like Reich, she researched far outside the borders of orthodox scientific research in the search for the constitution of the cosmic energy.

With Jung she shared the bonds of a deep spirituality, the belief in synchronicity, and the meaning of the archetypal power in the human unconscious. An English spiritualist medium even reassured her that Jung was her "spiritual leader" and lead and inspired her, what she received with initial scepticism, but then later willingly believed.

She borrowed Freud's model of psychological instances and the idea of psycho-sexual stages of development. Her basal therapeutic stance of the conscious non-intervention, the "let it happen" to which she encouraged her patients, reminds us of Freud's stance of the equitable and freely floating attention. However, her therapeutic programme was also in part diametrically opposed to Freud. To Freud's demand "where the "Id" is, the "I" should become" which he raised because he did not have great confidence in the unconscious, Gerda set up the trusting parole "where the "I" is, the "Id" must appear." Whilst the faustic Freud pleaded for the establishment of and consolidation of the "I-dam" against the destructive surge and clamour of the unconsciousness, Gerda Boyesen was animated by the idea of making the solidified and hardened "I" fluid once again, so that a better, more consistent synthesis of the personality parts can grow up within the newly free flowing life movement. Where Freud aimed in his edit at the healing affect of talking, Gerda warned against the "trap of words" and placed her trust more in the immediacy and authenticity of the body which can not lie.

One could almost say that she was joined to the psychoanalysis in a particular love-hate relationship. She never tired of castigating the Freudian process (and others) for its overemphasis of the intellectual and its body-distance, the interpretive arrogance and alleged ineffectiveness. On the other hand, she spoke with pride that her particular bio-dynamical work techniques facilitated a quazi "psychoanalysis of the body."

In 1980 Gerda married again, this time the American author Dan Smith, who remained her husband until her death. The distance to the extreme hype around the great Gerda Boyesen, which intermittently enabled her existence as the simple Mrs Smith was sometimes a welcome relief. But the retreat into private anonymity was not her thing. Even when she had exceeded the age of 80, she wanted to work and sought contact with her public.

Gerda Boyesen left behind her a rich quarry of original and creative ideas. Her writings resemble a treasure chamber, with many hidden pearls, which are yet to be appreciated and the value of which is yet to be discovered. The recognition of the established therapy circles remains denied to her, as with body psychotherapy in general, even though in her last publication, Gerda celebrated the discovery of the enteric nerve system, found in the intestine: the so called "stomach brain" as a late scientific appreciation and validation of her central psychoperistaltic concept.

And how could recognition from established therapeutic associations have been possible! She believed in the primacy of the body in overcoming psychiatric problems and trusted in the treatment of the body as the decisive psychotherapeutic technique. Gerda believed in the presiding of a cosmic energy and practiced aura techniques with immense sensitivity and intuition, guided by clear, self-developed theories. She believed in reincarnation and in the illumination-driven spirituality of the body. She believed in long-distance healing and radionics, which she also practiced. She believed in the medial communicable messages and inspiration from spirit beings.

Gerda's world was a world of miracles, the world behind the mirror, in which everything is augmented with magical significance. If you read her books, you can find formulations like "everything succeeded just like in a fairy story". In a tone of surprised amazement she reported exceptional events and unexpected assistance. Gerda loved to tell stories and she had many astonishing stories to tell. Gerda's world was that of exceptional synchronicities, close catastrophes, and the un-hoped for turns of fate and un-heard of and grandiose experiences. A few examples should suffice: barely arrived in London, with 400 English pounds on the stock exchange, she had 100 patients. Naturally, it was Sean Connery who called on her in order to offer to sell her his house. Of course it was a French Chateau in picturesque Burgundy in which the Boyesen family business was located for a short while. Of course she once made her arrival at the now legendary yearly summer retreats in this castle in a golden Rolls Royce. Of course she received a flat in Monaco by sheer chance. And her countless short case summaries often read like miracle cures. Yet she could also see the marvellous in the small and unimposing. Many of her stories told of apparently everyday events in which she was able to perceive bodily and psychodynamic connections which remained hidden to other less brilliant spirits. And she told her stories in a simple yet picturesque language. I was fascinated by her gift for beautiful, sensual body-near conception during her theoretical descriptions. Her theoretical concepts were just as full of awareness, truth, and precision as her touch.

I owe Gerda Boyesen a lot and am happy to have known her. Eleanor Roosevelt once said: "The future belongs to those who believe in the beauty of their dreams." The future belongs to you, Gerda.

One of Gerda's most important principles was that every therapy appointment should have a happy end. Although her last years were affected by serious illness, her adventurous, creative and full life was granted its happy end. Her daughter Ebba, who lovingly cared for and accompanied Gerda during the years in the hospital, reports that Gerda Boyesen consummated the passage to another dimension peacefully and in a blissful moment of letting go. In the presence of her granddaughter Vivia and in the protective arms of her daughter Ebba Boyesen, who sung a Tibetan mantra for her, Gerda Boyesen completed her journey through life on the late evening of the 29.12.2005.

Revisiting Gerda Boyesen's Theory of Psychoperistalsis

Carlien van Heel

Introduction

This article is based on my presentation at the 2nd Biodynamic Conference in London on 16 November 2014, entitled: "Revisiting Gerda Boyesen's Theory of Psychoperistalsis". My understanding of Boyesen's theory of psychoperistalsis has since deepened. I have added information on its significance in psychotherapy and the emphasis and layout of the material that was presented at the conference (section 2 and 3), has changed considerably.

This article has three sections. Section 1 will be descriptive. I will explain what psychoperistalsis is, why psychoperistalsis is important in psychotherapy and describe how we apply the theory of psychoperistalsis in Biodynamic psychotherapy and Biodynamic massage. This material was not presented at the conference. In section 2, I will present Boyesen's physiological and neurological understanding of psychoperistalsis. I have chosen 7 principles that underpin her theory of psychoperistalsis and I will link these principles to biological facts and current neuro-logical and physiological theories that, in my opinion, support her discovery.

The seven principles are:

1. Intestines are involved with emotional processes.
2. Peristaltic movement in the intestines is not only triggered by the presence of food.
3. Emotions move in the walls of the intestines.
4. Blocked emotions create not only muscle and respiratory tension and a thickening of connective tissue, but also stasis in the intestinal walls.
5. We can track or guide emotional processing through listening and following psychoperistaltic sounds.
6. Peristaltic movement can release internal pressure and help release a whole repression pattern in body and mind. The release allows a cleansing of body tissues.
7. When body tissues are cleared we can feel fluid streamings[1], which contributes to a sense of well-being.

The third part will describe Gerda Boyesen's professional development and the steps that led to her discovery of psychoperistalsis. There are footnotes for those not familiar with the terminology. I would like to thank Clover Southwell for her help with both the content and the editing of part 1.

1 Streamings - little rippling, tingling pleasure sensations within the body (Boyesen,1982).

The intestines and food digestion

There is great interest in which food and supplements support the digestive process in order to promote health and well-being and a lot of important research has been done. The right nutrition can help us recover from illness and support us in living healthier lives. I would like to clarify, however, that food consumption and the intestinal flora are not part of Boyesen's focus and therefore not part of this article. Boyesen's interest lies with the peristaltic movements of the intestinal walls and their link to the release of emotions and stress.

Part 1 What is psychoperistalsis?

Why is it significant in psychotherapy, what is its role in emotional processing and how do we work with psychoperistalsis in Biodynamic psychotherapy and massage?

1.1. What is Psychoperistalsis?

Gerda Boyesen (1922–2005) was a Norwegian psychologist and physiotherapist and the founder of Biodynamic psychotherapy and Biodynamic massage. She coined the word 'Psychoperistalsis' to describe the role intestinal peristaltic movements play in emotional processing. She discovered that the alimentary canal (the tubular passage of the digestive system) is involved in <u>every</u> emotion and stress experience. Boyesen found that, by listening to the sounds of the intestinal peristaltic movements, she could influence and stimulate the processing of these emotions, not only on a mental level, but also deep down in the tissues of the body. Boyesen felt that she had discovered the missing link between psyche and soma.

1.2. Why is psychoperistalsis significant in psychotherapy?

- In listening to peristaltic movements in the intestines we link to the underlying vegetative processes[2]. These are the processes that keep us alive; they make us grow and develop and ensure that our bodies heal when injured. We are hardly aware of these inner pulsations - the neural, hormonal and chemical exchanges, the fluid movements, the food digestion, the heart beating - yet these processes are fundamental

2 Vegetative processes - Life processes that are not subject to conscious control, like hear-beat, circulation, food digestion, hormone release, metabolic processes in cells. (Stauffer, 2005) 'Vegetative' is the Germanic word used by Wilhelm Reich and it is applied in most body psychotherapy traditions. In Anglo-Saxon literature the word 'autonomic' processes is used. (Heller, 2012).

to our existence. We are slightly more conscious of our breathing and can, to some extent, influence our breath. However, breathing will happen whether we direct it or not. It can be humbling and re-assuring to feel that life goes on no matter what we feel or think.

- In giving importance to the underlying vegetative processes and life force[3], we connect to a level of humanity that we all share, regardless of age, gender, race, skin colour, sexual orientation, religion, nationality, intelligence or wealth. Our childhood and life experiences can support or hamper this life force, but the inner design to grow and develop is in all of us.
- Intestinal peristaltic movements become active when the need for action or focus has passed. Peristaltic sounds herald and are part of the resting and integration phase, when body tissues get cleansed and the internal hormonal and chemical household gets back to homeostasis[4]. Gerda Boyesen found that the cleansing of body tissues eventually brought an amazing quality of fluidity and lightness to the body, something she called 'pleasure streamings'. Children often feel these pleasure streamings, but most adults have lost touch with this inner connection to spontaneity and aliveness. We can, however as adults, get to feel the underlying life force through our experience of streamings, once our body tissues are sufficiently cleansed. Boyesen discovered that this had far-reaching consequences. Through experiencing the streamings, we gain access to intuitive and essential levels that link us to all of humanity and beyond. She called this state 'The Primary Personality'[5]. Boyesen saw the reconnection to our essence[6] and 'Primary Personality' as the ultimate goal in psychotherapy and in life.

Gerda Boyesen found, in the peristaltic movement of the intestinal walls, a built-in recovery system. Psychoperistalsis is an accessible key to the whole autonomic, vegetative system. Not only could she track peristaltic movements through the stethoscope, she discovered that, through attuned attention and touch, she could influence the movements. By finding 'the key to opening the peristalsis', she could stimulate the parasympathetic process of release, cleansing and integration. She came to realise the huge importance of the cleansing and integration phase in psychotherapy. Cleansing of the body tissues, by our lymph vessels and veins, enables the digestion of mental and emotional stress. Clear tissues facilitate libido[7] flow throughout the body and these pleasure

7 Libido - a Freudian term used to describe a force that organises all of the dynamics of the organism and pushes it to maximise its pleasure in general and sexual pleasure in particular. (Heller, 2012).

sensations are the basis of our inner sense of happiness.[8]

[9]Cleansing takes place after the need for action has subsided. The cleansing process is governed by the parasympathetic branch[10] of the Autonomic Nervous System[11], which also stimulates psychoperistalsis. For more information on the physiological processes see part 2.

1.3. The role of psychoperistalsis in emotional processing

1.3.1. Boyesen's concept of the Emotional or Vasomotoric Cycle

Gerda Boyesen saw that each emotion goes through a cycle of arousal and wind-ing down. Each emotion involves myriad vegetative processes. Boyesen's core concept of the Vasomotoric or Emotional cycle describes an emotional impulse or response as happening on 3 levels: mental, physical (muscles) and vegetative. The three levels of the cycle correspond to the three embryonic layers: ectoderm – mental (brain, nervous systems, skin), mesoderm – muscles, (muscles, bones, connective tissue, blood and lymph vessels) and endoderm – vegetative (organs), from which our whole being develops. The three layers interlink and influence each other.

An emotional impulse or response, which is mediated by hormonal and/or neural processes (Damasio, 2004, 2000), will rise up in our body and mind and if it is allowed to be expressed or fully felt, then the emotion will subside and leave no traces. During the winding down process, which is governed by the parasympathetic branch of the Autonomic nervous system, our lymph vessels and veins, ideally, clear out the hormones and chemicals involved in the arousal. Our vegetative and muscular systems should revert back to an optimal state of homeostasis. In order for a full return to this optimal state of homeostasis to happen we might need to share the experience with a sympathetic friend or therapist so that we can fully integrate it. Eventually the whole experience should settle in our psyche and body. Boyesen called this

---

8 Autonomic Nervous System - the part of the nervous system that regulates individual organ function and homeostasis and, for the most part, is not subject to voluntary control (Stauffer, 2010).

9 Self-regulation – the ability to return to a state of inner balance and homeostasis.

10 Muscle armouring – the built up of chronic muscle tension that can lead to postural changes.

11 Vegetative tree - Boyesen's concept of the vegetative patterning of each uncompleted emotion all through the body. This patterning will always include stasis in the walls of the intestines. Releasing this stasis can free the whole vegetative patterning of a particular emotional event, and so complete an emotional cycle.

our built in self-regulation[12].

[13]If our expression or deeper acknowledgment is blocked then the cleansing process can't fully take place and the body makes a compromise. The emotional charge gets suppressed or deadened through muscle tension, which can lead to 'muscle armouring'[14], or, in some cases, muscle collapse (hypotonus). Our breathing may become limited and connective tissue thickens and encapsulates the charge (see part 2). Boyesen saw the encapsulating and clogged up connective tissue as 'Tissue armouring'. All this occurs way below our conscious awareness.

[15]This process of arousal and winding down is also applicable to daily stress and happens throughout the day. We may have to travel during rush hour or our boss might have been irritated with us. Life continually makes an impact on all aspects of our being. Sleep can be an opportunity for processing the stress and cleansing the tissues. However, often our pressured lifestyles give us little time to digest and clear our daily stress.

We all have many unfinished emotional and stress cycles in us, which will have left hormonal and chemical traces in our tissue as well as breathing and muscle constrictions. Unfinished emotional cycles are always waiting to complete. There is an innate movement towards completion, development and growth. Repressed emotions lie dormant, but once the right conditions are in place, an inner force will move towards completion of the Emotional cycle. This inner movement can also be released through massage.

The more traumatic the events we have experienced, the more protective repression patterns we will have to clear out. This can be a mammoth task and might not always be attainable. However, the ability to clear these patterns and re-connect with inner fluidity and therefore with the pleasure of being alive, is, in principle, part of our self-regulation mechanism and inherent in our biology.

Psychoperistaltic movements are part of the unwinding phase of the emotional

12 Therapeutic presence – an energetic resonance with the client, based on connection with life force energy, that generates and sustains the therapeutic process, far below interpersonal and transferential levels. (Southwell, 2007).

13 Essential and universal realm - realm that is experienced as connected to soul, spirituality.

14 Sympathetic arousal – arousal governed by the sympathetic branch part of the autonomic nervous system that takes over in fight-or-flight circumstances when an immediate and effective response is required.(Stauffer, 2010).

15 Embodiment – Being and feeling in one's body, aware of one's physical and physiological sensations cycle. The peristaltic sounds tell us that relaxation and clearing are taking place. Psychoperistalsis is therefore a valuable indicator of parasympathetic activity. Psychoperistalsis is an important part of our internal self-regulation system.

1.3.2. Boyesen's concept of the 'Vegetative tree'.

Boyesen came to realise that intestines are involved in every emotional cycle, in both the arousal and winding down process. The intestines are involved in the vegetative patterning in the body of each emotion (See part 2). A blocked emotion, therefore, not only creates muscle armouring, changes in breathing patterns and a thickening of connective tissue (Tissue armouring), it also creates a blocking, 'visceral armouring', in the walls of the intestines. Boyesen saw each emotion as one comprehensive vegetative patterning with 'branches' spreading all through the body. She called this the 'Vegetative tree'. [16]

A complex emotional pattern (vegetative tree) can release during a good psychotherapy session or a talk with an empathetic friend. Massage or movement can liberate this pattern by loosening muscles contractions or opening fluid blocks in connective tissue. There are several ways that can stimulate this full release – talking, laughing, being creative, music, dancing, sex, movement, exercise, relaxation, meditation, massage etc. However, in order for the 'vegetative tree' patterning to completely dissolve it will have to involve intestinal peristaltic movement which frees the fluid stasis, related to this particular pattern, in the walls of the intestines. In Biodynamic psychotherapy we are mindful to release all the three levels of the Emotional Cycle, so that the emotion or stress experience can move fully through and the whole 'vegetative tree' stasis in body and mind gets cleared and cleansed. In Biodynamic massage we can stimulate the psychoperistalsis more directly and can potentially unlock the unravelling of the 'vegetative tree'.

The cleansing of the body will bring relief and, eventually, a sense of embodiment and inner connection to oneself and to life as a whole.

1.4. How we apply our understanding of psychoperistalsis in Biodynamic practice.

1.4.1. Psychoperistalsis in Biodynamic massage

The clearest demonstration of Gerda Boyesen's theory of psychoperistalsis

16 Affective neuroscience – the study of the neural mechanisms of emotion. This interdisciplinary field combines neuroscience with the psychological study of personality, emotion and mood. (Wikipedia).

takes place during a Biodynamic massage session. We use the different psychoperistalt-ic sounds to guide the massage. We listen to the sounds by placing a microphone directly on our client's lower abdomen so that the tummy rumblings will be amplified through an electronic stethoscope. Practitioner and client can both hear the amplified sounds. The old fashioned stethoscopes, the ones Gerda Boyesen used, had to be placed directly in the therapist's ears.

In Biodynamic massage we are also guided by our other senses; particularly touch, as well as our energetic attunement and therapeutic presence. Our intention may be to give our client a sense of grounding and strength through softening or energising their muscles, or we may want to offer emotional support through our touch. Sometimes, we aim to help our clients sink into a deeper essential and universal realm. At these times we may have the peristaltic sounds going on in the background, but the sounds now are no longer of prime importance. The focus on the peristaltic sounds usually returns at the end of the massage when the person is resting on their left side. In this position the psycho-peristaltic sounds tend to come more easily and the client is then able to digest the impact of the massage.

We let the peristaltic sounds guide our work when we want to initiate para-sympathetic activity and cleansing of the tissues. As most of us have pressured lives where we are constantly switched 'on', in a state of sympathetic arousal, we can aim to 'tip' our clients' vegetative system into a parasympathetic state of relaxation and integration.

We can also follow the sounds in order to unlock an uncompleted emotional cycle. This may release a whole 'vegetative tree' patterning. The client will likely re-experience the previously suppressed emotional arousal and, this time round, may be helped to find a satisfactory completion.

1.4.1.1. Variety of Psychoperistaltic sounds

We can hear a wide variety of peristaltic sounds through the stethoscope. Watery sounds like babbling brooks or fast moving rivers; dry knocking sounds or the sound of dry pebbles tumbling down; sounds of creaky old doors starting to open, roaring lions, or the sounds of whistling winds. Tummy rumbling sounds can be assertive and flowing or hesitant and shy. In her article "Working with the stethoscope" (1996), Clover Southwell writes about a peristaltic sound that doesn't properly engage as 'skidding'. We won't follow these 'skidding' sounds, and will try to bring out sounds that are more connected and engaged.

Boyesen discovered that the flowing watery sounds indicated that the internal pressure in the body tissues was ripe for release. Emotional repression or too much stress can create an internal pressure. The dryer 'knocking' or 'creaky old door' sounds would indicate that a new layer of repressed emotional process was starting to surface. This could potentially increase the internal emotional pressure. By listening to and following these sounds, Boyesen was able to guide the therapeutic process. She could either encourage harmonisation by following the watery sounds which release pressure or she could choose to provoke and encourage repressed emotional material to surface by focussing on the dryer sounds. Boyesen would generally work with what was ripe for release (watery sounds), the layer that was closest to consciousness, so that the client would be able to integrate and process their emotions.

Clover Southwell gives lovely descriptions of how peristaltic sounds can be used to guide a process in her article "Working with the stethoscope" (1996).

> "With practice we learn that the belly sounds come as a very specific response to what our hands are doing in the massage. For instance, we move a hand slowly down a person's shin; at a precise moment, as our hands pass a precise spot, we hear a sound in the stethoscope, showing us that this particular spot in the body is now ready to discharge – change. Our next stroke can work precisely on the responding spot, to 'find' more sounds" (Southwell, 1996, pg1)

> "Apart from the fascination of the variety in the sounds, their precision is equally exciting. By paying attention to exactly which millimetre of the client is responding, and at exactly what depth, and to exactly what sort of touch, in which direction, we can go on an amazing energy dance with our client. When Mona Lisa Boyesen was working this way with me as a client, I used to feel perfectly 'tuned' by the end of a session, all harmony and sweet vibrations one week, all balanced strength and structure another week." (Southwell, 1996,p.2)

As described above, we carry different layers of repressed or blocked emotional processes in our body. Once we have cleared one layer and the watery sounds have emptied away, dryer knocking sounds might indicate that a new layer of repressed emotion is now getting ready to be worked with.

Not every massage will produce psychoperistaltic sounds. Sometimes, when clients are not very connected to their body and their self-regulation is impaired, it can take a few sessions, before the peristaltic sounds respond. Sometimes clients have too much stress, anxiety or grief in their lives and fear overwhelm if they let go. We then offer support for as long as it takes and try to find gentle ways of encouraging release.

I combine Biodynamic psychotherapy and massage in my own practice. My clients tend to come for regular weekly sessions and have busy daily lives. Alongside a psychotherapeutic process of gaining trust, awareness and insights, I use my understanding of psychoperistalsis and massage to help encourage cleansing, reconnection with one's sense of self and embodiment. This tends to be a gradual process. Now and then I might unlock a suppressed emotional cycle in the massage, which can then get worked through and integrated.

Gerda Boyesen was a master at unlocking uncompleted emotional processes. She could use the psychoperistaltic sounds in a very precise way. Her sessions often had a strong impact, helping a person to relive old emotional experiences in order to find a more positive outcome. Boyesen saw her clients mainly for short term block therapy or would work with people in (training) group settings, so strong impactful sessions were appropriate.

Below is an example from a presentation given by Gerda Boyesen at a conference in Vienna in 1997. It shows how Gerda Boyesen was searching for the opening of the psychoperistalsis and how the release of the peristaltic sounds enabled the whole vegetative anxiety pattern to dissolve.

The term Vegetotherapy relates to a Biodynamic method whereby the client is encouraged to feel and follow bodily sensations and impulses that are related to repressed emotions. The client often re-experiences the repressed event and is helped to find a more fruitful outcome to the old situation. This then allows a completion of the emotional cycle. Hormonal traces of the previously blocked emotion can now be cleared, connective tissue becomes more fluid and pulsation resumes. Vegetotherapy mainly happens lying down on a mattress, but is also possible in a chair or standing up. It generally does not involve direct touch, but here Gerda Boyesen completes the vegetotherapy session with massage.

> "A young woman who had worked with me in a deep regressive vegetotherapy on a mattress had experienced being in the bath with her mother when she was one and a half years old. She had fallen into the water and almost drowned when her mother went to answer the telephone. She was rescued but the experience left her with a lot of fear, which had come up during vegetotherapy. She still had tremendous fears and anxieties as the session neared its end. I searched for psycho-peristalsis but there was none. It was difficult to find the key to open it. Finally,

I found it. It turned out to be in the aura of the nose. When I worked there strong psycho-peristalsis came and she exclaimed:" Now I feel good and all my fear has gone". (Boyesen, 'Biodynamic psychotherapy and the Intestinal brain', Transcript of a talk at conference in Vienna, celebrating the centenary of Wilhelm Reich, 1997)

1.4.2. Psychoperistalsis in Biodynamic psychotherapy

In Biodynamic psychotherapy we don't work directly with the different psycho-peristaltic sounds. However, we are aware of the three levels of the Emotional or Vasomotoric cycle: the vegetative, muscles and mind levels and keep in mind the concept of self-regulation and the importance of completing and digesting an emotional process or stressful event.

During sessions we are attentive to arousal and relaxation states in our client and in ourselves. We are mindful of any word, gesture or breath impulse that brings a change. We regard these subtle movements as at least as important as the content of what the client says.

We consider a session where our client feels great as a session well spent, as we are tuned in to all the vegetative processes that are going on inside. We are not just looking for problematic issues.

We aim to create a space and opportunity for our client's inner subconscious intelligence to guide the process. The Biodynamic view is that there is a life force movement (based on vegetative processes) that will always try to move towards healing and fulfilment of one's potential. Our job is to help the client to trust this life force movement and to help them to align to it.

Familiarity with their own psychoperistaltic responses to their emotional states, makes clients more aware of their vegetative processes and their link to an organic inner intelligence.

The clearer we are, the more we can be in touch with this inner guiding force and the more we will feel present and fulfilled in our life.

1.4.3. Psycho-peristalsis as a self-regulation tool for psychotherapists

Psychotherapy sessions can be intense experiences for the psychotherapist. We are often witnessing enormous pain and struggle and this will, of course, have an impact on us. It is very important that we have time to process and digest these experiences and having awareness of one's own psychoperistalsis is a valuable tool. It helps us keep in balance. For myself, I notice that I can release mental or physical tension by opening my psychoperistalsis through relaxation, gentle stretching or self-massage.

I have dear memories of seeing Gerda Boyesen resting between sessions, stethoscope in her ears, crime novel in her hands, listening to her own psychoperistaltic sounds. She would 'digest' the impact of the previous session, so that she could remain in touch with her libido streamings and be refreshed for her next client.

Part 2 Boyesen's physiological and neurological basis of psychoperistalsis

Gerda Boyesen presented her work and theories in articles, but was reluctant to share her understanding of the physiology of her theories in much detail as her findings had not been taken seriously in Norway. Her daughter, Mona Lisa Boyesen, took it upon herself to present Boyesen's physiological theories in a series of articles entitled Psycho-peristalsis: Parts I – VIII, and in a later series of articles called Foundation for Biodynamic Psychology: Parts I – II. These articles were first published in the 1970's in 'Energy and Character', the Journal for Bio-energetic research', edited by David Boadella and in the 'Collected papers of Biodynamic Psychology', Volumes 1 and 2' (1978/1980). These are internal publications.

When Gerda and Mona Lisa Boyesen presented their physiological theories on psychoperistalsis, little was known about the Enteric Nervous System in the intestinal walls and about the important role of connective tissue in metabolic processing and encapsulating emotional charge. Since the 1970's and 1980's huge advances have been made in neuroscience, particularly in affective neuroscience, which looks at the neurology of emotions and at the impact of emotional trauma on brain and neural functioning.

I have chosen 7 principles that underpin Boyesen's concept of psychoperistalsis and I will link these principles to current theories and understanding that, in my opinion, support Boyesen's explanation of the role of psychoperistalsis in emotional processing.

The seven principles are:

1. The intestines are involved with emotional processes.
2. Peristaltic movement in the intestines is not only triggered by the presence of food.
3. Emotions move in the walls of the intestines
4. Blocked emotions create not only muscle and respiratory tension and a thickening of connective tissue but also stasis in the intestinal walls.
5. We can track or guide emotional processing through listening and following psychoperistaltic sounds.
6. Peristaltic movement can release internal pressure and help release a whole repression pattern in body and mind. The release allows a cleansing of body tissues
7. When body tissues are cleared we can feel fluid streamings, which contributes to a sense of well-being.

1. The intestines are involved with emotional processes.

Gerda Boyesen discovered the link between emotions and vegetative processes while she worked in the Aadel Bulow Hansen clinic. She writes in her book "Entre Psyche et Soma" (1985):

> "When we repress an emotion, we also inhibit the vegetative discharge". (Boyesen, 1985, p.32, French ed.p.39)

She realises that vegetative discharge is more fundamental to emotional processing than emotional release and discovers that Psychoperistalsis is an accessible key to the whole autonomic, vegetative system.

> "It seemed very clear to me that it was possible to dissolve neurosis right to its core, without encouraging crying or emotional release during the treatment. This is not to say that emotional discharge is not important, but it is not always necessary". (Boyesen, 1985, p. 34, French ed.p.41)

The intestines

Our digestive system, the ability to take in nutrients and expel waste products, is one of the most fundamental systems of the body. The digestive tube (endoderm layer) together with the neural tube (ectoderm layer) is the earliest of the embryonic organ developments, starting just 3 weeks after conception.

Nerve supply to the intestines

The intestines, more than any other organ in the body, have a huge nerve supply, similar to the brain. The intestines are connected to the rest of the body through 3 nerve supply systems.

1. The Vagus nerve, a hugely important cranial nerve connecting the intestines directly to the brain stem.
2. A range of Peripheral nerves that come out from the spine.
3. Its own Enteric Nervous System: a complete nervous system that can function independently from the brain. The ENS is embedded in the lining of the intestines.

When Boyesen wrote about her theories, information about the Enteric Nervous System was not yet published. Michael D. Gershon, M.D. (1998) author of 'The Second Brain - Your gut has a mind of its own' was one of the first people to write about the Enteric Nervous System as the gut's own independent nervous system.

Gershon states:

> "We have more nerve cells in our gut than in the entire remainder of our peripheral nervous system. The enteric nervous system is also a vast chemical warehouse within which is represented every one of the classes of neurotransmitter found in the brain. Neurotransmitters are the words nerve cells use for communicating with one another and with the cells under their control. The multiplicity of neurotransmitters in the bowel suggests that the language spoken by the cells of the enteric nervous system is rich and brain-like in its complexity. Neuroscientists, whose horizon ends at the holes in the skull, are continually amazed to find that the structure and component cells of the enteric nervous system are more akin to those of the brain than to those of any other peripheral organ." (Gershon, M.D., 1998, The Second Brain, p. xiii)

I would like to point out that in the above quote Gershon refers to the Enteric Nervous System and its vast chemical warehouse. There is also nerve supply to and from the intestines via the Vagus nerve and the Peripheral nerves. The nerve supply to and from the intestines and, subsequently, its connection to whatever is going on elsewhere in the body or brain is vast.

Neuroscientists like Antonio Damasio (2000, 2004, 2010) have shown that emotions are, in essence, neural and hormonal communications to the brain.

The neural connection in the walls of the intestines, as well as the nerves to and from the intestines suggest that it is highly likely that intestines are involved in emotional processes. (see also point 3)

Walter B. Cannon, professor of physiology of Harvard University was the first person to use Rontgen rays to study the movements of the intestines at the beginning of the 20th century. He describes in his book "The mechanical factors of digestion" (1911) how emotional disturbances in the animals he researched would stop the intestinal movements.

> "Even slight psychic disturbances were accompanied by stoppage of peristalsis". (Cannon, W, 1911, The mechanical factors of digestion, p.218)

Gerda Boyesen had similarly found that the peristaltic movements responded to her thoughts and emotions. (See part 3)

2. Peristaltic movement in the intestines is not only triggered by the presence of food.

There is evidence that there is a movement in the intestines that is not related to the breaking up or the movement of food down along the lumen.

<u>What creates movement in the intestines?</u>

1. Movement of fluid from inside the small and large intestines. The final breaking down of food happens in the small intestines. The blood circulation then picks up the nutrients through the walls of the small intestines and transports them throughout the body. In the large intestines the residual fluid is extracted in order to compact the non-digestible matter (faeces). This process is chemically mediated. No peristaltic movement is necessary for this process
2. A. Peristaltic movement that makes food move down along the lumen (the inside) of the gut. Different segments contract and fluid squirts in both directions. This is what we can hear.
   B. Peristaltic movement can happen without needing to be stimulated by the presence of food. This movement happens typically every hour, when relaxed. The Alimentary canal has its own pulse. (Stauffer, 2005, 2010; Gershon 1998; Cannon, 1911)

Point 2B is the movement we talk about when we talk about Psycho-peristalsis. This gut movement is not directly 'set off' by food digestion, but can, of course, involve food digestion. It is still not fully understood what stimulates this movement and to what purpose.

The peristaltic movements are controlled by the ENS and are also coordinated by direct cell-to-cell communication between smooth muscle cells. (Stauffer, 2010, p123). This cell-to-cell communication might be the same or an addition to what Gershon calls inter-neuron communication in the ENS (Gershon, 1998, p45)

Boyesen found support for her theory of psycho-peristalsis when she came across an article, published in Tidskrift Norske Laegeforen, 1964 by a Norwegian scientist and researcher Professor Johannes Setekleiv. Setekleiv discovered that fluid distension pressure in the lining of the walls of the guts could set of the second form of peristaltic movement. Setekleiv talked about the membrane potential of smooth muscle cells in the lining of the gut needing to be within, what he called, a certain 'zone of firing' in order to produce peristaltic movements. Overextension due to too much fluid pressure would render the smooth musculature hypotonic. The hypotonus in the smooth muscles prevents the intestines from bursting under too much pressure, a very useful way of neutralising an excess of inner emotional pressure. The smooth muscles go slack and peristaltic contractions are not possible anymore. Seitekleiv's theory of fluid pressure in the walls of the intestines fitted beautifully with Boyesen's theory of fluid stasis and visceral armouring in the alimentary canal.

Dr Michael Gershon describes how the neurotransmitter Serotonin, stimulates peristaltic movement. Serotonin is a neurotransmitter that contributes to feelings of wellbeing.

> "All the agreement about how serotonin starts peristaltic reflexes has been very gratifying.... Recently, moreover, serotonin's ability to initiate peristaltic reflexes has been a model that investigators are finding is applicable to other reflexes as well." (Gershon, M., 1998, the Second brain, p. 215)

Gershon's observation that serotonin release stimulates peristaltic movement makes me wonder whether massage, which is often pleasurable for the body, can stimulate serotonin production. We already know that attuned touch can stimulate the release of oxytocin, another well-being chemical. (Moberg, Kerstin Uvnas, 2011, 2013) The same might be true for serotonin. The majority of serotonin is created in the intestines.

"At the moment, there are more serotonin receptors in the gut than there are known functions of serotonin. Clearly, we still have no idea of what most of the enteric receptors for serotonin are doing." (Gershon,M. 1998, the Second brain, p.209)

3. ***Emotions move in the walls of the intestines.***

I have explained in point 1 that the intestines are very likely involved with everything that is going on elsewhere in the body and the brain, due to its huge nerve supply and that the Enteric Nervous system is embedded in the walls of the intestines.

Neuroscientist Antonio Damasio describes in his books 'Looking for Spinoza' and 'The Feeling of What Happens', what emotions are and where our sense of self comes from. Emotions are neural and hormonal communications to the brain and are part of homeostatic regulation. This is how life is organised, from simple single cell organism to complex organisms with brains like we humans have. All forms of life are geared towards survival.

There are several levels and each higher level incorporates the lower levels. The first level is a single cell organism. It consumes food, creates energy for movement and growth and disposes of waste products. Emotions are messages to the brain at a higher and more complex level and feelings are even more complex. Feelings create context around an emotion, by creating a particular mapping in the cerebral cortex of the brain. This gives us the chance to have choice about how to react to our initial emotional responses.

Damasio sees all these neural and hormonal messages as coming up from the depth of the body. He is not specific about emotions coming up the walls of the intestines, but the intestines are a very large organ (about 7 meters long) in the depth of the body cavity, travelling from the anus up to the mouth. He portrays the different levels of homeostatic regulation like an interconnecting 'tree'.

Damasio's 'tree' - levels of automated homeostatic regulation

Feelings

Social emotions
Emotions proper
Background emotions

Drives and motivations

Pain/Pleasure behaviours

Immune responses, basic reflexes, metabolic regulation

Level 5	Feelings - ability to create context around emotions
Level 4	Social emotions - (sympathy, embarrassment, shame, guilt, pride, jealousy, envy, gratitude, admiration, indignation, and contempt.) Emotions proper - (fear, anger, disgust, surprise, sadness, happiness) Background emotions - (feeling good, bad, somewhere in between)
Level 3	Drives and motivations (hunger, thirst, curiosity, exploration, play and sex). **The Libido drive is part of this level**
Level 2	Pain/Pleasure behaviours - withdrawing, contraction when pain, Reaching towards and expansion when pleasure.
Level 1	Every organism is geared towards survival, consuming food, creating energy for movement and growth and disposal of waste products.

(Damasio, 2003, pp.32, 37, 45)

Boyesen noticed, during her work in the Aadel Bulow Hansen clinic, that patients who had strong vegetative releases, like diarrhea or vomiting or strong emotional releases like sobbing and crying, would recover quicker from emotional distress. She was aware that we mainly express our emotions through our voice, the top end of the alimentary canal, while diarrhea happens at the other end of the alimentary tract. (see part 3)

Gerda Boyesen's idea that emotions travel up the walls of the intestines, as well as travelling up to the brain from other parts of the body, and being part of emotional patterning ('vegetative tree') seems to me very feasible.

4. Blocked emotions create not only muscle and respiratory tension and a thickening of connective tissue, but also pressure in the intestinal walls.

2.4.1. Muscle tension

Kathrin Stauffer (2010) gives a good description of how emotional process gets locked in by the muscles in the body.

"Again, the simplest way of thinking about muscles tension is to see it as embodying a conflict. Part of me wants to make a particular movement; another part of me wants to stop that movement. The muscles that would make the movement tense in the attempt, and the muscles that prevent the movement tense as well: the result is immobility in the corresponding part of the body. The great Wilhelm Reich (1933/1972) saw this as a basic mechanism of neurosis formation, because it fulfils all the requirements of a defence: It embodies the original desire as well as the inhibition, creates a layer of inactivated tissue around the tensed-up muscles, and at the same time binds large amounts of physical energy (required to hold all the tension in the muscles), which in turn decreases the anxiety provoked by the conflict " (Stauffer, K., 2010, Anatomy and Physiology for psychotherapists, p. 92)

Muscles and connective tissue are important in the process of repression. They hold back the emotional impulse. Chronic muscle tension can become muscle armouring, which can lead to postural changes in the body.

In addition, there will be a restriction in breathing (muscle contraction of inter-costal muscles and skeletal muscles involved in breathing) in order to hold down the emotional impulse. Shock will create a startle reflex pattern where the in-breath is held. Connective tissue holds the charged fluid by going fibrous.

2.4.2. How does connective tissue get blocked (Tissue armour)?

When there is an emotional updrift or stress, there is an activation of nerves sending signals to certain muscles to get ready for action as well as an increase of blood supply. The sympathetic nervous charge and hormones, like adrenaline, tighten the blood vessels to increase the blood pressure to the areas that need to be prepared for action. The extra blood supply fills the tissues around those particular muscles. If there is a conflict, expression or action will be blocked. The muscle tension can't be released (see Stauffer quote above) and the hormonal fluid that has swamped the area now gets stuck too. As well as fluid pressure, there are associated uncomfortable emotions that are difficult to bear. Our body therefore tries to deaden the area, so that we won't remain aware of these feelings. This blocking and deadening creates stagnation. Without pulsation or movement the lymph vessels and veins cannot clear the area and the fluid and hormonal and chemical remnants stay stuck in the connective tissue. The connective tissue initially becomes swollen with the fluid, but eventually will become more fibrous in order to bind the charge and fluid. This further hampers the cleansing process of the lymph vessels and veins.

2.4.3. Fluid stasis in the Intestinal walls

The walls of the intestines have 4 layers

1. The peritoneum is a layer of connective tissue that surrounds the outside of the guts.
2. The middle layer consists of two layers of smooth muscles. The long-itudinal muscles and the round muscles. Both these types of muscles are involuntary and influenced by the Autonomic Nervous System. They create the peristaltic movement. As described above, these smooth muscles can go hypotonic, if the fluid pressure is too intense and there is a risk of the walls bursting. This lack of tonus inhibits peristaltic move-ment.
3. The Submucosa is another layer of connective tissue, in which all the arteries, nerves (ENS), veins and lymph vessels are embedded.
4. The fourth layer is the lining of the guts (lumen). This is where nutrients are taken up by the blood circulation.

The surface of the lining of the guts has lots of folds, packing an incredible amount of surface area into a relatively small space. Michael Gershon says:

> "The surface of the small intestines is huge. Its area is magnified by a structure in which the surface folds, folds again, and then folds once more."
>
> The intestinal surface area is amplified by the structural folding to such an extent that the surface membrane of a centimetre of human intestine is enough to cover a doubles tennis court." (Gershon, M.1998,

The Second Brain, p.140)

The inside of the intestinal walls cover an incredibly large surface.

I find it interesting that the arteries, veins, lymph vessels and enteric nerves are all embedded in the submucosa layer, which is a layer of connective tissue. As I will expand on in point 6, connective tissue can switch from fibrous collagen to liquid fluid (gel to sol) and vice versa. When there is stasis in the walls of the intestines, I imagine the submucosa layer to go fibrous, to encapsulate the fluid and the emotional charge.

5. We can track and guide emotional processing through listening and following psycho-peristaltic sounds.

Tracking emotional processing in psychotherapy. Brain scans.

In psychotherapy, we try to help clients process and assimilate emotional experiences that they previously couldn't integrate. Thanks to neuroscience, we now know that psychotherapy helps build new neural pathways and maps in the cerebral cortex. (Damasio, 2000, 2004; Shore, 2003; Siegel, 2011) Brain-scans can shine light on how psychotherapy works. This re-wiring and re-mapping in the brain helps to create a different context around feelings. The next time a painful or scary feeling gets triggered, it might not be quite so entrenched and we may have tools to handle it better. This inner change is reflected by new neural pathways and maps in one's brain, and this can be seen in brain scans.

In Biodynamic psychotherapy we don't only focus on the brain, we focus equally on changes in the body. As everything is integrated, a different mapping in the brain will influence the physiology of the body just as changes in the body physiology will influence the brain.

Psycho-peristalsis as a tracking device

Boyesen saw the muscles as part of our conscious control, as they are controlled by our voluntary nervous system. We can consciously decide to move. The vegetative processes are controlled by our Autonomic Nervous System and are therefore outside of our conscious control and can be linked to unconscious processes. Chemicals and fluids are our basic internal make up, the undercurrent that influences all. Changes to these fluid movements, neural patterns or chemical releases will change how we feel.

Kathrin Stauffer says in her article 'On Peristalsis'

> "So if we want to communicate with a person's unconscious mind, one way of doing it is to communicate with their autonomic or spontaneous, physical processes. If, as a result of such communication, the way the fluids and chemicals move around my body changes, be it ever so slightly, I will have a profoundly different felt sense of myself and of the way I respond to a situation." (Stauffer, K., 2005, On Peristalsis, p1.)

Stauffer continues:

> "So if we want to work with these deeper unconscious layers of our souls, it makes sense to devise ways of following autonomic processes in the body. We like to speak of 'tracking' a process – that is, following one or several autonomic variables (say, skin colour or temperature, intestinal activity, or heartbeat) as a means of following what is happening in the soul of the person." (Stauffer, K., 2005, On Peristalsis, p2.)

Stauffer describes psycho-peristalsis as a useful tool for tracking our autonomic responses, i.e. our deeper unconscious layers. Psycho-peristalsis is only active when it is safe, when there is no need for a flight or fight response. It is an indicator of parasympathetic activity.

Boyesen became aware of how peristaltic movements respond to thoughts, moods and emotions. (See part 3). Peristaltic waves are therefore not just involuntary automatic processes; they are also influenced by emotional states. By following the sounds we can guide a therapeutic process.

Gerda Boyesen's concept of the 'vegetative tree' suggests that a change in the peristaltic movement, as an indicator of physiological changes, can, potentially, change other areas of the body that are related to a particular stress experience or emotional repression.

6. Peristaltic movement can release internal pressure and help release a whole repression pattern in body and mind.

Gerda Boyesen discovered, through observing her own and her patients processes, that by changing the fluid pressure in the walls of the intestines, through psycho-peristalsis, she could unlock and unravel an emotional process. Peristaltic movement releases fluid stasis in the connective tissue of the walls of the intestines. If this fluid stasis is linked to the repression of an emotional process then releasing the stasis in the walls of the intestines can potentially release the repression elsewhere.

The role of Psychoperistalsis in the clearing of emotional processes and the cleansing of tissues

I have shown in point 4 how a blocked emotion causes fluid stasis in the connec-tive tissue. This fluid stasis is full of hormonal and chemical substances that now cannot get taken up by lymph and veins, as the whole area has become stagnant. Lymph vessels and veins need movement or pulsation to be able to do their job. The lymph vessels and veins should constantly be clearing the basic metabolic waste products, expelled by cells, regardless of emotional charge. So all this cleansing is now restricted. Connective tissue will start to encapsulate the fluid so that it can contain the fluid and numb the emotional charge, which inhibits movement and pulsation even further.

There is a fluid form of connective tissue that surrounds all cells. This fluid form of connective tissue is called interstitial or intercellular tissue. It links each cell with blood supply. Arteries branch out into smaller capillaries, but not all of the capillaries can reach all of the cells. The exchange of oxygen and nutrients and clearing of waste products therefore happens in this intercellular tissue space. (see image) This process is called diffusion – nutrient rich blood passes through the walls of the capillaries into the intercellular fluid and these nutrients and oxygen are then absorbed through the cell membranes into the cell. In the same way, waste products are expelled by the cells into this intercellular fluid and are then taken up by lymph vessels and veins. If the area is deadened or restricted due to stress or emotional blocking, this whole exchange is hampered. Intercellular fluid is the fluid form of connective tissue.

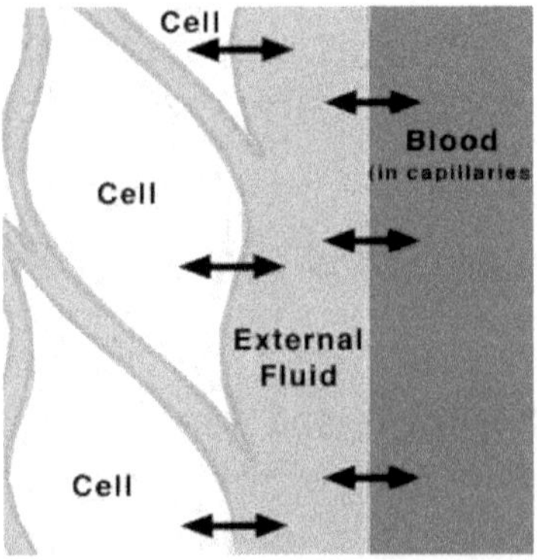

Picture of blood and cell (from James Goldberg Organelles Project on Liquid Bio Wiki)

When we massage or exercise we bring movement into the area again, which will bring it back to life. Unless the conflict is still active, the connective tissue will return to fluid and now the cleansing process can restart. Old fluid and hormonal waste products are absorbed through the lymph vessels and the veins and cell pulsation is re-established. The tissue can get cleansed and basic cell pulsation can resume.

Connective tissue

In his book 'Job's body' (1987), Dean Juhan gives an excellent description of the changeable qualities of connective tissue.

> "A transparent fluid ground substance is found to one degree or another in all of the body's connective tissues, and it may be thought of as the basis for the production of all their other forms. This viscous liquid, much like raw egg whites in appearance and consistency, surrounds all the cells in the body, and is part of the internal ocean". (Juhan, D. 1987, Job's body, p.64)

Connective tissue however exists not just in fluid form. It can have different consistencies. Connective tissue is everywhere in the body. Until recently, when scientists dissected a body, they would cut out all the connective tissue and what would be left to investigate would be muscles and bones. Now with 3D imaging, we can appreciate how huge the connective tissue network is. Connective tissue connects everything. When Boyesen wrote her theories, the extent of the connective tissue network and its ability to change texture had not yet been fully understood.

> "Just beneath the skin it forms an envelope that wraps the body as a whole. Beneath its outer layer it organizes the muscles into functional groups, wraps each individual muscle, and also honeycombs the interior of the muscle belly with supporting septa. It gathers the ends of the muscles into tendons, and tendons blend into the fibrous sheath that covers the bones, the periosteum; the periosteum is continuous with the ligaments, and even with the inner coating of the hollow bones, the endosteum." (Juhan, D., 1987, Job's body p.75)

> "Connective tissue binds other specific tissues into their organ shapes and supplies them with vessels and ducts. It ties these organs together, and suspends them in their proper relationships in the body cavities. It forms the walls of the blood and lymph vessels, it surrounds these vessels and it anchors them into place among the muscles, bones and organs. It anchors the nerves in the same fashion." (Juhan, D, 1987, Job's body p.75).

> "In short, connective tissue constitutes the immediate environment of every cell in the body, wrapping and uniting all structures with its moist, fibrous cohering sheets and strands". (Juhan, 1987, Job's body p.76)

The network of Connective tissue all through our body supports Boyesen's concept of the 'vegetative tree'. Not only are the intestines connected to everywhere through the huge nerve supply, they are also connected to everywhere and everything through the connective tissue network. Connective tissue is a like a spider web throughout the body. If you pull one corner it will affect the other areas.

> "The connective tissue fluid is produced in specialised cells called fibroblasts. Fibroblasts also produce the long white fibres of collagen. These tough strands give all the organs and other tissues its shape, resilience and strength. The fibres can be arranged in any kind of way. The fibres themselves are not living and have no nucleus. The fibroblasts cells can travel quickly through the whole body and play a key element in wound healing. (Juhan, 1987)

Connective tissue and Thixotropy

> Connective tissue can change consistency and can take on varying degrees of fluidity, The process of consistency change from viscosity to fluidity, and vice versa, is called thixotropy. Thick tough fibres can soften and become more porous. (Juhan, 1987)

The opposite effect can also happen whereby connective tissue glues more and more together, by collagen fibres linking together in what is called hydrogen bonds. It is these ever tighter hydrogen bonds that create stiffness. This is also how connective tissue encapsulates emotional charge.

Due to the Thixotropic nature of connective tissue, movement and touch can have a big impact on the quality, permeability and fluidity of connective tissue. Connective tissue can also be influenced by energy fields.

> "This thixotropic effect provides one of the cornerstones for effective bodywork. Since connective tissue is largely non-living, it is the mechanical motion and friction caused by muscular activity, which provides much of the energy and warmth that maintains its fluid qualities. When a part of the body loses some degree of movement and vitality through trauma or disuse, it will not be as inviting, as comfort-able, perhaps not even as possible to move that part with the vigor it requires to keep the connective tissue warm, moist, and resilient". (Juhan, 1987, p.69)

Connective tissue and the cleansing of the tissues.

It is clear that a lot of chemical activity goes on in the interstitial/intercellular fluid through the diffusion process of nutrients and waste products, passing from blood vessels to tissue cells and back again, and due to hormonal and chemical remnants that have been brought there to get tissue ready for action or expression. As this intercellular fluid is part of connective tissue and connective tissue is a network of fluid and fibres all through our body, the change from tough fibres to fluidity will increase the nourishment of cells and the cleansing process in that area. It is very likely to influence a shift in the consistency of connective tissue elsewhere too. Once the cleansing can resume our whole body chemistry will work better, which will result in an overall feeling of well-being and lightness.

The emotional stasis in the intestinal walls is held by the connective tissue layer (submucosa). It makes sense to me to think that peristaltic movement will soften this connective tissue layer and this new fluidity will stimulate the cleansing of the submucosa layer. This will influence both the nerves in there, as well as bring movement to other areas of connective tissue elsewhere in the body.

7. When body tissues are cleared we can feel fluid streamings, which contributes to a sense of well-being.

Boyesen found, through her personal experience and through work with her patients, that as bodies became more fluid and cleansed, people would experience pleasure sensations throughout their body. She felt that these streamings were connected to the movement of libido, the inner life force and called them libido streamings. She realised that these libido streamings were part of our basic human condition. Most adults have lost touch with the connection to our libido force. Boyesen linked the losing touch with the libido force, to the development of neurosis, which deadens and blocks our body tissues and therefore inhibits cell pulsation and fluidity. Her therapeutic aim was to reestablish this inner connection to the life force streamings. She discovered that these libido streamings gave not only an inner sense of pleasure and harmony, but would also stimulate creativity, love and a deeper sense of meaning and connection to all of life. She called this being in touch with one's 'Primary personality'.

> "By the Primary Personality, I mean a person who does not withdraw or encapsulate their Life Energy and its associated "streamings" — the little rippling, tingling sensations within the body that tell us we are alive; a

process that usually happens during childhood. It is a person who is in touch with his or her "libido" circulation; the pleasure that is derived from being in one's environment and obtained from participation in any situation; and who will not betray this in themselves or deny it for themselves or others. There is a natural joy in life, a euphoria that is also practical and pragmatic. It is grounded. (Boyesen, G. 1982, The Primary Personality,p4, article in Journal of Biodynamic Psychology, no. 3, winter, 1982)

I imagine the experience of 'streamings' to be linked to a free flow of fluids through the cells and tissues. A cleansing process that can be stimulated by the movement of psycho-peristalsis.

Movement therapist like Emily Conrad (Continuum concept) and Bonnie Bainbridge Cohen (Body Mind Centering) discovered the same principles through their movement practices. (Conrad, 2007 ; Bainbridge Cohen, 2008) They followed the same organic vegetative movements in the body, as Boyesen did through following psycho-peristalsis. Yoga practices, and energetic movements like Tai chi and Qigong follow very similar principles. The deeper we follow the life pulsation movements and the autonomic, vegetative processes, the closer we will get to optimal metabolic processing, cleansed pulsating tissues and pleasure streamings.

Boyesen put these vegetative streamings into the context of psychotherapy, linking body and mind in its fullest sense.

Part 3 Gerda Boyesen's professional journey and how she discovered psychoperistalsis

3.1. Boyesen's professional development

Gerda Boyesen (1922-2005) lived in Norway until 1969. She was married and had three children, all of whom have become body psychotherapists in their own right[17]. Boyesen studied psychology and worked as a psychologist in a psychiatric hospital in Oslo. She was in Reichian training analysis with Ola Raknes, a student of Wilhelm Reich. Boyesen also trained as a physiotherapist

17 Ebba Boyesen, Mona Lisa Boyesen and Paul Boyesen were Gerda Boyesen's colleagues and are all accomplished body psychotherapists and international trainers. Ebba and Mona Lisa Boyesen are directors of ESBPE – Europaische Schule fur Biodynamische Psychologie in Germany. Paul Boyesen is the founder of Psycho-Organic Analysis in France.

and treated psychiatric patients with specialised neuro-muscular techniques, in the Aadel Bulow Hansen clinic. The Aadel Bulow Hansen clinic was linked to the psychiatric practice of Dr. Trygve Braatoy. Braatoy was also a student of Wilhelm Reich and of Otto Fenichel. Reich had lived in Norway between 1934 and 1939 and his Norwegian students influenced Boyesen's professional development. Boyesen combined psychotherapy and massage in her own private practice.

Gerda Boyesen came to London in 1969 and was welcomed into the thriving therapy community as a neo-Reichian therapist. She met John Pierrakos, David Boadella and Jay Stattman and included some of their techniques in her therapeutic approach. Boyesen's clinical work expanded into teaching and she established her own form of Body psychotherapy, which she called Biodynamic psychotherapy. She opened a training centre in West London and people from all over the world came to train with her. She taught Biodynamic psychotherapy all over Europe and continued to teach until her death in 2005.

I will now describe how Gerda Boyesen developed her concept of psychoperistalsis. Boyesen developed most of her theories while living in Norway, by closely observing her own and her patient's processes.

3.2. Boyesen's discovery of the concept of psychoperistalsis

The neuro-muscular treatments at the Aadel Bulow Hansen clinic had a strong effect on the patients. Boyesen became aware that patients who had vegetative discharges after the massages, like diarhea or vomiting or strong emotional reactions like screaming or sobbing, recovered quicker from emotional distress. Release through the mouth or anus, at both ends of the alimentary canal, seemed to aid the therapeutic process. Boyesen thought of talking therapy as a gentler form of release via the mouth and wondered whether there could be a gentler form of release at the other end of the alimentary canal. This was the first link she made between emotions and the intestinal tract.

Boyesen writes:

> "I knew that emotional material could be discharged at two levels: from above, in an ascending motion through the oral system, and from below, descending through the anal system. Since there were also two forms of discharge from the oral system – the strong, tearful form, and the gentle, verbal form – it seemed to me that the anal system must work in the same way. I was familiar with the strong form of descending, anal discharge – diarrhoea – but now I began to wonder

> what the corresponding gentle form of downward discharge might be. " (Boyesen, 1985, p.67, French ed. p.78)

Boyesen received the same neuro-muscular massages herself from Aadel Bulow Hansen and these massages provoked emotional processes in her too. She felt a strong internal pressure coming up the alimentary canal that was pushing for expression. For almost a year she felt the need to scream, but was not able to find the opportunity to do so. Then, one day, she felt an inner switch, thanks to a tummy rumbling, and the strong internal pressure suddenly turned into a pleasurable sensation. She understood that this inner switch was potentially an amazing therapeutic tool. The intestinal movement had released the internal emotional pressure.

Boyesen writes in her book:

> "First of all, this energy rose up through the emotional channel with an urge to find expression; when I was unable to express it, it went back down again, rippling down my body like a mild, warm breeze. While it was thrusting its way upwards, it could provoke screams and emotional discharges; but it could also reverse its direction into a harmonising, descending movement that dissolved the tension completely. This is how I discovered what I call the "fountain" or the "melting principle"". (Boyesen,G., 1985, Between Psyche and Soma, p. 69., French ed.p.80)

Boyesen then became aware, in her own and her patients' body, that once the muscles started to soften, fluid would accumulate in the connective tissue around the muscles. Boyesen's once beautifully shaped legs had swollen and no amount of Bulow Hansen massage could make the fluid stasis disappear. She decided to see Dr. John Olesen, a medical doctor in Copenhagen, who worked with fluid retention. Dr. Olesen emphasised the importance of the cleansing function of the veins and the lymphatic system. His hypothesis was that most somatic disorders were caused by a malfunction of the venous blood circulation, due to inadequacy of the vein pump. Veins and lymph vessels need movement to help facilitate the uptake of waste products. Dr. Olesen made the fluid stasis in Boyesen's legs disappear through working on the connective tissue which stimulated the lymph and venous uptake of waste products. His work greatly influenced Boyesen's later theories of tissue armour, visceral armour and the Vasomotoric or Emotional cycle.

Boyesen was now aware that apart from muscle armour, there could also be fluid blocks in the body (tissue armour) holding emotional charge. She developed massages that worked on connective tissue, like the membrane that envelops the muscle fibres. This is how she discovered psycho-peristalsis.

> "I now began working on the surface of the muscle membrane only. As I did so I noticed an intriguing phenomenon: quite loud gurgling noises - the sounds of peristalsis - could be heard from my patients' abdomens. Each time that I worked in this way, I now heard the same story: my patients told me how they clearly felt the inner pressure from which they were suffering diminishing during the massage, and, little by little, they felt their anxiety slipping away. Their psychosomatic ailments and muscular pain also disappeared, and they began to discover and delight in a new sensation: their bodies were filled with delicious feelings of pleasure and sweetness that seemed to flow through every single cell." (Boyesen, 1985, pp.65,66, French ed. p. 76,77)

There was a clear link between the release of fluid stasis and intestinal peristaltic movements.

Boyesen became more and more intrigued and discovered that she could listen to peristaltic sounds with the use of a stethoscope. From then on she didn't stop exploring what influenced the sounds. She discovered that emotions and states of mind would influence the peristaltic movements.

> "Though the peristaltic waves were sensitive to interference, they only reacted to disturbances in my emotions. Demands, anticipation, insecurity, ambivalence - these all broke the flow of the waves, whereas neutral disturbances such as traffic noise, the radio, unfamiliar voices and so on did not " (Boyesen, 1985, p.77, French ed.p.88)

As the sounds were clearly influenced by emotional states Boyesen called these peristaltic movements – 'Psychoperistalsis'.

Boyesen realised that by listening to the peristaltic sounds she could monitor whether the massage was getting too provocative for her patients and, if so, she could adjust her technique and work for harmonisation rather than provocation. The psychoperistalsis would provide her with feedback and made her very accomplished at fine-tuning her treatments.

> "This discovery made my work with my patients much easier; now I

could regulate my massage to produce a more dynamic or more gentle effect. My technique became extremely precise, as I learned how I could lead my patients' awareness into deeper layers, or simply dissolve the layers that were "ripe" and closest to the ego. Working in this way, guided by the peristaltic sounds (to which I later gave the name of "psycho-peristalsis"), I could also treat cases of depression and hysteria which we were not allowed to treat with Aadel Bulow-Hansen's methods. But with my new massage method I could simply choose how deep I wanted the effects of my work to go." (Boyesen, 1985, p.70, French ed. p.81)

Conclusion

Gerda Boyesen devised, in Biodynamic psychotherapy and Biodynamic massage, a therapeutic modality that is closely aligned to organic life processes in body and psyche. There is simplicity to her methods, as the focus is on allowing and supporting these natural life force movements, yet her work is also rich and complex. Her theories can be hard to explain. I hope that this article manages to convey the therapeutic value of a core aspect of her work, namely psychoperistalsis. I believe that the new discoveries in neuroscience and physiology offer valuable explanations as to why psychoperistalsis can be seen as an important tool in psychotherapy and healing. A tool that Gerda Boyesen understood deeply and was able to apply with great skill.

Carlien van Heel, April 2015

Bainbridge Cohen, Bonnie. 2008. Sensing, Feeling & Action. Northampton, MA: Contact Editions.

Boyesen, Gerda. 1980. The Primary Personality and it's Relationship to the Streamings, 11-20, The Collected Papers. London: Biodynamic Psychology Publications

Boyesen, Gerda. 1980. Psycho-peristalsis Part III: A Case History Of A Manic Depressive, 45-54. The Collected Papers. London: Biodynamic Psychology Publications.

Boyesen, Gerda. 1982. The Primary Personality. Journal of Biodynamic Psychology, 3-8 (Ed. Young, C). London: Biodynamic Psychology Publications.

Boyesen, Gerda. 1982. The Dynamic Of Psychosomatics. Journal of Biodynamic Psychology, 55-72 (Ed. Courtney Young).

Boyesen, Gerda. 1985. Entre Psyché Et Soma. Paris: Payot.

Boyesen, Gerda, 1997, Biodynamic psychotherapy and the intestinal brain, transcript of presentation given at conference of centenary of Wilhelm Reich, Vienna

Boyesen, Mona-Lisa. 1980. Psycho-peristalsis: The Abdominal Discharge Of Nervous Tension, 21-32, The Collected Papers. London: Biodynamic Psychology Publications.

Boyesen, Mona Lisa, 1980. Psycho-peristalsis Part II: Emotional Repression As A Somatic Compromise: Stages In The Physiology Of Neurosis, 33-44, The Collected Papers. London: Biodynamic Psychology Publications.

Boyesen, Mona-Lisa. 1980. Psycho-peristalsis Part IV: Dynamics Of The Vasomotor Cycle: Nuances Of Membrane Pathology According To Mental Condition, 55-67, The Collected Papers. London: Biodynamic Psychology Publications.

Boyesen, Mona-Lisa. 1980. Psycho-peristalsis Part V: Function Of The Libido Circulation, 68-75, The Collected Papers. London: Biodynamic Psychology Publications.

Boyesen, Mona-Lisa. 1980. Psycho-peristalsis Part VI: Bio-Physical Aspects Of Libido Circulation, 76-82, The Collected Papers. London: Biodynamic Psychology Publications.

Boyesen, Mona-Lisa. 1980. Psycho-peristalsis Part VII: From Libido Theory To Cosmic Energy, 83-92, The Collected Papers. London: Biodynamic Psychology Publications.

Boyesen, Mona-Lisa. 1980. Psycho-peristalsis Part VIII: Self-Regulation And The Streamings, 93-100, The Collected Papers. London: Biodynamic Psychology Publications.

Boyesen, Gerda and Boyesen, Mona-Lisa. 1980. Foundation For Bio-dynamic Psychology Part I: Spontaneous Movements And Visceral Armour, 123-132, The Collected Papers. London: Biodynamic Psychology Publications.
Boyesen, Gerda and Boyesen, Mona-Lisa. 1980. Foundation For Bio-dynamic Psychology Part II: Cries From The Guts, 133-140, The Collected Papers. London: Biodynamic Psychology Publications.

Cannon, Walter. B, 1911, The Mechanical Factors of Digestion, International Medical Monographs, general eds Dr Leonard Hill, F.R.S. and Dr. William Bulloch, Boston Massachusetts

Conrad, Emilie. 2007. Life On Land: The Story of Continuum. Berkeley,CA: North Atlantic Books.
Damasio, Anthony. 2004. Looking For Spinoza. London: Vintage, Random House.
Damasio, Anthony. 2000. The Feeling Of What Happens. London: Vintage, Random House.

Gershon, Michael. 1998. The Second Brain: Your Gut Has A Mind Of It's Own. 2nd ed. New York: Harper.

Heller, Michael C. 2012. Body Psychotherapy: History, Concepts,Methods. New York: W.W. Norton.

Juhan, Deane. 1987. Job's Body: A Handbook For Bodywork. New York: Station Hill.

Lee, Robyn, 1985, Tissue theory in relation to Biodynamic Massage, Transcript of theory talk, Sydney

Moberg, Kerstin Uvnäs. 2011. The Oxytocin Factor: Tapping The Hormone Of Calm, Love and Healing. London: Pinter and Martin Ltd.

Schore, Allan N. 2003. Affect Regulation And The Repair Of The Self. New York: Norton.

Setekklieiv, Johannes. 1980. The 'Spontaneous' Rhythmical Activity in Smooth Musculature, Journal of Biodynamic Psychology,72-82. (Ed. Iain St. John) London: Biodynamic Psychology Publications.

Siegel, Daniel. 2011. Mindsight: Transform Your Brain With The New Science Of Kindness. London: Oneworld

Southwell, Clover, 1982, Biodynamic massage as a therapeutic tool (Training material)
Southwell, Clover, 1996, Working with the stethoscope, (Training material)
Southwell, Clover. 2007. The Biodynamic Therapeutic Presence. (Training material)

Stauffer, Kathrin A. 2005 On Peristalsis (Training material)
Stauffer, Kathrin A. 2010. Anatomy And Physiology For Psychotherapists: Connecting Body And Soul. New York: Norton

Further Literature / Publications by and related to Gerda Boyesen
compiled by Dorian Boyesen

[Source: Wikipedia DE https://en.wikipedia.org/wiki/Gerda_Boyesen, 04.11.2021]

Publications

- Boyesen, Gerda; Boyesen, Mona Lisa, "Biodynamische Theorie und Praxis", in: Hilarion G. Petzold [Ed.], Die neuen Körpertherapien, 1st ed. Paderborn: Jungfermannsche Verlagsbuchhandlung, 1977, pp. 140-157

- Boyesen, Gerda; Boyesen, Mona Lisa, Biodynamik des Lebens: Die Gerda-Boyesen-Methode - Grundlage der biodynamischen Psychologie, Essen: Synthesis, 1987, 183 p.

- Boyesen, Gerda, Über den Körper die Seele heilen: Biodynamische Psychologie und Psychotherapie, Munich: Kösel, 1994 (7th ed.) ISBN 3-466-34167-1

- Boyesen, Gerda, Über den Körper die Seele heilen: Biodynamische Psychologie und Psychotherapie, Kiel: Boyesen Verlag, 2019 (1st ed.) ISBN 978-3-944225-02-9

- Boyesen, Gerda; Leudesdorff, Claudia; Santner, Christoph, Von der Lust am Heilen: Quintessenz meines Lebens, Munich: Kösel, 1995, ISBN 3-466-34323-2

- Boyesen, Gerda, Entre psyché et soma, Payot, 1996 ISBN 2-228-89064-2

- Boyesen, Gerda; Bergholz, Peter, Dein Bauch ist klüger als du, Hamburg, Miko-Edition, 2003 ISBN 3-935436-13-0

[Source: https://afkp.org/biodynamik-veroeffentlichungen, 04.11.2021]

80. Boyesen, Gerda, Boyesen, Mona Lisa (1977b): Foundations for Biodynamic Psychology Part I: Spontaneous Movements and Visceral Armour, in: Energy and Character, The Journal of Bioenergetic Research, Vol. 8, No. 1, 1977, S. 32-41, und in: Biodynamic Psychology: Collected Papers, 1 Aufl., London: GBI, 1980, S.123-132

81. Boyesen, Gerda, Boyesen, Mona Lisa (1977c): Foundation for Biodynamic Psychology Part II: Cries from the Guts, in: Energy and Character, The Journal of Bioenergetic Research, Vol. 8, No. 2, 1977, S. 62-69, und in: Biodynamic Psychology: Collected Papers, 1 Aufl., London: GBI, 1980, S.133-140

82. Boyesen, Gerda, Boyesen, Mona Lisa (1980): Biodynamic Theory of Neurosis, in: Ian St. John [Hrsg.], Journal of Biodynamic Psychology, No.1, London: Biodynamic Psychology Publications, S. 57-71

83. Boyesen, Gerda (o.J.): Physiatrie: Periostmassage, in: International Foundation for Biodynamic Psychology [Hrsg.], unveröffentlichtes Manuskript (Trainingspapier), 8 S.

84. Boyesen, Gerda (1981a): Appendix. Are we all survivors of cot death, in: Courtenay Young [Hrsg.], Journal of Biodynamic Psychology, No.2, London: Biodynamic Psychology Publications, 1981, S.103-108

85. Boyesen, Gerda (1981b): Introduction, in: Courtenay Young [Hrsg.], Journal of Biodynamic Psychology, No.2, London: Biodynamic Psychology Publications, 1981 , S.3

86. Boyesen, Gerda (1982a): Masochism, in: Courtenay Young [Hrsg.], Journal of Biodynamic Psychology, No.3, London: Biodynamic Psychology Publications, 1982, S.109-122

87. Boyesen, Gerda (1982b): The Dynamic of Psychosomatics, in: Courtenay Young [Hrsg.], Journal of Biodynamic Psychology, No.3, London: Biodynamic Psychology Publications, 1982, S. 55-72
• Boyesen, Gerda, Die Dynamik der Psychosomatik, in: Studientexte in Biodynamischer Psychologie II (Ausbildungstexte), La Salle: Gerda Boyesen Institute, 1984, 23 S. und in: David Boadella, Bernhard Maul [Hrsg.]: Energie & Charakter, Zeitschrift für Biosynthese - Somatische Psychotherapie, Vol. 27, Heft 14, 1996, S. 70-85

88. Boyesen, Gerda (1982c): The Primary Personality, in: Courtenay Young [Hrsg.], Journal of Biodynamic Psychology, No.3, 1. Aufl., London: Biodynamic Psychology Publications,1982, S. 3-8
• Boyesen, Gerda, Die Primärpersönlichkeit, in: Einführungstexte in Biodynamischer Psychologie (Ausbildungstexte), La Salle: Gerda Boyesen Institute, o. J., 7 S.

89. Boyesen, Gerda (1985a): Bio-electricity and psychosomatic symptoms. Vortrag vom 26.09.1985, unveröffentlichtes Vortragstransskript

90. Boyesen, Gerda (1985b): Prevention of neurosis. Vortrag vom 24.04.1985, unveröffentlichtes Vortragstransskript

91. Boyesen, Gerda (1985c): The aim of psychotherapy. Vortrag vom 28.02.1985, unveröffentlichtes Vortragstransskript

92. Boyesen, Gerda (1985d): Tragic and trivial levels in life and in psychotherapy. Vortrag vom 14.03.1985, unveröffentlichtes Vortragstransskript

93. Boyesen, Gerda (1985e) : Entre Psyche et Soma, 1. Aufl., Paris: Payot,

Boyesen, Gerda (1987a): Über den Körper die Seele heilen: Biodynamische Psychologie und Psychotherapie, München: Kösel, 197 S.

94. Boyesen, Gerda, Boyesen, Mona Lisa (1987): Biodynamik des Lebens: Die Gerda-Boyesen-Methode - Grundlage der biodynamischen Psychologie, Essen: Synthesis, 1987 , 183 S.

95. Boyesen, Gerda (1987b): Die Methode der biodynamischen Entspannung, in: Boyesen, Gerda und Mona-Lisa, Biodynamik des Lebens: Die Gerda-Boyesen-Methode - Grundlage der biodynamischen Psychologie, 1. Aufl., Essen: Synthesis, 1987, S.7-23 (geringfügig überarbeitete Fassung von 7)

96. Boyesen, Gerda (1987c): Transference in Biodynamic psychology. Interview mit Michael Heller am 14.11.1986, in: Adire, Nr. 2,3, 171-177

97. Boyesen, Gerda (1988): Über die Biodynamische Psychologie, in: Deutsche Gesellschaft für Biodynamische Psychologie [Hrsg.], DIALOG Biodynamische Psychologie, Zeitschrift für Biodynamische und Transformationelle Psychologie, Bd.1, Heft 1, Oldenburg: Transform, 1988, S. 32-40

98. Boyesen, Gerda (1995a): Interview mit Christian Bartuska. Über ihre Pläne, Gruppenarbeit, Aura, Übertragung, Nachnähren, und ozeanisches Gefühl. Gespräch vom 9.2.94 in Wien, in: Bartuska, Christian und Gabriele [Hrsg.]: Zeitschrift für Körperpsychotherapie, Bd. 1, Heft 2, 1995, S. 12-23,

99. Boyesen, Gerda (1995b): Interview mit Christian Bartuska II. Sie spricht über Mißbrauch, sexuelle Revolution, Übertragung und ihre eigene Therapie. Gespräch vom 9.2.94 in Wien, in: Bartuska, Christian und Gabriele [Hrsg.]: Zeitschrift für Körperpsychotherapie, Bd. 1, Heft 3, 1995, S. 16-29,

100. Boyesen, Gerda (1995c): Psychotherapie und Spiritualität, in: Zundel, Edith und Pieter Loomans [Hrsg.], Im Energiekreis des Lebendigen: Körperarbeit und spirituelle Erfahrung, 1. Aufl., Freiburg Basel Wien: Herder, 1995, S. 176-185

101. Boyesen, Gerda, Leudesdorff, Claudia, Santner, Christoph (1995): Von der Lust am Heilen, München: Kösel, 175 S.

102. Boyesen, Gerda (1996): Ein Aspekt in der Psychotherapie. Vortrag bei "The World of Psychotherapy", 1.st Congress of the World Council of Psychotherapy WCP, Wien, 30.6. – 4.7. 1996, Audiokasstte, Münsterschwarzach: Vier-Türme-Verlag

103. Boyesen, Gerda (1997a): Biodynamische Psychologie und Psychotherapie, in: Muths, Christa [Hrsg.]: espacio time, Lebendige Integration von Körper, Geist und Seele zum Erfahren des Seins., Jg. 3, Heft 1, 1997, S. 14-16

104. Boyesen, Gerda (1997b): Gerda Boyesen und Christa Muths im Gespräch, in: Muths, Christa [Hrsg.]: espacio time, Lebendige Integration von Körper, Geist und Seele zum Erfahren des Seins., Jg. 3, Heft 2, 1997, S. 16-19

105. Boyesen, Gerda (2000): Biodynamic psychotherapy and the intestinal brain, in: Energy and Character, International Journal of Biosynthesis, Vol. 30, No. 2, 22-28

106. Boyesen, Gerda (2001): Body Psychotherapy is a Psychotherapy, in: Heller, Michael (Hrsg., 2001): The flesh of the soul: The body we work with. Selected papers of the 7 th congress of the European Association of Body Psychotherapy , 33-43

107. Boyesen, Gerda, Bergholz, Peter (2003): Dein Bauch ist klüger als Du, Hamburg: Miko-Edition

108. Boyesen, Joelle (1991): Eros und Liebe in der therapeutischen Übertragung, in: Deutsche Gesellschaft für Biodynamische Psychologie [Hrsg.], DIALOG Biodynamische Psychologie, Zeitschrift für Biodynamische und Transformationelle Psychologie, Bd.3, Heft 1, Oldenburg: Transform , 61-82

109. Boyesen, Mona Lisa (1973): The basic trust, in: Energy and Character, The Journal of Bioenergetic Research, Vol. 4, No. 1, 1973 , S. 32

110. Boyesen, Mona Lisa (1974a): Psycho-peristalsis: The Abdominal Discharge of Nervous Tension, in: Energy and Character, The Journal of Bioenergetic Research, Vol. 5, No. 1, 1974, S. 5-16 , und in: Biodynamic Psychology: Collected Papers, 1 Aufl., London: GBI, 1980 , S.21-32
• Boyesen, Mona-Lisa, Psychoperistaltik I: Die Entladung nervöser Spannung über den Unterleib (nach Aufzeichnungen von Gerda Boyesen), in: Boyesen, Gerda und Mona-Lisa, Biodynamik des Lebens: Die Gerda-Boyesen-Methode - Grundlage der biodynamischen Psychologie, 1. Aufl., Essen: Synthesis, 1987 , S.43-61

111. Boyesen, Mona Lisa (1974b): Psycho-peristalsis Part II: Emotional Repression as a Somatic Compromise: Stages in the Psychology of Neurosis, in: Energy and Character, The Journal of Bioenergetic Research, Vol. 6, No. 3, 1974, S. 9-20, und in: Biodynamic Psychology: Collected Papers, 1 Aufl., London: GBI, 1980, S. 33-44
• Boyesen, Mona-Lisa, Psychoperistaltik II: Emotionale Unterdrückung als somatischer Kompromiß: Stadien der Physiologie der Neurose (nach Aufzeichnungen von Gerda Boyesen), in: Boyesen, Gerda und Mona-Lisa, Biodynamik des Lebens: Die Gerda-Boyesen-Methode - Grundlage der biodynamischen Psychologie, 1. Aufl., Essen: Synthesis, 1987, S. 63-82

112. Boyesen, Mona Lisa (1975a): Psycho-peristalsis Part IV: Dynamics of the Vasomotor Cycle: Nuances of a Membrane Pathology according to Mental Condition,

in: Energy and Character, The Journal of Bioenergetic Research, Vol. 6, No. 2, 1975, S. 45-59, und in: Biodynamic Psychology: Collected Papers, 1 Aufl., London: GBI, 1980, S. 55-67
• Boyesen, Mona-Lisa, Psychoperistaltik IV: Die Dynamik des vasomotorischen Zyklus (nach Aufzeichnungen von Gerda Boyesen), in: Boyesen, Gerda und Mona-Lisa, Biodynamik des Lebens: Die Gerda-Boyesen-Methode - Grundlage der biodynamischen Psychologie, 1. Aufl., Essen: Synthesis, 1987, S. 99-123

113. Boyesen, Mona Lisa (1975b): Psycho-peristalsis Part V: Function of the Libido Circulation, in: Energy and Character, The Journal of Bioenergetic Research, Vol. 6, No. 3, 1975, S. 61-68, und in: Biodynamic Psychology: Collected Papers, 1 Aufl., London: GBI, 1980 , S. 68-75
• Boyesen, Mona-Lisa, Psychoperistaltik V: Die Funktion der Libidozirkulation (nach Aufzeichnungen von Gerda Boyesen), in: Boyesen, Gerda und Mona-Lisa, Biodynamik des Lebens: Die Gerda-Boyesen-Methode - Grundlage der biodynamischen Psychologie, 1. Aufl., Essen: Synthesis, 1987, S. 125-137

114. Boyesen, Mona Lisa (1976a): Psycho-peristalsis Part VI: Biophysical Aspects of Libido Circulation, in: Energy and Character, The Journal of Bioenergetic Research, Vol. 7, No. 1, 1976, S. 31-37, und in: Biodynamic Psychology: Collected Papers, 1 Aufl., London: GBI, 1980, 76-82
• Boyesen, Mona-Lisa, Psychoperistaltik VI: Biophysische Aspekte der Libidozirkulation (nach Aufzeichnungen von Gerda Boyesen), in: Boyesen, Gerda und Mona-Lisa, Biodynamik des Lebens: Die Gerda-Boyesen-Methode - Grundlage der biodynamischen Psychologie, 1. Aufl., Essen: Synthesis, 139-151

115. Boyesen, Mona Lisa (1976b): Manuel de Bio-Release, in: unveröffentlichtes Manuskript (Trainingspapier), Ewijckshoeve: Institut de Psychologie Bio-dynamique, 45 S.

116. Boyesen, Mona Lisa (1976c) Psycho-peristalsis Part VII: From Libido Theory to Cosmic Energy, in: Energy and Character, The Journal of Bioenergetic Research, Vol. 7, No. 2, 1976, S. 38-47, und in: Biodynamic Psychology: Collected Papers, 1 Aufl., London: GBI, 1980, 83-92
• Boyesen, Mona-Lisa, Psychoperistaltik VII: Von der Libidotheorie zur kosmischen Energie (nach Aufzeichnungen von Gerda Boyesen), in: Boyesen, Gerda und Mona-Lisa, Biodynamik des Lebens: Die Gerda-Boyesen-Methode - Grundlage der biodynamischen Psychologie, 1. Aufl., Essen: Synthesis, 1987, S.153-169

117. Boyesen, Mona Lisa (1976d): Psycho-peristalsis Part VIII: Self Regulation and the Streamings, in: Energy and Character, The Journal of Bioenergetic Research, Vol. 7, No. 3, 1976, S. 40-47, und in: Biodynamic Psychology: Collected Papers, 1 Aufl., London: GBI, 1980, 93-100

• Boyesen, Mona-Lisa, Psychoperistaltik VIII: Die Selbstregulation und die Ströme (nach Aufzeichnungen von Gerda Boyesen), in: Boyesen, Gerda und Mona-Lisa, Biodynamik des Lebens: Die Gerda-Boyesen-Methode - Grundlage der biodynamischen Psychologie, 1. Aufl., Essen: Synthesis, 171-183

118. Boyesen, Mona Lisa, Orgonomy Massage: Four different approaches in biodynamic vegetotherapy, in: unveröffentlichtes Manuskript (Trainingspapier), o.J. , 2 S.

119. Boyesen, Mona Lisa (1977): Bio-Release, in: Energy and Character, The Journal of Bioenergetic Research, Vol. 8, No. 3, S. 66-69, und in: Biodynamic Psychology: Collected Papers, 1 Aufl., London: GBI, 141-144

120. Boyesen, Mona Lisa (1978): Bio-Release Part II: The Startle Reflex Pattern and Organic Equilibrium, in: Energy and Character, The Journal of Bioenergetic Research, Vol. 9, No. 2, 1978, S. 72-75, und in: Biodynamic Psychology: Collected Papers, 1 Aufl., London: GBI, 145-148

121. Boyesen, Mona Lisa (1979): Ausgewählte Texte in Biorelease (von dem Biorelease Handbuch), in: unveröffentlichtes Manuskript (Trainingspapier), La Salle: Biorelease Foundation, 61 S.

122. Boyesen, Mona Lisa, Intention (1980): in: International Foundation for Biodynamic Psychology [Hrsg.], unveröffentlichtes Manuskript (Trainingspapier), 1980 , 9 S.

123. Boyesen, Mona Lisa, Mobilisation (1981a): Mobilisation, harmonisation, vitalisation, in: International Foundation for Biodynamic Psychology [Hrsg.], unveröffentlichtes Manuskript (Trainingspapier), 4 S.

124. Boyesen, Mona Lisa (1981b): The Infant and the Alpha, in: Courtenay Young [Hrsg.], Journal of Biodynamic Psychology, No.2, London: Biodynamic Psychology Publications, 1981 , S. 60-102

125. Boyesen, Mona Lisa (1982a): Alpha Nursing in: Courtenay Young [Hrsg.], Journal of Biodynamic Psychology, No.3, London: Biodynamic Psychology Publications, 1982, S.151-154

126. Boyesen, Mona Lisa (1982b): Der Säugling im Alpha-Rhythmus, in: Rudi Scholz & Peter Schubert [Hrsg.]: Körpererfahrung, 1. Aufl., Reinbek bei Hamburg: Rowohlt, 1982 , S.254-288
• Auch in: David Boadella und Bernhard Maul [Hrsg.], Energie und Charakter, Zeitschrift für Biosynthese u. Somatische Psychotherapie, 26, Nr. 12, Berlin: Verlag Bernhard Maul, 1995, S. 31-61

127. Boyesen, Mona Lisa, Voet, Hanskim (1982): Biorelease Instructor Handbook, La Salle: International Foundation of Biodynamic Psychology, 1982, 58 S.

128. Boyesen, Mona Lisa (1985): Methoden und Ansätze in Biorelease und Biodynamik, in: unveröffentlichtes Manuskript (Trainingspapier), 1985, 2 S.

129. Boyesen, Mona Lisa (1986): Das Öffnen der Psychoperistaltik und die Verteilung der Energie durch Exitbereiche: Grundprinzipien der Psychoperistaltik-Behandlung mit dem Stethoskop, in: unveröffentlichtes Manuskript (Trainingspapier), 1986 , 4 S.

130. Boyesen, Mona Lisa, Gromann, Petra, Richter, Andreas (1987): Biorelease Handbuch - Teil 1: Grundlagen der Biorelease Methode, Altneudorf: Gerda Boyesen Institut, 1987, 30 S.

131. Boyesen, Mona Lisa, Voet, Hanskim (1987): Biorelease: Instruktoren-Handbuch, Hamburg: Gerda Boyesen Institut, 50 S.

132. Boyesen, Mona Lisa (1990):, Transfer and counter transfer between man and woman in the massage work, in: unveröffentlichtes Manuskript, S.1-13
• Boyesen, Mona Lisa (1990) Übertragung und Gegenübertragung zwischen Mann und Frau in der biodynamischen Massage, in: Deutsche Gesellschaft für Biodynamische Psychologie [Hrsg.], DIALOG Biodynamische Psychologie, Zeitschrift für Biodynamische und Transformationelle Psychologie, Bd.2, Heft 1, Oldenburg: Transform , S. 83-96

133. Boyesen, Mona Lisa (1995): Erogenetik: Neue Aspekte in der Biodynamischen Psychologie, in: Zundel, Edith und Pieter Loomans [Hrsg.], Im Energiekreis des Lebendigen: Körperarbeit und spirituelle Erfahrung, 1. Aufl., Freiburg Basel Wien: Herder, 1995, S.186-219

134. Boyesen, Mona Lisa (1996): Die vier Kategorien emotioneller Körpersymptome, unveröffentlichtes Trainingspapier, 5 S.

135. Boyesen, Mona Lisa (1997): Der erogenetische Aspekt der Libidodynamik, in: GBP e.V. (Hrsg., 1997): Biodynamische Arbeit mit Kindern. Beiträge der 1. Fachtagung der GBP in München, 8.-10.11.1996, S. 27-37, Ulm: Eigenverlag

136. Boyesen, Mona Lisa (1998): Das erogene Kind. Die Libidodynamik in der oralen Phase, in: GBP e.V. (Hrsg., 1998): Berührung. Sexualität. Missbrauch. Beiträge der 2. Fachtagung der Gesellschaft für Biodynamische Psychologie/Körperpsychotherapie (GBP e.V.) in Hamburg, 14.-16. November 1997, S. 29-58, Ulm: Eigenverlag

137. Boyesen, Mona Lisa (1999): Der Stammbaum des Wissens. (Erweiterte Ausgabe des Vortrages vom 15. 11. 1998), in: GBP e.V. (Hrsg., 1999): Kreativität- Transformation, Spiritualität. Beiträge der 3. Fachtagung der Gesellschaft für Biodynamische

Psychologie/ Körperpsychotherapie (GBP e.V.) in Köln 13.-15. November 1998, Köln: Eigenverlag, S. 109-152

138. Boyesen, Mona Lisa (2001): Frühstörungen und ihre körperlichen Auswirkungen, unveröffent lichtes Arbeitspapier, 5 S.

139. Mona Lisa Boyesen (2006): Der erogenetische Aspekt der Libidodynamik, in: Energie & Charakter, 37, 30, 52-59

140. Mona Lisa Boyesen (2009): Organische Selbstregulationaus der Sicht der Biodynamischen Psychologie, in: Thielen Manfred (Hrsg., 2009): Körper – Gefühl – Denken. Körperpsychotherapie und Selbstregulation, Gießen: Psychosozial Verlag, 103-112

141. Boyesen, Mona Lisa (2010): Die Erogenetik, in: GBP e.V. (Hrsg., 2010): Perlen des Lebens und Selbst-Wert-Schöpfung, Beiträge der 11. und 12. Fachtagungen, Stuttgart: Books on Demand, 11-32

142. Boyesen, Mona Lisa (2013): Blitzlicht über die Biografie der Biodynamik, in: GBP e.V. (Hrsg., 2013): Lust am Heilen – Lust am Leben, Beiträge der 15. Fachtagung, Norderstedt: Books on Demand, 9-19

143. Boyesen, Mona Lisa (2017): Das ödipale Rätsel, in: GBP e.V. (Hrsg., 2017): Eros und Psyche – oder die Entfaltung der Libido. Beiträge der 19. Fachtagung 2016 in Goslar, Norderstedt: Books on Demand, 102-112

144. Boyesen, Mona Lisa & Freudl, Peter (1999): Tiefenpsychologisch fundierte Biodynamische Körperpsychotherapie, in: Handbuch für ganzheitliche Therapie und Lebenshilfe, Gschwend: Verlag Drei Sterne, 34-38

145. Boyesen, Mona Lisa & Boyesen, Ebba (2004): Eröffnungsreden anlässlich der Tagung der GBP 2003 in Göhrde, in: GBP e.V. (Hrsg., 2004): A Visit of Unity. Beiträge der 7. und 8. Fachtagung der Gesellschaft für Biodynamische Psychologie/ Körperpsychotherapie (GBP e.V.) in Munzingen und Göhrde, 17.-20.05.2002 und 24. - 26.10.2003, Linden: Eigenverlag, 45-57

146. Boyesen, Paul (o.J.): The psychoorganic cycle, in: unveröffentlichtes Manuskript (Trainingspapier), o.J. , 2 S.

147. Boyesen, Paul (1987): Transference and projection, in: Adire, 2,3, 221-226

148. Boyesen, Paul (1988a): Die Aufgabe der Psychotherapeuten, in: Deutsche Gesellschaft für Biodynamische Psychologie [Hrsg.], DIALOG Biodynamische Psychologie, Zeitschrift für Biodynamische und Transformationelle Psychologie, Bd.1,

Heft 1, Oldenburg: Transform, 1988 , S. 7-8

149. Boyesen, Paul (1988b): Die Psychoorganische Analyse, in: Deutsche Gesellschaft für Biodynamische Psychologie [Hrsg.], DIALOG Biodynamische Psychologie, Zeitschrift für Biodynamische und Transformationelle Psychologie, Bd.1, Heft 1, Oldenburg: Transform, 1988 , S. 47-64

150. Boyesen, Paul (1990a): Von der Biodynamik zur Psychoorganischen Analyse, in: Deutsche Gesellschaft für Biodynamische Psychologie [Hrsg.], DIALOG Biodynamische Psychologie, Zeitschrift für Biodynamische und Transformationelle Psychologie, Bd.1, Heft 1, 1. Aufl., Oldenburg: Transform , 1990, S. 41-46

151. Boyesen, Paul (1990b): An die Deutsche Gesellschaft für Biodynamische Psychologie, in: Deutsche Gesellschaft für Biodynamische Psychologie [Hrsg.], DIALOG Biodynamische Psychologie, Zeitschrift für Biodynamische und Transformationelle Psychologie, Bd.2, Heft 1, Oldenburg: Transform, 1990, S. 7-11

152. Boyesen, Paul C., Huber, Hans-Georg (1991): Eigentlich möchte ich ..., München: Kösel

153. Boyesen, Paul (1991a): Das Wort und sein Körper, in: Deutsche Gesellschaft für Biodynamische Psychologie [Hrsg.], DIALOG Biodynamische Psychologie, Zeitschrift für Biodynamische und Transformationelle Psychologie, Bd.3, Heft 1, Oldenburg: Transform, 1991, S. 83-115

154. Boyesen, Paul, (1991b): Mißbrauch in der Therapie, in: Deutsche Gesellschaft für Biodynamische Psychologie [Hrsg.], DIALOG Biodynamische Psychologie, Zeitschrift für Biodynamische und Transformationelle Psychologie, Bd.3, Heft 1, Oldenburg: Transform, 1991 , S. 8-17

157. Boyesen, Paul (1994): Die fünf Phasen der Geburt, in: Deutsches Institut für Psychoorganische Analyse, Basistexte Psychoorganische Analyse, Heft 3, 1994, S. 6-24

158. Boyesen-Centre (1981a): The Functioning of the Stress Mechanism (according to Frederic Vester), in: International Foundation for Biodynamic Psychology [Hrsg.], unveröffentlichtes Manuskript (Trainingspapier), 1981 , 4 S.

159. Boyesen-Centre (1981b): Boyesen-Centre, in: Courtenay Young [Hrsg.], Journal of Biodynamic Psychology, No.2, London: Biodynamic Psychology Publications, 1981, S. 149

Search query by Dorian Boyesen in the EABP Bibliography of Body-Psychotherapy - special thanks to Courtenay Young for this

Search results for *Gerda Boyesen*:

33 books/chapters found, shown in order of relevance

Book: The collected papers of Biodynamic Psychology: Vol 1 & 2 , Boyesen, Gerda; Boyesen, Mona-Lisa; Boyesen, Ebah et al. - 1980

Chapter: Foundation for bio-dynamic psychology: Part II: Cries from the guts , Boyesen, Mona Lisa; Boyesen, Gerda - 1980

Chapter: Foundation for Bio-dynamic Psychology: Part 1: Spontaneous movements and visceral armour , Boyesen, Mona Lisa; Boyesen, Gerda - 1980

Chapter: Psycho-peristalsis Part IV: Dynamics of the vasomotor cycle: Nuances of membrane pathology according to the mental condition , Boyesen, Moan-Lisa - 1980

Chapter: Psycho-peristalsis, part VII: Self regulation and the streamings , Boyesen, Mona-Lisa - 1980

Chapter: Psycho-peristalsis: The abdominal discharge of nervous tension , Boyesen, Mona-Lisa - 1980

Chapter: Psycho-Peristalsis Part II: Emotional repression as a somatic compromise: Stages in the physiology of neurosis , Boyesen, Mona-Lisa - 1980

Chapter: Internal organismic pressure , Southwell, Clover - 1980

Chapter: Psycho-peristalsis, Part VI: Bio-physical aspects of libido circulation , Boyesen, Mona-Lisa - 1980

Chapter: Psycho-peristalsis, Part VII: From libido theory to cosmic energy , Boyesen, Mona-Lisa - 1980

Chapter: Psych-peristalsis, Part V: Function of the libido circulation , Boyesen, Mona-Lisa - 1980

Chapter: Flesh, energy and orgonotic contact , Boadella, David - 1980

Chapter: The primary personality and it , Boyesen, Gerda - 1980

Chapter: Experiences with dynamic relaxation and the relationship of its discovery to the Reichian view of vegetotherapy , Boyesen, Gerda - 1980

Chapter: The chemistry as armour: Part I: Adrenaline as an agent of neurosis , Surendra - 1980

Chapter: Bio-release Part II: The startle-reflex pattern & organic equilibrium , Boyesen, Mona-Lisa - 1980

Chapter: The essence of energy distribution , Boyesen, Ebba - 1980

Chapter: The energy distribution treatment , Southwell, Clover - 1980

Chapter: Psycho-orgastic vibrations: A standing exercise in ecstacy , Boyesen, Ebba - 1980

Chapter: Psycho-peristalsis: Part III: A case history of a manic-depressive , Boyesen, Gerda - 1980

Chapter: The scope of energy distribution , Lee, Robyn - 1980

Chapter: Bio-release , Boyesen, Mona Lisa - 1980

Chapter: How I developed Biodynamic Psychotherapy , Boyesen, Gerda - 2006

Book: Entre psyche et soma , Boyesen, Gerda - 1985

Book: Life in movement: The evolution of the personality from the perspective of biodynamic psychology. , van Schie, Lenie - 1999

Book: The charge of consciousness: Energy, chemistry and the dynamics of the brain , Boadella, David - 1979

Chapter: The primary personality and its relationship to the streamings , Boyesen, Gerda - 1991

Book: Introduction to psychosomatics , Holman, Paul - 1979

Book: Leven in beweging: De evolutie van persoonlijkheid benaderd vanuit de biodynamische psychologie , van Schie, Lenie - 1999

Chapter: Zwischen roehrentierchen und bewusstseinswesen das menschenbild in der koerperpsychotherapie , Thielen, Manfred - 1994

Chapter: Was sollte die koerpertherapie von der psychoanalyse lernen? ,

Moser, Tilmann - 1994

Chapter: The model of humans in body oriented psychotherapy, Thielen, Manfred - 1994

Chapter: What should body oriented psychotherapy learn from psycho-analysis? Moser, Tilmann 1994

47 journal articles found, shown in order of relevance

The healer: In memory of Gerda Boyesen, Burns, Richard - 2006

Personal reflections on Gerda Boyesen 1922-2005, Westland, G. - 2006

The life and work of Gerda Boyesen, van Heel, Carlien - 2006

History of Biodynamic (Psychology): Interview with Gerda: 1st part: Gerda in Norway, Gabler, Miriam - 2003

Cries from the guts. Foundation for Biodynamic Psychology: Part 2., Boyesen, Mona Lisa & Gerda - 1977

The dynamics of psychosomatics, Boyesen, Gerda - 1982

Foundation for Biodynamic Psychology: Part 1 Spontaneous Movements and Visceral Armour, Boyesen, Mona-Lisa and Gerda - 1977

History of Biodynamic (Psychology): 2nd part: London - birth, formation and development, Gabler, Miriam - 2003

The primary personality, Boyesen, Gerda - 1982

On the enjoyment of healing: An obituary of Gerda Boyesen, Freudl, Peter - 2006

The infant and the alpha: Appendix - Are we all survivors of cot death ?, Boyesen, Gerda - 1981

History of Biodynamic (Psychology): 4th part: London - following(s), Gabler, Miriam - 2004

Historique: rencontre avec Gerda : 1, Gabler, Miriam - 2003

Masocism and masochistic energy - an insight, Boyesen, Gerda - 1982

Biodynamic Psychotherapy and the intestinal brain, Boyesen, Gerda - 1999

Transference, resonance and interference., Boadella, David - 1982

History of Biodynamic (Psychology): 3rd part: London - following(s), Gabler, Miriam - 2004

Report of the Down to Earth Festival, Cotter Dam, Canberra and 1st International Healing Conference at the Australian National University, Canberra 10-14 December 1976, Eedy, Peter - 1977

Flesh, onergy and orgonotic contact, Boadella, David - 1977

Biodynamic massage: The interface with psychotherapy, Westland, Gill - 2004

Psycho-orgastic vibrations, Boyesen, Ebba - 1978

The essence of therapy, Boyesen, Ebah - 1981

Psycho-Organic Analysis, Blamauer, Richard - 2003

Firing zones, muscle tone, and the orgasm reflex, Boadella, David - 1981

Albert Abrams - a prophetic genius, Mayor, David - 1981

The embodied politics of intention, therapeutic intervention and artistic practice, Bonenfant, Yvon - 2006

Bio-release, Boyesen, Mona-Lisa - 1977

The essence of energy distribution, Boyesen, Ebba - 1977

The infant and the alpha, Boyesen, Mona Lisa - 1981

Historique de la Biodynamique: 3, Gabler, Miriam - 2004

Historique de la Biodynamique: 2, Gabler, Miriam - 2003

Historique de la Biodynamique: 4, Gabler, Miriam - 2004

What therapy means to me, Young, Heather - 1981

Stimulating the feeding rhythm in the newborn, Boyesen, Mona Lisa - 1982

The use and abuse of language in therapy, Young, Courtenay - 1981

Irritable Bowel Syndrom (Part 2), Fovargue, Lindsay - 2006

Self-help for angina sufferers, Nunneley, Peg - 1981

The energy distribution treatment, Southwell, Clover - 1977

Respondability - the way of the heart, Winkler, Dana - 1981

A translucent turtle ascends to the stars, Heuer, Gottfried - 1981

Biodynamic Massage as a therapeutic tool - with special reference to the biodynamic concept of equilibrium, Southwell, Clover - 1982

Communication, intention and attention: An essay, Nunnelley, Peg - 1982

On the shift of paradigms from Characteranalytic Vegetotherapy, Bioenergetic Analysis and Psychoanalysis to Existential Characteranalytic Vegetotherapy., Gronseth, Rolf - 1998

Learning from the East: Shared treasurers, Martin, Vicki - 2006

Eutonie from the viewpoint of functional relaxation and concentrative movement therapy, Fuchs, Marianne - 1977

Zwischen Passivitaet und Eigenbewegung Koerperpsychotherapie mit Frauen, Grossmann, Margit - 1998

Body therapy with women, Grossmann, Margit - 1998

1 websites, shown in order of relevance

Building Bridges and Celebrating Diversity, Conference Recording -

[Source: http://bibliography.eabp.org/result.php?q=Gerda+Boyesen&searchBtn=Search, 14.11.2021]

Further research on the EABP website: https://eabp.org/research/

GBP e.V. (Professional Association for Biodynamic Psychotherapists in Germany) https://www.gbpev.de/gerda-boyesen-eine-kurzbiografie/, 25.01.2022, by Ebba Boyesen and Thomas Haudel.
https://www.gbpev.de/glossar/, 25.01.2022
https://plus.wikimonde.com/wiki/Analyse_psycho-organique
https://everybodywiki.com/Analyse_psycho-organique

Afterword

My first memories of Gerda are of a most wonderful, fun and flamboyant grandmother. We had an incredibly strong bond, and she was my world as a child.

Through my mother Ebba & my grandmother Gerda I feel I was given a solid foundation and a strong sense of self in my early years.

It wasn't until being an adult and mother that I trained as a bio-release massage practitioner myself that I truly realised what a pioneer Gerda had been in her field.

Luckily times and mindsets are changing and the notion that we heal in a holistic way, is becoming increasingly accepted. As is the understanding that our psyche, body & soul are all interconnected in the search for optimal health.

Making her book "Between Psyche & Soma" seems as relevant today as it did when it was first published.

She embodied her methodology right until her last breath as she peacefully let go of life in a very biodynamic and orgonic way, accompanied by myself and my mother Ebba.

Vivia de la Chesnais, Gerda's granddaughter

With this book, the long-awaited introduction to "Biodynamic Psychology" developed by Gerda Boyesen is available.
It has two essential foundations:
1. the Vegetotherapy of Wilhelm Reich, and
2. massage, which works like a psychoanalysis.
By working with the body a dynamic process is set in motion, which works out the neurosis and transforms the psyche. This subtle (cf. *soft)* method is integrating the views of the three Greats of Psychotherapy - Freud - Jung - Reich - and has frequently proven itself reliable for treating personality disorders and psychosomatic illnesses and leads towards personal development.
In an autobiographical narrative, Gerda Boyesen shows how Biodynamic Psychology developed theoretically and practically in the course of more than thirty years of clinical and private practice. Numerous examples and classic case-histories illustrate this lively account / chronicle.
Her daughters, Ebba & Mona Lisa, and her son, Paul Boyesen, joined her in 1969 in London, and all contributed, and still do, to the field of Body-oriented Psychotherapy and Psychoanalysis. Mona Lisa even coined the terms "Biodynamic Psychology" and "Psychoperistalsis" and developed the method "BioRelease", Ebba invented "BirthRelease" and extended Reich's Segmental Armoury Theory from 7 to 12, so as to include the whole leg and feet segment, and Paul founded Psycho-Organic Analysis (POA).
Biodynamic Psychology is one of today's most effective psychotherapeutic therapies and is offered by a considerable number of therapists worldwide. Gerda Boyesen, was born in 1922 in Bergen, Norway; died December 29th, 2005 (aged 82) in London, England; psychologist, physiotherapist, analysis and training in Vegetotherapy (with Ola Raknes) and in therapeutic massage (with Aadel Bülow Hansen); lived in London since 1968; founded the Centre for Bioenergy 1972 (from 1974: Gerda Boyesen Centre); taught and practiced her methods in all Western European countries and internationally.

www.ingramcontent.com/pod-product-compliance
Lightning Source LLC
Chambersburg PA
CBHW050523240926
51846CB00003B/674
* 9 7 8 3 9 4 4 2 2 5 0 3 6 *